D1246374

CONTRARY COUNTRY

CONTRARY COUNTRY

A Chronicle of Vermont by
RALPH NADING HILL

Illustrated by George Daly

SHELBURNE MUSEUM PUBLICATIONS

SHELBURNE, VERMONT

To Carl and Betty Carmer

BOOKS BY RALPH NADING HILL

THE WINOOSKI (*Rivers of America*)
CONTRARY COUNTRY
SIDEWHEELER SAGA
WINDOW IN THE SEA
YANKEE KINGDOM: *Vermont and New Hampshire*
(*Regions of America*)
THE COLLEGE ON THE HILL: *A Dartmouth Chronicle*
VERMONT: *A Special World* (*Co-editor*)
VERMONT ALBUM
LAKE CHAMPLAIN: *Key to Liberty*
For younger readers:
ROBERT FULTON AND THE STEAMBOAT
THE DOCTORS WHO CONQUERED YELLOW FEVER
Fiction
THE VOYAGES OF BRIAN SEAWORTHY

ISBN 0-8289-0211-9

© Copyright 1950, 1961 by Ralph Nading Hill; 1982 by the Shelburne Museum
First Edition published in 1950 by Rinehart & Company, New York and Toronto.
Second printing, 1951
Second Edition published in 1961 by Stephen Greene Press
Brattleboro, Vermont, 1961
Third Edition, The Shelburne Museum, Shelburne, Vermont 1982
All rights reserved. Printed in the United States of America.
Library of Congress Catalog Card Number: 50-12397

82 83 84 85 86 87 9 8 7 6 5 4 3 2

Foreword

No commonwealth, unless it is Texas, is presumed to have a more widely acknowledged personality than Vermont. If this statement is false it is up to skeptics to prove it. In doing so they must reckon with several hundred thousand fanatic Believers, native and foreign, and refute the testimony set forth in one of the largest bibliographies of any state in the Union.

Of course it is not fair for Vermontophiles just to say that they have religion on their side. It is not enough to propound such intangibles as: "When you cross the border from New York you can *see* the difference. Vermont is greener and has more Rare Birds per county."

One must look to the geography and history of the Green Mountains for telling evidence of the state's uniqueness. Nature carved Vermont, like an old breadboard, into many small valleys. Each will comfortably hold and support just so many people. Because the individual is set as dramatically against the landscape as the four seasons he can never be lost sight of. In a suburban era of Togetherness this is a precious natural advantage, one that goes far to explain this country's true heritage of independence. Certainly one must take into account the vital and uncompromising race which settled the New Hampshire Grants and set up a thorny mountain republic that fought the Revolutionary War more or less on its own terms and is still doing pretty much as it has a mind to.

In this book, written 32 years ago, my intention was to show that Vermont has a distinctly private flavor, although I was not then sure and am not now whether it is more a state of mind or a thesis, scientifically arrived at. It has been said that history is the sum of innumerable biographies. If it follows that the character of a state is a compound of the faiths and follies of its people it is clear that Vermont is much richer in the variety of its human experience than many of its larger neighbors.

The citizens both native and adopted who appear in these pages, and

v

the events in which they took part, were not chosen because they are all historically important but because they are the kind of people and events that have always been characteristic of Vermont—and because Vermont is what they made it.

Oakledge   Ralph Nading Hill
Lake Champlain, Vermont
September, 1982

Contents

I. Tremors Under
the Timberline

WHEN Doomsday comes perhaps countries and states will stand along with men before the bar of judgment. If this occurs, it will be entertaining to know what disposition is made of Vermont, the state conceived in controversy between New Hampshire and New York, and reared in rebellion.

Fires of rebellion, which flamed for a hundred years, have not gone out. Embers of protest still smolder in town meetings, under the dome of the state capitol and in phrases spoken by Vermont legislators in Washington. Visitors to the Green Mountains find Vermonters chemically unable to endorse the popular view on any subject from politics to the weather. It is dangerous in Vermont, they have found, to suggest that it is a nice day—even if it is a nice day—for the Vermonter will surely qualify such a categorical statement. Politically the nation has been out of step with this northcountry never-never land of eternal Republicanism—of liberal Republicans and conservative Republicans. Vermont liberals are not really liberal, nor are the conservatives really conservative. They are simply conservative in some things and liberal in others.

The spore of rebellion is implanted deeply in this resistant people whose ancestors first came to till a resistant soil. Perhaps because Vermont has so clearly diverged from twentieth-century streamlined living, the trait of waywardness has recently been the subject of intense rediscovery by transplants and humorists, as if it were a new phenomenon on the landscape of New England. But it is not really new. The particular brand of nonconformist known as the Vermont Yankee has, like live oak, been curing for several centuries—even before the first Vermonters trekked west from New Hampshire and north from Connecticut.

First came the frail ship *Speedwell* bearing Martin Pring, on a search for sassafras. There was none—but this voyager out of Bristol was one of the first Englishmen to appraise the jagged coast of Vermont's mother colony, New Hampshire. The Frenchman, Champlain, was next. Then in 1614 Captain John Smith dropped anchor within the saltswept outposts of rock that guard New Hampshire's wedge of seacoast. Smith took a crude map of the coast and a description of the country back to Britain. Prince Charles named it New England.

Forty English knights, noblemen and gentlemen gathered at Plymouth in 1620 to establish the Council for New England under guidance of the King. Within a decade the knives of royal land speculators began to carve up the distant Indian terrain. They had received from his Majesty grants for a great slice of country that had "lakes which tend toward California in the south sea on the west thereof; on the north-east is the great river of Canada . . . the air thereof is pure and wholesome, the country pleasant, having some high hills full of goodly forests and fair vallies, and plains fruitful in corn, vines, chestnuts, walnuts, and infinite sorts of other fruits; large rivers well stored with fish, and invironed with goodly meadows full of timber trees. One of the great lakes is called the lake of the Iroquois, which, together with a river of the same name, running into the river of Canada, is 60 or 70 leagues in length. In the lake are four fair Islands, which are low and full of goodly woods and meadows, having store of bucks, beavers and other sorts of beasts, which come from the main land to the said islands; the rivers which fall into the lakes have in them good store of beavers, of the skins of which beast, as also of the elks, the savages make their chiefest traffick."

The English came off the sea and up into New Hampshire from the nursling settlements of Massachusetts. They were a strange assortment, even for the New World—refugees from Europe, and refugees from the refuge of southern New England.

"Resolved," they declared, "that the Earth is the Lord's and the inheritance thereof.

"Resolved: That the inheritance belongs to the Saints.

"Resolved: That we are the Saints."

By the middle of the 1600s their patchwork towns—Portsmouth, Dover, Exeter and Hampton—were busy with land vendors, fishermen, trappers, "Anabaptists, Antinomians, Quakers, free thinkers and free lances." Thus by 1640 agents of staid Massachusetts reported to their worried governor that the New Hampshire people were "ripe for our government. They grone for Government and Gospel all over that side of the Country. Alas! poore bleeding soules."

Though the mountains and wooded valleys of the New Hampshire mainland invited the oppressed and the disgruntled and impoverished of Massachusetts and southern New England, those who tramped north in the 1600s did not find all the freedom they sought. Two British empire builders, Captain John Mason and Sir Ferdinando Gorges, had received immense grants of land from the Council for New England which they dominated. For ninety years the fortunes of the people who lived on the land depended upon the whims of the

landowners and their heirs. Mason and Gorges were hand in glove
with the King in Council, so when New Hampshire became a province separate from Massachusetts in 1679 the royal governors who
arrived to rule were bitterly resisted by the raw and clamorous settlers.
The people succeeded in remolding the province according to their
own designs. By the early 1700s their resistance had worn out the heirs
and assigns of Mason and Gorges and the unsettled land was divided
into separate farmsteads.

The spirit of opposition to the governors was tested severely by the
conflict between the English and French. Four dreary wars endured
from 1680 to 1763. Here clashed the builders of empire: France thrust-
ing from Canada south along Lake Champlain, and England, northwest from her colonies on the Atlantic. Yet the grueling demands of
Britain's war against France seemed to toughen the spirit of Yankee
rebellion against England—a resistance heightened by the appearance
of new and discordant groups. In 1722 the Scotch-Irish arrived to
settle the New Hampshire town of Londonderry. These "rigid Presbyterians, followers of Oliver Cromwell, enemies of the Church of
England, and of Popery, lovers of learning and liberty" brought to
this country more than the Irish potato. They readily fused themselves
with the tough core of independence possessed by the westward-ex-
panding peoples of inland New Hampshire.

The Revolutionaries migrated both north and west, imperceptibly
at first, and then with growing momentum at the close of the French
and Indian War. An air of dignity had settled on the Connecticut
and Massachusetts towns and the countryside along the New Hampshire coast. Fortunes in shipbuilding and trading endowed Portsmouth
with graceful mansions, with leisure and with conservatism. The social climate of the coast country was no longer agreeable to the ad-
venturous, the radical, the poor and the persecuted. The Anti's and
the Isms now seemed to languish here.

North and west they migrated—first into the empty Cohos (pine
country) land by the Connecticut, and then beyond that broad stream
into the wilderness of the Green Mountains.

II. Vox Clamantis in Deserto

None know, nor can any, without Experience, well conceive of the Difficulty of Educating an Indian. They would soon kill themselves with Eating and Sloth, if constant care were not exercised for them—at least the first Year. They are used to set upon the Ground and it is as natural for them as a seat to our Chlidren—they are not wont to have any Cloaths but what they wear, nor will they, without much Pains, be brot to take Care of any. They are used to a Sordid Manner of Dress and love it as well as our Children to be clean. They are not used to any Regular Government. The sad Consequences of which you may a little guess at. . . . They have never been used to the Furniture of an English House and dont know but that a Wine glass is as strong as an Hand Iron.

AFTER trying for seventeen years to Christianize the savages Eleazar Wheelock was forced in 1761 to so harsh a judgment. But an agent of the Great Awakening who had already saved many souls would not quickly conclude that it was the color of a man's skin that plagued his experiments. The fault might sooner lie with methods used. To remove a young Indian from his tribe, to efface childhood impressions and teach him to walk not only Christian but English paths, was a challenging task that needed further pursuit.

Wheelock's interest had been awakened by his early success with Samson Occom, who was born a Mohegan in 1723 and remained a savage until he was sixteen. The boy had learned some English while still with the tribe and had received permission to attend Wheelock's informal preparatory school in Lebanon, Connecticut. He passed four fruitful years in the minister's immediate family. Hopeful that he might spend his whole life educating savages, Wheelock one day passed the collection basket in a Connecticut church for funds to start

5

the project. The returned basket contained only a bullet and a gunflint, stark evidence "that there were many in the colonies of the opinion that the only good Indian is one who is dead."

Determining to admit Indian boys and girls to his school and to support them with his own funds, Wheelock shortly learned that the young redskins who followed Occom were not of the same caliber. Of one he remarked, "I have taken much pains to purge all the Indian out of him, but after all, a little of it will sometimes appear."

By 1760 Wheelock was teaching eight Indians in his Lebanon "tenement," with classrooms on the first floor and lodgings above. Since they paid nothing for room, board or education, Wheelock shortly found his philanthropy too expensive. If his school was to continue he needed outside funds. He therefore sent his model product, Occom, to Britain to acquaint the English with the idea of an American Indian college.

The Church of England was not interested, but Occom's dignified manner did win the attention of many individuals, among them Lord Dartmouth, who appeared to Occom as a "worthy Lord indeed . . . a Christian Lord and an Uncommon one." From such men in England and Scotland—and even from the King, who gave £200—Occom received donations of nearly £11,000. Meanwhile Wheelock was succeeding in a less notable way in his appeals to the governors and legislatures of the American colonies. In 1769 his dream of a formal Indian school finally became real. Since it was the first adventure of its kind to approach success, it gained wide notice not only in America but abroad. The prospect of civilizing the savages had long filled the dreams of empire builders in France and England. Although the trail of French Jesuit missionaries among the Indians had been marked with blood and violence, and though early British efforts had likewise failed, it was clear that the European nation which won the loyalty of the Indians would be the one to direct the destinies of America. Wheelock was not unaware of this; his Indian school was no less rooted in religious motives than in a desire to serve the mother country.

"In rideing last week to New London," wrote John Smith, a Boston merchant, "I turned some miles out of my way to see Mr. Wheelock's Indian School, nor do I Repent my Trouble. I had heard in general that it consisted of Twenty or more Indian Boys & Girls of the Mowhawks & other tribes of Indians . . . I reached his House a little before the Evening Sacrifice, & was movingly Touched on giveing out the psalm to hear an Indian Youth set the Time, & the others following him, and singing the Tenor and Base with remarkable Gravity. . . .

"I omit Mr. Wheelock's prayer & pass to the Indians; in the morning . . . on Ringing the Schoolhouse Bell, they Assemble at Mr. Wheelock's House about 5 o'clock with their Master; who named the Chapter in Course for the Day, and called upon the near Indian who read 3 or 4 Verses . . . and so on till all the Indians had read the whole chapter. . . . And it is really charming to see Indian youths of Different Tribes and Languages in pure English reading the word of God . . .

"In passing some Days after that through the Mohegan Country, I saw an Indian Man on horseback, whom I challenged as Mr. Occom & found it so. There is something in his mien & Deportment both amiable & venerable & though I had never before seen him, I must have been sure it was he. . . ."

Funds came, but they did not bring the new school's goal any closer to fulfillment in the eyes of its founder. Indians who had graduated and had been sent out as missionaries among the Iroquois shortly returned to tribal living or fell under the influence of alcohol.

"There have been near forty," wrote Wheelock in 1771, "who were good readers, writers and were instructed in the principles of the Christian religion and were sufficiently masters of English grammar, arithmetic and a number . . . considerably advanced . . . in Greek & Latin. . . . Behaved well while . . . with me and left my school with unblemished character. . . . Many of them [went] at once into . . . business . . . as school masters and interpreters; but [because of] their want of fortitude to resist those fashionable vices which were rampant among their tribes . . . not more than half . . . preserved their characters unstained. Some . . . are sunk down into as low, savage and brutish a manner of living as they were . . . before. . . . And six of those who did preserve a good character are now dead."

Eleazar had included English boys in his Lebanon seminary to serve as missionaries to the Indians but by 1770, when he decided to move his school away from that town, he had begun to change his mind about devoting all his efforts to the Indians. Thus the original purpose of his seminary gradually became secondary to the teaching of white youths.

Wheelock received several offers of large, free tracts of land when his decision to move became definite. Albany proposed as a site a square in the city overlooking the Hudson. Samson Occom wanted the school on Long Island so that students could provide their own nutriment with oysters and clams. Ohio, then a wilderness, begged for attention. Stockbridge and Pittsfield, Massachusetts, made good offers, and the New Hampshire governor, Benning Wentworth, with other individuals in that province promised an estimated 15,000 acres.

The spot finally chosen in the township of Hanover lay on a pine-darkened plateau above the banks of the Connecticut. On both sides of the river lay hardy new settlements. The Indian tribes of the Algonquins were abundant to the north in Canada; and these Wheelock planned to draw upon for his school. Moreover the settled clergy of southern New England had not inhibited the wilderness with religious tradition. Wheelock yearned for the northern woods where Dartmouth College—with the first charter in America that excluded none because of race or religion—might prosper.

Early in 1770 the axes of Eleazar Wheelock's task force began to bite into trunks of white pine as tall as any in New England—two hundred seventy feet, some of them—for scores of decades a roof of impenetrable green under the Hanover sky. Ax and horsepower cleared six acres that first summer and shelters went up for Wheelock's family and the students. The rough dwellings were nearly completed when they had to be torn down and moved some distance southward to the third well which had finally produced water. Late in the summer Mrs. Wheelock arrived in a student-driven English chariot that had somehow survived ruts, stones and corduroy roads; and Eleazar's nephew brought one hundred pounds of tobacco, pipes, coffee and brandy, if not the celebrated "gallons of New England rum."

Brown worms, striped with black and yellow, many nearly four inches long, attacked the crops which Wheelock needed so badly. A

Thetford minister said there were so many that he could not touch the ground without touching a worm. He had seen ten bushels in one pile. They filled the trenches which had been dug around fields to trap them, their advancing legions passed over the bodies of the trapped and blanketed the houses inside and out. A few people saved enough corn for seed. The ensuing winter was heartless, and the next June boughs and stumps were still frozen in a matted tangle and there were six inches of ice in front of the college door. The brush was still too green to burn, too great in quantity to be carried off, the stumps too resistant to be pulled, and the ground so fertile that second growth was almost impossible to discourage. Nevertheless the work of clearing other tracts continued.

"You will consider that I am Wholly alone in the Whole affair," Wheelock had written before leaving Connecticut. "Whatever concerns the Missionaries, School Masters in the Wilderness—the Collegians— the Male and female Schools at Home—all lie upon me—and besides all this I can't yet get my people willing that I should be discharged from my care of them—besides the Business of my Farm upon which I chiefly depend, and God, for the support of my Family."

In Hanover now, at sixty-one, his burden was heavier. He was not only the father of eleven children, president, professor and spiritual leader, but fund-raiser, contractor, builder and business agent. Yet neither these responsibilities nor his advancing years could suppress his zeal for educating Indians. With a new territory and a new source of redskins (the Algonquins) to draw from, he began bringing them in from Canada until there were nearly as many in Hanover as there had been in Connecticut. His lack of success with the Algonquins, however, was as complete as it had been with the Iroquois, and the American Revolution all but ended his efforts in their behalf.

The departure of the Indians brought hardship to Eleazar and to Dartmouth because the large foreign fund was intended for teaching Indians. The English remonstrated against using the money for whites, while the Scottish directors allowed only the interest to be spent. Disciplinary problems also harried Wheelock, who had gradually become absolute monarch of all the activities of the school and of the town which was growing on the Hanover plain. When, at the first

Commencement, all the cooks became drunk, Eleazar had to face the task of providing personally for the guests, among whom was Governor John Wentworth, nephew of the former New Hampshire governor, Benning Wentworth. He had tried to cope with the liquor problem by bestowing the sole innkeeper's license on his bookkeeper; but the court granted another license to John Payne, who saw to it that the students, including the Indians, were amply supplied. This resulted in a skirmish, with Wheelock keeping a sharp surveillance on Payne's tavern and Payne, in retaliation, tearing down the college gates.

The students' food was apparently inferior and on one occasion a sample of bread was smuggled to Portsmouth so that the trustees could savor its wretched quality. As a result of this agitation Wheelock was censured by the governor: ". . . your provision for the students is extremely bad, their entertainment neither clean, plentiful nor wholesome, tho' the price and expense exceeds for comfortable living, that youths are thereby unhealthy and debilitated, their constitution impaired and their friends and parents highly disgusted."

To which Wheelock replied:

"Everything has been done that was doable for the comfort and health of the Scholars. As to their diet I have plenty of Good Pork, Beef, fresh meat all the winter and as often since as it co'd be had. They have had wheat or Indian puddings & butter or sauce as often as they pleased excepting a few days we were out of Butter and it could not be had. We have had a fullness of sugar & molasses, chocolate and tea when it could be had. . . . They have had pea, rye or wheat coffee. They have not had a fullness of milk. My cows had the horn distemper this spring, & some died & others almost as good as dead. I have sent to Conn. for more. They have had for sauce peas, potatoes cabbage & turnips (in the season of them) & plenty of greens the best that this country affords. Several sorts of food they reject with an outcry such as peas & pork cooked by the best skill of our country. Fresh meat broth they wholly refuse nor have the Cooks dared to offer it to them more than two or three times for the twelve months past and then it raised a hideous clamor. Sometimes the cooks have made mistakes and the scholars have not been dealt with as they ought to have been. Last week there was a gross mistake made, the pudden was not well salted. Upon the clamor I went over to see & found that part of the pudden was too fresh & the other part too salt. The cook told me her salt was too coarse and the pudden not sufficiently stirred after the salt was in which she readily confessed about through very great hurry. They have steadily had good bread & generally of late since we have had malt have had good common beer. . . ."

Perhaps the rough terrain and the sharp winters encouraged the vein of rebellion that ran through some of Dartmouth's early students. The most singular example of a student who found it impossible to conform was John Ledyard, the son of an old Connecticut friend of Wheelock. Young Ledyard arrived in Hanover in 1772 in an ancient sulky drawn by a rheumatic horse. The carriage, loaded with calico for stage curtains and other necessaries of the theater, was no less peculiar than Ledyard, whose dress bid "defiance to symmetry of proportion and to the fashion of the times. . . . The stage," says Jared Sparks, "was fitted up and plays were acted, in which Ledyard personated the chief characters. *Cato* was among the tragedies brought out upon his boards and Ledyard acted the part of old Syphax, wearing a long gray beard and a dress suited to his notion of the costume of a Numidian prince . . ."

The obligation of freshmen to blow the conch shell calling the students to classes was regarded as unjust by Ledyard, and when his turn came he produced weird effects that unstrung the authorities of the college. Among various petitions whose circulation Ledyard encouraged, was one asking permission for students "to spend certain leisure hours in stepping the minuet & learning to use the sword." He had been in college only part of his freshman term when he departed and for three and a half months wandered among the tribes of the Iroquois. His final exploit, after being criticized by Dr. Wheelock for squandering the small patrimony that had been intended for his tuition, was his almost legendary trip down the Connecticut in a dugout. Helped by friends he cut down a large tree and hollowed it out. With a bearskin and a supply of dried venison aboard, a shelter of willow twigs at one end and Ovid and the Greek Testament to occupy odd moments, Ledyard shoved off in secrecy and soon floated out of Dr. Wheelock's jurisdiction. He had a narrow escape at Bellows Falls and after several days' journey managed to reach Hartford, one hundred forty miles downstream. There he penned a combination indictment of, and farewell to, Dartmouth College. He went to sea with Captain Cook, wandered in Russia and Siberia and finally died in an expedition to Africa. A stone erected where he cut down the tree bears the inscription, "His was the Dartmouth Spirit."

In 1774 hostility against Great Britain prompted the leaders of New Hampshire towns to organize at Exeter the first provincial congress in the country—the first step taken by any of the colonies toward statehood. Across the Connecticut the Allen brothers engaged in busy seed-planting that would soon bear the fruit of an independent republic—Vermont. The virus of revolution also infected the officials of Dartmouth College, for the state congresses at Exeter in 1775 did not allow Hanover enough representation. The College party soon began to imagine a state of their own—a Connecticut valley state, of which Hanover would be the geographical and political center.

The western boundary of New Hampshire had been in doubt for two centuries. What would happen to Vermont was anyone's guess. New York claimed all of it. The Vermonters, with the Allens at the helm, were steering a course through perilous shoals of Yorkers. In the southeastern communities of their claimed state the Vermonters were exerting a most feeble control over dissident patches of Yorkers who had settled there under New York land grants and were claiming the authority of that state.

After protesting the encroachment of New York on the Green Mountain territory to the west, the New Hampshire government of John Wentworth had now all but given up. Colonel Jacob Bayley, a prominent settler on the opposite bank above Hanover, had reported to Wheelock:

"When Gov. Wentworth came up to the first Commencement he was at my house, and appeared to be very jealous to get the lands on the western side of Connecticut River added to the Province of New Hampshire, and desired my assistance in the affair and when he took his leave he gave me his hand and added that he would use his utmost efforts to recover the aforesaid lands. In about two months afterward

I received a letter from Gov. Wentworth in the following tenor, viz., that I must make the best terms I could with New York . . . in consequence of which my quiet was very much disturbed, and to such a degree that I immediately took my horse and rode to Portsmouth, and enquired of the Governor the reason of his writing in the manner as has been related. But I could not get that satisfaction from the Governor that I desired and Expected; but he rather seemed to put me off . . . the reason of which I could not learn. Being still perplexed, I mounted my horse and rode to New York. When I arrived there, the Secretary smiled, and addressed me in the following manner: 'What! you are come now; now you are obliged to come, for your Governor is come before you, and now you are come.' Says I, 'What do you mean by your Governor's coming, I don't understand you.' 'Here,' says he (handing me a letter), 'you may see what I mean.' The contents of which were thus, viz.: that if the Governor of New York would grant patents to the Governor of New Hampshire of those five hundred acre lots which old Governor Wentworth had reserved for himself in every town on the western side of the river when he gave charters of said towns, then he, viz., Governor [John] Wentworth would be contented to resign his claim to those towns and would exert himself no more to have them revert to the Province of New Hampshire. . . .'"

As pioneer distances went, Hanover was a long way from the settled towns of the New Hampshire seacoast. It was at an even greater ideological distance. The interior towns were teeming with an assortment of rebels, atheists and refugees whose ideas were mountains removed from those of the landed gentry along the seacoast. With the people and land of the whole area all the way to New York in a state of revolutionary flux, the College party felt the chances were good that they could step in and pluck their Connecticut valley state from under the noses of the warring factions. It little disturbed their vision that to create it they would have to take about half of the land of present New Hampshire and all of Vermont west to the Green Mountains. The river, placid and broad, tended to weld together the people of the hillsides that sloped down to each bank. A Connecticut River state was natural and logical. To make this ideal a reality, Wheelock's son-in-law, Bezaleel Woodward, with his usual enterprise assumed the role of political strategist for the College party.

On July 31, 1776, eleven Connecticut River townships met in Hanover to protest that their say in the New Hampshire provincial government at Exeter was not representative enough. Wheelock, moving in the background of this conclave, secretly engaged in bringing the broth to a boil. Six months later the towns in western New Hampshire were refusing to pay taxes or join in the assembly at Exeter. By 1778 the success of the College party was such that the people on both sides of the Connecticut were eager for a separate state embracing the river communities. In Vermont the Allens (in danger of losing the eastern half of their new republic) intensified their endeavors to hold the dikes against the floodtide of land-claiming states, or would-be states, whose number Eleazar had now increased by one.

The dikes soon crumbled and the Vermont republic, much against the will of its leaders, was inundated by sixteen of Wheelock's New Hampshire townships. These towns had proposed to the Vermont assembly that they be admitted to Vermont. For Wheelock and the College party this strategy was sound. Relations with the Exeter government would be completely severed. With Vermont enlarged by adding New Hampshire territory, the political center of the new republic would have to move east to the Connecticut valley—perhaps, Wheelock hoped, to Hanover.

Because the Vermonters in the river townships were more numerous than those in the towns of the Allens' Bennington party, the sixteen New Hampshire towns were admitted. Dartmouth College in 1778 thus became a Vermont college and Eleazar Wheelock was made a Vermont justice of the peace. But Ethan and Ira Allen, who hoped to make the Vermont republic the fourteenth state, at once went on the warpath against the sixteen added towns, for surely the New Hampshire leaders of the Exeter government, having lost their Connecticut River territory, would retaliate in Congress. They would block Vermont's chances for statehood. Ethan, after a trip to Philadelphia, reported to the Vermont Council, "From what I have heard and seen . . . it is my opinion that except the State recede from such union immediately, the whole power of the Confederacy of the United States of America will join to annihilate the State of Vermont to vindicate the right of New Hampshire." Ira Allen wrote the New Hampshire governor that the Dartmouth College group were "a few Restless, uneasy Men not having the good of either of the States at Heart, but their own private Interest and Emoliment." Ethan called them "a Petulent, Pettefoging, Scribbling sort of Gentry, that will Keep any Government in hot water till they are thoroughly brought under by Exertions of Authority."

The hostility of the Allens and the hostility of New Hampshire leaders at Exeter, who were getting ready to force the wandering townships back to the home fold, proved too much for the College party. They were not able to prevent the Vermont legislature from voting in February 1779 to reject their sixteen towns. The rub for the Vermonters was that when the sixteen New Hampshire towns withdrew, they took ten Vermont river towns with them. A snowstorm of leaflets followed, containing denunciations and counter-denunciations with anonymous signatures such as Pacificus and Republican. Much less wary of the mixed metaphor than the College party, officials of the New Hampshire government (whose wandering towns were at the moment preparing to become independent of everyone) said of Eleazar: ". . . By this single blow of the clumsy fist of this dabbler in politics, the glorious fabric of American Independence will be laid prostrate, jumbled into a heap of sand, without any cement to hold it together."

Wheelock's son-in-law went to Philadelphia and poured forth his grievances to Congress. Along the banks of the river there were conventions and committee meetings galore. Colonel Jacob Bayley, smarting under the slap administered by the Allens to the Connecticut towns, proposed that all of Vermont "be connected and confederated with the State of New Hampshire." This respected soldier had never quite made up his mind. As Charles M. Thompson says, "He was for New Hampshire, then for New York, then Vermont, then for a valley state separate from both New Hampshire and Vermont, then for New Hampshire enlarged to include all Vermont east of the Green Mountains." He wanted a state controlled neither by the seacoast conservatives nor by the rabble of the Allen party.

Meanwhile in 1779 the College faction was supporting New York claims in Vermont west of the Green Mountains—for it hoped to take the rest of the state east to the river, together with all the New Hampshire towns that would secede.

By 1779 a lifetime of exertion had worn out Eleazar Wheelock, whose troubles in founding his wilderness college had been clearly beyond the endurance of one man. With the coming of the Revolution the fragile pipe line through which he had been siphoning funds from Europe had collapsed and the war had succeeded in draining off the Dartmouth student body. Wheelock was tired and sick. Rancor against those who disagreed with him about what was good for the college and the town had involved him in a dispute over whether or not there should be a general inoculation against a smallpox epidemic.

His duties as minister, teacher and administrator had continued beyond an age—sixty-nine—where he could physically bear them. The political project of which the College party had dreamed—that Dartmouth be the center of an illustrious political state in the bright valley of the Connecticut—was not fulfilled, nor did it bear immediate prospect of fulfillment. Wheelock's favorite task, that of elevating the Indians—an ideal to which he had devoted his utmost energy—was a failure. There were now only a few Indians in Hanover. Toward these, equally with the white students, however, he still directed his care and concern.

"My family & School are in want of Cloathing," he wrote in 1778 to John Phillips, his friend and benefactor. "Your generous Nephew Sent Seasonable relief to Some of my Charity Schollars as to woolen, but the necessity remains not less as to linnen; to supply which we have cut up all the Sheets, Table Cloths, under beds Towels etc. which could be spared in the House, to cover their nakedness, and have now Scarce a whole linnen garment in the house and most of them Such as you would not think worth taking from the floor unless for a papermill."

On March 29, 1779, he wrote a lifelong friend: ". . . I have been a long time in a very low state and my case of late has been esteem'd desperate by my Physicians; but, by the pure mercy of God, I am so far reviv'd as to be able unassisted more than by my staff, to walk from my bed to the fire, and back again, and to sit in my chair near half my time."

The end came on April 24. They buried him near the college in a

wooded graveyard and set up a stone on which these words were
carved:

BY THE GOSPEL HE SUBDUED THE FEROCITY
OF THE SAVAGE AND TO THE CIVILIZED HE
OPENED NEW PATHS OF SCIENCE

TRAVELER
GO IF YOU CAN AND DESERVE
THE SUBLIME REWARD OF SUCH MERIT

The death of Eleazar Wheelock in 1779 did not end the struggle of the
College party for a Connecticut valley state free of both New Hampshire and Vermont. After the sixteen wandering New Hampshire
towns had been turned away from Vermont, they boldly announced
their claim to the entire valley on both sides of the Connecticut. To
retaliate against the College party—and against the Vermont republic
for having started the sixteen towns on the road to autonomy—the New
Hampshire government at Exeter now again asserted its claim to every
acre of land all the way to Lake Champlain. This was painful to the
Allens, who had hoped that by sending the sixteen towns back home
to New Hampshire, that state would help Vermont to be admitted to
the Union. Yet the Allens could rationalize that one reason their republic had so far prospered was that Congress had as yet been unable
to decide for any one of the various claimants—New York, New
Hampshire, Massachusetts, and now the college with its proposed valley state, New Connecticut.

The hopes of the College party waxed and waned, and waxed again
in 1781 when on January 16 it was able to assemble the representatives
of forty-three river towns at Charlestown. A free Connecticut valley
state was not yet politically possible. However the convention did rec-
ommend that all of Vermont be annexed to New Hampshire. If this
were to come about, the New Hampshire capital would have to move
west to a point nearer the center of the enlarged area—to Hanover, the
Dartmouth strategists hoped. Concurred in by many of Vermont's
river towns, the vote was carried. The Vermont republic thus faced
its hour of greatest peril. Ira Allen, dispatched to Charlestown to do
whatever was wise and possible, arrived after the voting. To achieve
one of the most remarkable diplomatic feats of his life, he rallied the

delegates to a course of action diametrically opposed to the one they had just taken. They voted the following morning not to annex Vermont to New Hampshire, but the New Hampshire towns to Vermont. Thus the towns east of the Connecticut once again became Vermont towns and Dartmouth College a Vermont college. This arrangement was satisfactory to Dartmouth leaders, for with the addition to Vermont of the New Hampshire towns, the capital of Vermont would have to move *east* to Hanover. But the hopes of the Dartmouth strategists were once again dashed by the Bennington party of the Allens. Barely in control of the Vermont legislature, they succeeded in granting admission to some New York towns on the west of their republic to counterbalance the New Hampshire towns on the east, so that the seat of power remained where it was—with the Allens.

The wailing of New York and New Hampshire leaders echoed through the halls of Philadelphia and stirred Congress to a new peak of frustration. General Washington suggested that if Vermont would return the annexed towns to New York and New Hampshire, Congress would admit it as the fourteenth state. In 1782 the Vermont legislature, looking forward to statehood, returned the towns, much to the mortification of the Dartmouth leaders who were once again back where they had started with their valley state. Bezaleel Woodward, spokesman of the College party in the political arena, began to pay more attention to his position as professor, trustee and treasurer of Dartmouth College. Not that Hanover and the towns immediately around it had given up hope. They continued their meetings until 1784 when Woodward appeared as Hanover representative in the New Hampshire legislature at Exeter. Then everyone knew that the fight was at last over—the fight for an independent valley state.

Upon the death of his father in 1779 John Wheelock, the second of Eleazar's four sons, had become president of Dartmouth. Dignity and understanding, qualities which the passing years presumably impart to men, were lacking in this twenty-five-year-old. Sensing his inadequacy as spiritual and educational mentor, he sought to endow himself with suitable qualities by artificial means. He ordered students to remove their hats when passing within six rods of him, to stand when addressing him, and neither to talk nor sit until invited to do so. When addressing the students Wheelock stood extremely erect and spoke in a high-pitched voice. According to a member of the class of 1804 it was Wheelock's custom "to speak in a stiff and affectedly elevated style, to assume some empirical airs of the polite gentleman; to exact attention from others and to pay for them by making superfluous bows, and lighting up his face with smiles, while he gracefully lifted and waved his tricornered beaver . . ."

As for bowing, it is related that he never allowed another man to have the last bow. On one occasion he was "put to the test by a person of some assurance who undertook to compete with him in a contest of politeness. He accordingly took his leave, bowed himself out of the mansion, and continued to bow as long as he was upon the premises, but the President followed him to the gate and remained in possession of the field."

George Ticknor, a member of the class of 1807, wrote that "Dr. Wheelock was stiff and stately. He read constantly, sat up late and got up early. He talked very gravely and slow, with a falsetto voice. [Daniel] Webster could imitate him perfectly. . . . I saw a great deal of him . . . but never felt the smallest degree of familiarity with him, nor do I believe that any of the students did. They were generally very awkward, unused to the ways of the world. Many of them when they went to the President on their little affairs did not know when the time had come for them to get up and leave him. He was very covetous of his time, and when the business was settled . . . he would say, 'Will you sit longer or will you go now?' It was a recognized formula and no young man that I ever knew of ever sat longer after hearing it."

Wheelock's learning, at least at the beginning of his presidency, was naturally not much greater than that of his seniors, and, because he was superficial and often illogical, he leaned heavily on books or prepared texts. His pompous manner provided the students with much secret amusement.

As presiding officer of special college programs, the president liked to proclaim the order of events in Latin, and on one occasion when an interval of music was due, he announced, "Musica expectatur." The students failed to respond. He uttered the words loudly twice more;

and when the awkward pause persisted Wheelock lost his temper and boomed at the musicians, "Play up!"

While offering the prayer in chapel one day Wheelock used material he had absorbed from a recent medical lecture to exclaim in all seriousness: "Oh, Lord, we thank Thee for the oxygen gas, for the hydrogen gas, for the mephitic gas, we thank Thee for all the gases. And we thank Thee for the cerebrum, for the cerebellum, for the medulla oblongata."

Despite his peculiarities the younger Wheelock was able to sustain the school financially in its early period of travail and to maintain the high standards of scholarship established by his father. Ephraim Smedley in the class of 1793, who not only read but meticulously set down how much he had read, tells us that his record in the sophomore year was 7,913 pages; and he moralizes thus concerning it, "A very small number of pages to read but a few well attended are better than a large number slightly run over." He died at the end of that year.

The course for the spring term of the freshman year was: *The Iliad,* Coleridge's *Introduction to Greek Classic Poets;* Bojesen's *Manual of Greek & Roman Antiquity;* Cicero, *Tusculan Quest;* Prose Composition (Arnold); Geometry (Loomis). Rhetoric with weekly themes rounded out the schedule. There were no electives. The students were ordinarily up at five o'clock, or on winter mornings "as early as the President could see to read the Bible." After prayers in the frigid chapel came the first recitation and breakfast. A study period was next, then a second recitation, followed by dinner, study, afternoon classes, and finally evening prayers (as late as the president was able to see). Sunday's four compulsory religious exercises were as drab as a conference with President Wheelock.

College rules prohibiting drunkenness, riotous meetings, indecent clamor, disorderly night-walking, firearms, public parties and entering taverns, were designed to reduce life on the Hanover plain to monastic sobriety. The records—particularly those of the late 1780s and '90s, when a wave of unchristian rebellion rolled over the campus—show an astonishing reaction to Wheelock's blueprint. Students stole hens and cooked them in their rooms, blew the doors off a building with a cannon, captured and hid the president's stuffed library bird, and demolished the old Commons Hall. "The stage at that time exhibited scenes wounding to Christian piety, and to which modesty was indignant. In a quarrel on the stage one would stab the other and he would fall as dead, wallowing in blood from a concealed bladder, which was wittingly punctured by the point of a sword. A student would take the stage, assuming to be a preacher, and with a pious tone would barbecue Scripture, with a view to shower contempt upon unlearned ministers. One of these young preachers, in executing his purpose, said that 'Nebuchadnezzar's fundament was het seven times hotter than ever it was before . . .'!"

Peace veiled the campus for a brief period following the agitation for a Connecticut valley state, but in the last of the 1790s it was rent by a struggle that almost ruined the college. Since the affair of the eastern townships, Dartmouth had not been popular with the state government of New Hampshire. There had been trouble over certain New Hampshire lands which the college had improved and later had lost to settlers supported by the state of New Hampshire. On the campus John Wheelock was spoiling for a fight with several of his trustees, among whom was Judge Nathaniel Niles, a theologian, lawyer, doctor, inventor and poet from West Fairlee, Vermont, a man who had served as Vermont legislator, supreme court judge and Congressman. Niles was warlike and no less accustomed to domineer than Wheelock. Moreover the judge was a strong Hopkinsian Calvinist and Wheelock, like his father, was a New Light. Religious differences could not be tolerated. They hated each other.

At first, however, the crisis had nothing specifically to do with Niles or other disgruntled trustees. It started when Wheelock, unable to dictate all the policies of the Hanover church, withdrew the students and Professor Smith, the college-supported minister. This left the church without a pastor for two months in 1797; but the difficulties were presently patched up and combined services in the church for the students and townspeople were resumed. In 1804 the board of trustees appointed Roswell Shurtleff to the chair of religion. As a faculty member his duties were to lecture regularly and fill in as minister. The presumption was that he would also take over as minister of the Hanover church, since the prosaic Smith, who for twenty years had preached his parishioners to sleep, was retiring as professor of divinity. Because they considered Smith too much of a religious handy man for Wheelock, the people gladly summoned Shurtleff to their pulpit. Not trusting Shurtleff, Wheelock announced that Professor Smith would not step down from the pulpit after all. Rather, he decreed, the two men would serve as co-pastors.

A schism in the church developed rapidly. Wheelock, Smith and a few residents of Hanover claimed jurisdiction as members of what they called the original church, and Shurtleff, with a large number of disgruntled parishioners, objected to Wheelock's attitude of righteousness. Breastworks were thrown up and all newcomers to Hanover were, like fraternity pledges, courted by one or both of the opposing camps. Since the towns were adjacent, the people of Hartford across the river in Vermont were members of the Hanover church; but the Vermonters had not attended regularly. Wheelock now gathered the Vermont members into his fold so that those who held his point of view in the Hanover church might be in a majority and outvote the others. The conflicting parties therefore became known as the Hartford branch and the Hanover branch. ". . . Now there was a division among the people, some saying this must not be, for our sacred body will come to naught, if we transfer our government from an Elder to a Beardless Youth, so Johannes Maximus sent messengers to the half tribe on the other side of Jordan . . . saying prepare yourselves for the battle and come over this side the Jordan to defend mine annointed against the mocking of the heathen and the raging of the undevout."

Try as it would the Hanover branch was unable to get rid of Professor Smith, owing to the efforts made on his behalf by Wheelock's Hartford branch. The cleavage widened to a gulf. In 1805 the Hanover branch seceded and set up its own church with Shurtleff as minister. John Wheelock stayed with the Hartford group, which had more members in Vermont than it did in Hanover. Both bodies owned the Hanover meetinghouse; both had a right to meet there. This brought further trouble.

Adamant in his efforts to dominate the church and cripple the Hanover branch if possible, John Wheelock placed the matter before Dartmouth's board of trustees. They did not wish to become involved. Neither did the Vermont members of Wheelock's Hartford branch, whom he had been using as tools: the fight therefore narrowed to one strictly between Wheelock and the Hanover church. Yet because Wheelock *was* the college and insisted upon enlisting the trustees in his service, the board finally had to consider the matter. Wheelock supposed that they would decide in his favor since most of them were friendly toward him; but they agreed not only that there should be no restriction on Shurtleff's preaching but also that both branches of the church should have the right to use the meetinghouse. This decision rankled Wheelock and made him more determined than ever to gain his ends. His objectives and the means employed to achieve them were so unworthy that, when Professor Smith died in 1809 and new men joined the board of trustees, he lost control of that body. He now had no means of blocking the appointment of faculty members who disagreed with his point of view and shortly found himself opposed by the trustees and, in addition, by a majority of the faculty. They steadfastly insisted that the college should use no coercion in religious matters and that the Hanover minister should not be financially dependent on the college in the future.

Wheelock now openly attacked Shurtleff for being delinquent in college duties and in his preaching and accused the board of trustees of misusing funds. The trustees replied that they had "long labored to restore the harmony which formerly prevailed in this Institution, without success: and it is with reluctance they express their apprehension, that if the present state of things is suffered to remain any great length of time, the College will be essentially injured."

With an air of persecution Wheelock made his grievances known by writing and sending out pamphlets hostile to his board of trustees. The newspapers and political parties entered the fight and soon the original issue was clouded. In a larger sense it had become Federalist against Democrat and Calvinist against Evangelical, but it was really Wheelock against the trustees. All the sundry factions aligned themselves with one side or the other until, in 1815, the college issue dominated the politics of New Hampshire. In August of that year the Dartmouth trustees met and resolved "that the appointment of Dr.

John Wheelock to the presidency of this college by the last will of the Rev. Eleazar Wheelock, the founder and first President of this College be . . . disapproved, and it is further Resolved that the said Dr. John Wheelock . . . be removed . . ."

His dismissal and the appointment of Francis Brown, a minister from Yarmouth, Maine, as president made a martyr out of Wheelock. Thus many New Hampshire individuals and groups who might have been against him rallied to his defense out of sympathy. The Federalists generally upheld the board of trustees and called the Democrats, who were for Wheelock, "villains" and "French Jacobins." Having been rejected by the voters for supporting the unpopular War of 1812, the Democrats were using the college affair as a means to return to power. They denounced the Federalists and supporters of the trustees as "infuriated bigots of popery in the dark ages," and "the gangrened persecutors of President Wheelock." There were also the religious arguments, many of which were contrary to fact. The Democrats were making Wheelock appear to be a religious and political liberal, while actually he was neither.

Northern-state Federalists met at Hartford, Connecticut, in 1814-15 to consider the estrangement of New England from the Union because of their bitter feeling against a war that had eclipsed their region's trade. The college case thus became deeply involved in the war's fortunes. So thoroughly did the War Hawks succeed in rousing the electorate's sympathy for John Wheelock, that, when the war was over and the Federalist party doomed, the Democrats returned to power in New Hampshire by a large margin. Meanwhile an impartial report of the entire college affair—in the form of an investigation upon which Wheelock had insisted while still president—reached the legislature. It was more than a little critical of his actions and embarrassed his Democratic friends to such an extent that they strove to have it suppressed. They succeeded in pigeonholing it in a committee which reported that the real trouble with Dartmouth lay in the charter, which should be changed. The legislators refused to hear the trustees' side of the story and voted to change the name from Dartmouth College to Dartmouth University. They also voted to increase the number of the board from twelve to twenty-one, the added members to be named by the governor and council. The purpose of these measures was to enable Wheelock to gain control of the board of trustees.

By 1817 the legislature had firmly established Dartmouth University and had installed John Wheelock as president. Brown, meanwhile, had been invited to become head of Hamilton College at a much larger salary than he was receiving at Hanover. However he was so determined that the college should prevail over the university that he resolved to stay on and fight. Thus there were two separate colleges on the Hanover plain, each with its own professors, students and schedule —a situation loaded with possibilities for strife. University agents at once broke into the chapel, removed the college's lock and installed one of their own. They forced entrance to Dartmouth Hall and replaced the old lock to the bellroom with one of their own. They did the same in the museum, the library and the philosophy hall.

In order that the college might have a sympathetic representative in the legislature, its students invaded the Hanover town meeting, claiming they were residents of the town and entitled to vote. The local government (which was under the control of Wheelock) was unable to exclude them, but made the student-voters discharge other duties of freemen—working on the town roads and drilling with the militia.

After they seized the college library, agents of the university later tried to take possession of the several-thousand-volume libraries of the two literary societies, the United Fraternity and the Social Friends. Fearing for the safety of their books, the two societies had appointed committees of safety, and Rufus Choate, librarian for the Friends, had quietly rented a room near his own to which he had removed most of the volumes. The United Fraternity shortly followed suit and had transferred about eight hundred of its books when the university faculty got wind of this secret operation. Henry Hutchinson, university inspector of buildings, gathered a posse of two professors, five students and ten villagers and trooped first to the rooms occupied by the Social Friends. Finding the door locked and unable to batter it in by running against it, Professor Dean directed one of the party to chop it down with an ax, while the rest stood by with clubs. The racket brought the students rooming near by to the scene along with the entire membership of the United Fraternity, who had been meeting downstairs. When they found the university posse armed with clubs, they quickly snatched sticks from the firewood stacked in the hall. One of their number, in a stern voice heard all over the vicinity, boomed, "Turn out, Social Friends, your library is broken open!" In a distant room one student "heard Oliver's ringing voice distinctly," and with his roommate was soon at the scene where "we found Coffin still cutting away at the door, and Hutchinson giving orders. Profs. Dean and Carter were also present with Bissell and Cook and 3 shoemakers and others unknown to fame. The first sensible speech I heard was from one of the shoemakers who addressed his associates saying, 'It appears to me we are in a cursed poor scrape. I had rather be in a nest of hornets than among these college boys when they get mad and roused up.'"

The university party displayed their determination with poised clubs and an upraised ax but were shortly outnumbered by the surrounding group of college adherents. One by one the members of the university posse passed through an indignant gantlet of college boys—the professors first and then the others under an arch of uplifted clubs.

John Wheelock did not live to enjoy his new prominence as president of Dartmouth University. He died in April 1817 of "dropsy of the chest"—confident to the last in the justice of his cause and the belief that the university would win. His passing was not honored with the sorrow that had attended the death of his father. The faculty and students had always regarded him with varying degrees of dislike because he had never cast off the cloak of formality which he had acquired as a young man. His love of property and his quickness to foreclose on mortgages alienated the townspeople. He had even been at odds with his own brothers. If he had died a year previously, the entire college affair might have been peacefully settled, but the rancor he had caused was now too deepseated.

The case of Dartmouth College versus Dartmouth University shortly reached the courts. Daniel Webster, '01, had been engaged by Brown to defend the college's position that legislative tampering with the charter of a private institution and the establishment of the university was unconstitutional. The case was heard in the state court and the college cause was lost. Refusing to cease operations, however, the college authorities conducted their classes as usual and appealed to the Supreme Court of the United States. If that tribunal sustained the decision of the lower court, the college would have to close. Formidable John Wheelock and his allies in the legislature, which had changed the charter and created the university, would thus be vindicated.

The college never lost hope although the litigation was rapidly draining its meager funds. In the incisive legal mind of Daniel Webster, in the eloquence and indomitable spirit of Black Dan, the college hopes were rooted. At thirty-six he was already known not only as a clever politician but also as a lawyer who clearly possessed qualities of greatness. His love of his alma mater had filled his defense of the college in the lower court with that animation characteristic of great speeches and writings. But he had lost. The arguments of the university proponents on this occasion were, according to Webster, "able, ingenious and plausible"—although incorrect. Now, in March 1818, as he summoned all his energy for the Supreme Court trial, the existence of the college was at stake and Daniel Webster's reputation at a turning point.

The capitol at Washington had been razed by the British. The trial therefore began in the rented house where the Supreme Court was sitting. In the words of Rufus Choate:

"Mr. Webster . . . scarcely looked at his brief, but went on for more than four hours with a statement so luminous and a chain of reasoning so easy to understand, and yet approaching so nearly to absolute demonstration, that he seemed to carry with him every man of his audience without the slightest effort. . . . It was hardly eloquence in the strict sense of the term; it was pure reason. Now and then for a sentence or two his eyes flashed and his voice swelled into a bolder note, as he uttered some emphatic thought but he instantly fell back into the note of earnest conversation, which ran throughout the great body of his speech. . . . I observed Judge Story sit, pen in hand, as if to take notes. Hour after hour I saw him fixed in the same attitude; but I could not discover that he made a single note.

"The argument ended. Mr. Webster stood for some moments silent before the court while every eye was fixed intently upon him. At length, addressing Chief Justice Marshall, he said—'This, sir, is my

case. It is the case not merely of that humble institution, it is the case
of every eleemosynary institution throughout our country, of all those
great charities founded by the piety of our ancestors to alleviate human
misery, and scatter blessings along the pathway of human life. It is
more. It is in some sense the case of every man who has property of
which he may be stripped—for the question is simply this: Shall our
state legislature be allowed to take that which is not their own, to turn
it from its original use, and apply it to such ends or purposes as they,
in their discretion, shall see fit? Sir, you may destroy this little institution; it is weak; it is in your hands. I know it is one of the lesser
lights in the literary horizon of our country. You may put it out, but
if you do you must carry through your work. You must extinguish,
one after another, all those great lights of science, which, for more
than a century, have thrown their radiance over the land! It is, sir, as
I have said, a small college, and yet there are those that love it . . .'

"Here the feelings which he had thus far succeeded in keeping down,
broke forth. His lips quivered; his firm cheek trembled with emotion;
his eyes were filled with tears; his voice choked, and he seemed struggling to the utmost simply to gain the mastery over himself which
might save him from an unmanly burst of feeling.

"The court-room during those two or three minutes presented an
extraordinary spectacle. Chief Justice Marshall, with his tall, gaunt
figure bent over as if to catch the slightest whisper, the deep furrows
of his cheek expanded with emotion, and eyes suffused with tears; Mr.
Justice Washington at his side with his small emaciated frame, and
countenance more like marble than I ever saw on any human being . . ."

Of the court's decision Chancellor Kent wrote that "it did more
than any other single act . . . to throw an impregnable barrier around
all rights . . . derived from the grant of government, and to give . . .
inviolability to the literary, charitable, religious and commercial institutions of our Country."

On the day the court handed down its decision Joseph Hopkinson
sent a letter to President Brown of the college. "I would," he wrote,
"have an inscription over the door of your building, 'Founded by
Eleazar Wheelock, refounded by Daniel Webster.'"

III. By Dint of Labor

SETH HUBBELL would have been better off if he had never chosen to move to Vermont. This Connecticut son of misfortune was the father of five girls under ten. It is doubtful if his troubles in moving north would have been any fewer if he had had the help of five boys over ten.

In February 1789, accompanied by his wife and two eldest daughters, an ox team and a horse, he left Connecticut for the Vermont town of Wolcott, where he had spent the previous summer clearing the wilderness. Within a hundred miles of his goal one of the oxen "failed," as he described it in his autobiography. Unhitching the ailing beast he harnessed himself to the yoke in its place and labored slowly forward until he reached a point where the sick animal refused to go any further. Forced to leave his ox without provision for its food in the care of a man in Johnson, he forged ahead to Esq. McDaniel's in Hyde Park, where the road ended. Eight miles ahead in deep woods under four feet of snow lay Wolcott—his destination.

Hubbell was now forced to do something about the sick ox back in Johnson. In Cambridge he found a man who would give him some hay. Loading it on his back a bundle at a time, he trudged back and forth daily to Johnson, five miles away, for ten days. On the tenth day the ox died. Returning to Hyde Park he made preparations, with another family named Taylor, for an assault on the trackless forest, which took place April 6 on snowshoes. In this manner the first settlers founded the town of Wolcott, eighteen miles from the nearest settlement with the exception of two families in Hyde Park. Hubbell had no money to get food or equipment; yet he managed to keep his family alive on moose meat bought from an Indian and carried five miles on his own back, and a half-bushel of wheat received in exchange for an animal skin.

The growing season of 1789 allowed mere subsistence in the settled southern towns of Vermont. In the untamed northern area even day-to-day survival was uncertain. With a great deal of pain Hubbell was forced to ration his daughters' food—he now had all five of them in Wolcott. Yet if food had been his only problem life would have been much simpler. He had thought that fifty acres would be given to him for helping settle the town, but now he found that he had to buy his land and sacrifice his few animals, including a treasured cow, in payment. In the fall he was fortunate enough to secure a second cow, which he reported was lost the following June in a "singular accident." This cow had had a calf which died the next fall "by being choked." The fate of three other cattle he had obtained was equally black. One was killed while fighting, another was found dead in the yard and the third, a young bull, was "hooked" by his neighbor's ox. Hubbell had heard that a merchant in Haverhill was buying snake-root, so with his two eldest daughters he "dug and dried a horse-load and carried this new commodity to the merchant but this was like most hearsay reports . . . he knew nothing about this strange article, and would not even venture to make an offer; but after a long conference I importuned with the good merchant to give me a three year old heifer for my roots. I drove her home and with joy she was welcomed to my habitation." This cow survived.

Hubbell had first arrived in Wolcott armed only with an ax and an old hoe, with which he managed to clear two acres of forest. When he was too tired to work he would catch a trout from the waters of the Lamoille River flowing beside his clearing; broiling it over coals he would eat it and then set to work again. He could not obtain a single potato plant. He secured eight quarts of seed corn by swapping it for two and a half yards of whitened linen at a neighbor's twenty miles away. The corn froze in an early frost. The second summer he went to help with the harvest near Lake Champlain, where he earned a half-bushel of green wheat. After a variety of delays and disappointments he returned with it to his starving family. "I . . . was welcomed home with tears," he wrote. "My wife baked a cake, and my children again tasted bread."

The next winter he secured twelve bushels of corn, as many of potatoes, and one of wheat, obtained largely on credit. The Cambridge man from whom he purchased the grain kindly volunteered to carry it to the mill. The miller not only offered to grind it toll-free, but loaned him his oxen to transport the heavy load to Hyde Park. At the same time Hubbell agreed to carry a half-hogshead tub to Johnson for another man. The month was March, it was raining and the ice was rotten on the tributaries of the Lamoille. He reached Brewster's Branch with his sled, potatoes, grain, oxen and half-hogshead tub, to find the river deep, fast-running and nearly free of ice. Leaving half the bags on shore, he placed the other half in the tub and led the oxen into the water. Soaked to the middle and shocked with cold, he reached the opposite bank. There he emptied the tub, put it on the sled again and started back across the stream. However the tub had no weight now and the force of the current swept it off the sled and carried it twenty rods downstream, with Hubbell holding on to it grimly. Finally he struggled to the shore and returned with the tub to the waiting oxen, where he filled it with the rest of the grain and crossed safely. After traveling three or four miles he put up for the night.

The next morning he came to the Lamoille, which was covered with ice. The thaw had weakened it but he still considered it safe. When he was about halfway across, the ice began to settle under the oxen. Hubbell jumped from the sled, pulled out the pin that held the yoke, and managed to drag the sled back to safety on the shore. By the time he returned to the oxen they had sunk down with the ice and were now swimming in the icy current.

"I could do nothing but stand and see them swim round—sometimes they would be nearly out of sight, nothing scarcely but their horns to be seen—they would then rise and struggle to extricate themselves from their perilous situation. I called for help in vain; and to fly for assistance would have been imprudent and fatal. Notwithstanding my unhappy situation, and the manner by which I came by the oxen &c. I was not terrified in the least—I felt calm and composed;—at length the oxen swam up to where I stood and laid their heads on the ice at my feet. I immediately took the yoke from off their necks; they lay still till the act was performed, and then returned to swimming as before. By this time they had made an opening in the ice as much as two rods across. One of them finally swam to the down stream side, and in an instant, as if lifted out of the water, he was on his side on the ice, and got up and walked off; the other swam to the same place and was out in the same way. I stood on the opposite side of the opening and saw with astonishment every movement. I then thought, and the impression is still on my mind, that they were helped by supernatural means; most certainly no natural course could produce an effect like this: that a heavy ox six and a half feet in girth, can of his own natural strength heave himself out of the water on his side on the ice, is too extraordinary to reconcile to a natural cause:—that in the course of Divine Providence events do take place out of the common course of nature, that our strongest reasoning cannot comprehend, is impious to deny; though we acknowledge the many chimeras of superstition, ignorance and barbarism in the world; and when we are eye witnesses to such events, it is not for us to doubt, but to believe and tremble."

By dint of labor also far beyond the natural and ordinary, Hubbell managed to carve a farm and a living for his family out of the wilderness.

In 1806 his wife and one daughter died in a sickness that swept through the entire family. Because of debts resulting from the epidemic he lost his hard-won farm. Nevertheless he was permitted to stay on it and work the land. He married again and had seventeen children in all, including thirteen daughters, forty-seven grandchildren, and, up to the time he wrote the sketch of his life, six great-grandchildren, "making," he recorded, "my posterity seventy souls."

IV. The Caliphs of Cumberland

E VEN after the English Crown freed the corrugated land between Lake Champlain and the Connecticut from the claims of the Dutch and the French, his various Majesties never knew just what to do about it. The Allen brothers trooped north out of Litchfield County, Connecticut, in the early 1770s and relieved first the Crown, then the states of New Hampshire and New York from the responsibility of deciding. Their struggles to found the Republic of Vermont are well chronicled. Although the Allens deserve the upstage-center treatment history has accorded them, their operations obscure a comedy of errors that took place in the valley of the Connecticut before, during, and after the Revolutionary War.

In addition to the pamphlet war of Eleazar Wheelock for a Connecticut valley state with its capital at Hanover, there was also the thunder of Ethan Allen's forge as he hammered the Green Mountain lands into a republic. Deep in Vermont along the Connecticut's west bank there were distraught groups of Yorkers who fancied that they were living in the state of New York. Then there was the New Hampshire government at Exeter, which claimed that its western boundary was Lake Champlain.

The King raised the curtain on the first of many acts and countless scenes in 1764, when he decided that the orphan terrain between the lake and river belonged to New York. Four years later New York organized the New Hampshire Grants into a county called Cumberland, and sent in its officers and magistrates. John Wentworth, the indignant governor of New Hampshire—whose portly Uncle Benning had first laid out townships and granted the land in these western hills—resolved somehow to get even.

There were abundant straight pines of first growth in Cornish and Windsor—more than enough to meet the demands of his Majesty's shipyards—and Uncle Benning had not previously made an issue of cutting trees. Thus the settlers who had received their grants from New Hampshire had been busy in the clearings, and the logs were piling up on the riverbank, awaiting their turn at the sawmills. But now that New York had moved in, John Wentworth, governor and also surveyor-general of his Majesty's woods, saw a chance to make political capital across the river in the busy forests of the Grants.

Captain William Dean and his sons William, Jr., and Willard, were partisans of New York in the log-house community of Windsor, which was overwhelmingly sympathetic to New Hampshire. In the fall of 1768 Dean, with his sons, was busy felling pines, some of them reportedly oversize. His neighbors informed Governor Wentworth what the three Yorkers were doing and in January 1769 Wentworth hurried from Portsmouth through three hundred miles of snowbound forests to the site of Dean's operations. Tranquilly passing on the way piles of illegitimate logs cut by settlers faithful to New Hampshire, the governor viewed with an alien glare Dean's fallen pines. Finding three oversize logs, he started to prosecute at once through the Admiralty Courts.

In the absence of Captain Dean, William, Jr., and Willard were arrested and marched to New York, where their father joined them to await trail by the Admiralty Court. The political overtones of their case were soon to be heard. Wentworth knew that the English admiralty, with courts independent of New York or any province, would judge the dispute. He hoped it would find Dean guilty under the terms of the New Hampshire land patents. "If a patent issued by New Hampshire was valid enough to deprive Dean of his land, it was also valid enough to sustain a New Hampshire land title." This was what Wentworth was thinking. What he did not suspect was that John Kempe, New York proctor in the admiralty, also owned land in Cumberland County, as did many of his friends. Thus Kempe was as much against having the case come to trial as Wentworth was for it.

The case was tried in a stalemated and sterile atmosphere. Dean was fined £850 which he never paid. He and his sons served a jail sentence that was no hardship owing to the sympathy and aid of fellow Yorkers. The admiralty, paying the costs of the case, failed to judge whether Dean's land was properly New York or properly New Hampshire. Unless Wentworth was merely satisfied to decrease the number of New York sympathizers on the west bank of the Connecticut by three, his efforts must have given him scant satisfaction.

In such a way, at any rate, did the felling of a few oversize pines by three obscure woodsmen introduce the first episodes of a tumultuous border war in the valley of the Connecticut. Inflammatory incidents followed each other until, in 1772, the embattled counties between New York and New Hampshire were in a ferment. In May of that year Westminster was selected as the seat of New York power in Cumberland County, and a spot near the meetinghouse was picked as a site for the courthouse. On a wide avenue between the hills and the river the clapboarded building went up, its hewn timbers supporting a gambrel roof and a cupola. Forty feet square, with a twelve-foot aisle through the middle of the first story, the completed structure housed a tavern, bar and jail, besides the spacious courtroom on the second floor.

Near the courthouse was the Congregational church, whose ponderous sounding board above the pulpit had been described as "a massive affair—like a stemless toadstool." In front of the pulpit were the deacons' benches, with long whips conveniently at hand for driving out Sunday-meeting dogs. In a small room under the pulpit, the people of Westminster stored the village powder and lead, and were thus simultaneously prepared for any eventuality, whether in heaven or on earth.

The building of the courthouse raised the temperature of New Hampshire partisans. Here in wood and glass stood undeniable proof of New York's will to administer the affairs of Cumberland County. In this building the tight-lipped clique of New York magistrates now plotted vengeance against the obstreperous claimants of New Hampshire, not caring if their cases were maljudged or their laws maladministered so long as they weakened the opposition. The judges and their minions labeled the people "the mob" and the settlers under New Hampshire called the judges "the court party" and "Tories." It became evident, as the early 1770s progressed, that there was more here than a fight for land. New York, a stronghold of British colonial government, was trying to force an alien and aristocratic philosophy of large landholding on a county of small farmers raised in independence and rebellion.

By 1775 the General Assembly of New York had rejected the Continental Congress, while the New Hampshire faction of wayward Cumberland County adopted it with enthusiasm, promising henceforth to have no dealings with any colonial province in North America. They meant specifically, of course, that they would have no dealings with New York.

Early in March of 1775 forty men appeared in Chester at the house of Judge Chandler and advised him to suspend the court, to which he replied that there was a murder case which ought to be tried. The men said that they suspected the court was planning to sit under the armed protection of the New York sheriff. Chandler promised that there would be no guns at Westminster, and with this assurance the forty men departed. At first they resolved to take Chandler's word that the court would use no force, but hearing rumors that the Tories intended to plant armed guards in the courthouse, they decided to take possession of the building themselves.

The Tories, now aware of the intentions of "the mob" or Whigs, determined to take countermeasures. On March 13, the day before the session was scheduled to begin, the high sheriff began to recruit men from as far south as Brattleboro, and soon had assembled twenty-five followers, armed with clubs. As they marched north, others carrying rifles joined them. Meanwhile anti-Yorkers had gathered in Westminster. Seizing sticks from Azariah Wright's woodpile on the afternoon of the thirteenth, they entered the courthouse one hundred strong, planning to remain there throughout the night. Shortly before sunset the New York sheriff marched into town from the south with his posse of sixty or seventy men, halted in front of the courthouse door and commanded the inmates to get out. There was no reply.

The sheriff then ordered a proclamation of the King to be read, which he followed with an ultimatum that unless the mob quit the building within fifteen minutes he would "blow a lane" through them. The defenders answered that they planned to stay but that the Yorkers could come in if they left their guns outside. They said that since their intentions were peaceful they would be glad to have a parley with the sheriff. Had the sheriff, they wanted to know, come for war? Samuel Gale, clerk of the court, waved his pistol and shouted: "Damn the parley with such damned rascals but by this!" A heavy exchange of oaths followed.

"You'll be in hell before morning!" warned one of the sheriff's party.

"If you try to come into the building," hollered a carpenter from Dummerston, "you'll be in the same place in fifteen minutes!"

The sheriff's party withdrew briefly. Seeing this, three Whigs presently came out for a conference with the Yorkers. When they were again told that they were "damned rascals," they returned to the courthouse. Later the defenders received Judge Chandler and asked whether he would meet their spokesmen to discuss the opening of the court. The judge said that the question was whether or not the King's business should be done, and that he could not discuss that. Admitting that the Tories had brought rifles without his consent, he promised to disarm them and agreed that the Whigs should occupy the building until morning when the court would receive their arguments. Thus assured, the defenders emerged from the courthouse, leaving only a few men on guard. The New York sheriff now quickly rounded up his force and arrested all the Whigs he could find, after which he and his men repaired to the royal inn to celebrate the coup. Here they drank heavily to George III and castigated the rebels of New England for their hostility to such edicts as the Stamp Act.

Hours later the sheriff sent small groups, properly bolstered by punch and inflammatory talk, out of the inn and up the hill to the courthouse. They moved forward stealthily under cover but their bayonets caught the light of a low moon. Realizing they were discovered, the sheriff announced that he would enter by force if necessary, and he climbed up the steps to the door. The guard pushed him back but he and his men forced their way up the steps again. The sticks from Azariah Wright's woodpile now began to fall about the Yorkers' heads and shoulders, with little effect, however, except to enrage the rum-laden attackers. The sheriff ordered his men to fire. Three triggers were pulled and the answering bullets passed over the guards' heads and entered the ceiling of the first floor. The second volley, which was lower, forced the defenders back into the interior. The Tories now surged into the building, firing and slashing their way with rifles and swords, and in the darkness of the passageways within "did most cruelly mammoc" the small defending guard. The battle was brief. Ten Whigs were wounded, seven made prisoners and a few escaped through a side entrance.

The Tories now crowded into the bar on the first floor and continued their drinking, the jailer filling their bowls until morning. The wounded were thrown into two cold cells where they suffered throughout the night, enduring the drunken taunts of the victors. Daniel Houghton from Dummerston lay on the floor, mortally shot. Riddled by five bullets from Tory guns, William French, a twenty-one-year-old farmer, was dragged, still living, into the crowded cell. Through the bars the Tories shouted that there should be forty more like him— that his friends would be in hell before the next night. Even as he fought for his last few breaths, they made "sport for themsleves at his dying motions."

The court opened on schedule the next morning. It adjourned until three—then adjourned forever. By afternoon four hundred men from both sides of the river had converged upon Westminster. They liberated the prisoners, seized the Tories, judges and accomplices and herded them into the courtroom where the blood of last night's skirmish was still wet on the floor. Spreading into the hinterlands, the news of the preceding night's events brought a multitude of angry farmers to Westminster. One man announced with a fiendish grin that "his flesh crawled to be tomahawking." Some wanted to burn down the courthouse and string up the sheriff, but Colonel Benjamin Bellows, for whom Bellows Falls is named, insisted that the prisoners be protected, and began an orderly investigation. While this was going on, Robert Cockran came over the mountains with forty Green Mountain Boys, and five hundred additional soldiers fully armed crowded into the village. Fortunately their tempers subsided to a degree that allowed fair treatment of the prisoners. A committee representing all factions inside and outside Cumberland County ruled that the New York leaders be lodged in the Northampton, Massachusetts, jail pending a fair trial. Meanwhile they were put on public exhibition in the courthouse to be viewed by hundreds of people.

The astonishing news that William French and Daniel Houghton had died of their wounds swept over the countryside until not a backwoodsman in Cumberland County remained ignorant of the manner of their death. But no one in those early days of March 1775 knew that the rifles which spoke that night at the courthouse under a waning moon were among the first to be fired in the American Revolution.

The rutted streets and modest frame houses of Windsor were dark with the twilight of a summer storm and the representatives could not go home. They stayed through the afternoon and heard the constitution read, paragraph by paragraph. By the time the storm had carried its noisy baggage of thunder, lightning and rain beyond the bordering mountains of the Connecticut, the constitution had been adopted and Vermont was a republic.

The drama of that July afternoon in 1777 might have produced stirring events in the Connecticut valley but, in retrospect at least, the tenor of the following years was that of low comedy.

"We . . . shall forward to the Assembly of the pretended State of Vermont," declared Cumberland County Yorkers, "a protest against erecting the Grants into an independent government . . . and also one copy thereof to his Excellency Governor Clinton, and another to the press for publication. . . . We think it the duty of every friend of independence of America, more especially in the Grants, to use their most strenuous efforts to suppress or check this offspring of anarchy . . ."

At the height of the American Revolution the "New York malcontents," as Ethan Allen called them, were refusing to share in the new government. They were still disrupting sessions of the courts with bludgeon-carrying posses, declining to pay taxes or to serve in the state militia.

The greatest single troublemaker in Cumberland County—a man who perhaps more than any other kept the Republic of Vermont from early statehood—was plump, bald Charles Phelps, "a notorious cheat and nuisance to mankind," according to Governor Chittenden. Phelps had secured a grant from the governor of New Hampshire and moved to Marlboro in 1764, when it was just a name on the land. For some years he supported the New Hampshire cause, saying, "I would as soon put manure in my pocket as a commission from New York." During the Revolution, though, he switched to New York. Phelps had an incisive legal mind whose edge he kept sharpened in the largest private library for miles around. He made the fullest possible use of his research—four hours of argument in the courtroom, they say, would just bring him "to the threshold of his argument." Phelps's everyday dress was slovenly but on such occasions as his appearances before Congress, representing Cumberland County for New York, he wore "the finest linen, frilled at wrists and bosom with the most costly cambrics; golden buckles to his stock, costly gems for buttons to his wristbands; deep blue broadcloth coat of the finest and firmest material; buff vest and small clothes, with bands at the knee secured with golden buckles. . . . And then the wig: that ample, full-bottomed, full-powdered wig, of the style of Louis XIV or George II, to which add the brilliant on his finger and the rings in his ears; the whole being surmounted with the tasteful *chapeau-de-bras* with buttons of gold . . ."

Phelp's interests radiated from his library, which filled a room at the end of the first floor of the preposterously large building in which he lived. Raised between 1770 and 1772 at the expense of the proprietors of Marlboro, it became known as "the meetinghouse," though the only people who met there were the members of Phelps's family. Standing forlornly in the middle of a stump-infested field, the house boasted, besides the library on the first floor, a windswept hall with folding doors at each end. There were also four sleeping rooms, a dining hall, kitchen and parlor. Horsepower mills for grinding corn had been installed in the basement, while on the second and third floors there were unfinished dormitories and lecture rooms for a proposed college. In the interim this section was filled with hay. There were no windows or chimneys. The whole was barnlike, drafty and ill-furnished, but an eminently satisfactory establishment in the eyes of the peculiar individual who dwelt therein.

When Phelps's wife, the mother of seven children, died in 1775 the squire plucked another from an old Boston family named Eustis. Apparently Phelps first sought the hand of this lady's aunt. She declined but suggested that he meet a visiting niece, the widow of a man named Kneeland. An introduction was immediately arranged and Phelps at once proposed marriage. The young lady, blushing from shock, requested a week to think it over, but Phelps made it clear that it was now or not at all. After an interval of modest dickering the lady agreed, and this notice appeared forthwith:

"Married, by the Rev. Mr. ――――, according to the forms of the venerable Church of England, the Honorable Charles Phelps, late one of his Majesty's Justices of the Common Pleas, *a gentleman of uncommon politeness,* to the interesting and accomplished Mrs. Anstis Eustis Kneeland, relict of Mr. Kneeland, late of Boston, printer, after a romantic courtship of 24 hours."

With her silks, gold bracelets, chain and jeweled locket around her graceful neck, and "heavy establishment in her girdle," Anstis was thus spirited away to Phelps's lonely and eccentric meetinghouse in

Marlboro, there to become his partner in uncertainty and strife.

Prior to 1781 Phelps's political agitation, first for Massachusetts and later New York, had not boomeranged. On January 1 of that year, however, he was drafted. He refused either to serve or pay the fine, and when Abel Stockwell attempted to force payment, he was vigorously thrashed by Phelps and his son, Timothy. Stockwell returned, seized Phelps's cows, placed a £20 fine on Timothy and warned that if this was not paid, Timothy would be subject to the whipping post, which he shortly erected in Marlboro. While his trial for assault on Stockwell was pending, the state seized sixty acres of his land. When his case came up in August Phelps defended himself in a long-winded and self-righteous manner, saying he had attacked Stockwell in order to protect his property, which was being "wrenched from him by force and arms." He declared that he was a subject of New York, without protection, and therefore by the "laws of nature and nations" had to defend himself as best he could. The court fined him $500.

This caused Phelps neither sorrow nor repentance. He redoubled his activities on behalf of New York with countless letters, remonstrances and memorials such as: *Reasons to Induce His Excellency the Governor, Judge Morris, the Attorney-General and the Council of Appointment to go into Cumberland and Gloucester Counties to Appoint Civil and Military officers for the complete organizing them, and instituting civil and military government and Courts of Justice, as fully to all intents and purposes as in any other counties in the State.* If New York bolstered its rightful authority in Cumberland County with force, it would unquestionably "sink the hearts and deaden the resolution of all the Vermont party; intimidate their guilty and dejected minds; enfeeble their resolutions against us, and wholly enervate all their ambitious, indignant, avaricious and despotic designs, so arrogantly formed against us . . ."

New York at last decided to act and appointed Phelps and fourteen others as justices of the peace in Cumberland County, with power to arrest threatening troublemakers and to scrutinize armed forces raised against the New York inhabitants. Timothy Phelps, who was as ardent a Yorker as his father and the possessor of a vicious temper, received the post of high sheriff of the county. One day soon after his appointment, while he was feeding his oxen with a pitchfork, a Vermont constable arrived with his deputies to attach the oxen for taxes. Timothy raised the pitchfork and, when the constable kept on coming, bashed him to the ground with a single blow while the deputies retreated in terror.

With mounting confidence Charles Phelps wrote the New York governor that the Vermonters "dare not meddle with us Yorkers," but suggested that General Washington order four cannon sent to Brattleboro to strengthen their position. In June of 1782 Vermont passed a law to abolish the Cumberland County faction. Phelps must have known that the ice on which he skated was thin, because the Yorker towns at a meeting in July sent Governor Clinton a plea that the New York militia be sent in case the Vermonters crossed the mountains.

On Monday morning, September 9, two hundred militiamen, assembled by exasperated Vermont under Ethan Allen, marched for the houses of the blacklisted Yorker agitators. A detachment of forty under Ira Allen proceeded to the Marlboro house of Timothy Phelps. With her maid, her son, John, and a ten-year-old almshouse boy named Caleb Pond, Mrs. Phelps was doing her washing in Mill Brook when the mounted Vermont posse, glittering with swords and led by Colonel Williams, a neighbor of Phelps, splashed into the fordway. Mrs. Phelps came resolutely forward on seeing the colonel, a dashing Revolutionary soldier who had been selected by Allen to lead the attack because of his familiarity with the neighborhood.

"Colonel Williams," she said, "you grieve and amaze me. I had not expected such meanness and treachery from a friend like you." While Williams blurted out an apology, the almshouse boy slipped off unnoticed to warn Timothy Phelps, who betook himself to a hiding place. Colonel Williams had meanwhile shamefacedly withdrawn and left Allen and the posse guideless, but they shortly found the house. Riding around their target several times with military pomp, they dismounted and, finding the front door bolted, forced it in. When Mrs. Phelps returned she found the house filled with soldiers. "Cowardly miscreants!" she cried, and began a scornful harangue. With Phelps nowhere to be found and Mrs. Phelps chastising them, the soldiers began to fidget and to glance uneasily at one another. When they asked her to lead them to her husband, she took up a heavy kitchen fire shovel and started chasing them around the room, shouting to them to get out. All of the posse, and even Mrs. Phelps, sensed the ludicrous in the mêlée that followed and they were soon laughing heartily. As soon as Mrs. Phelps assured them her husband was not at home they bowed respectfully and departed.

By the time the sun went down, however, Timothy Phelps was in Vermont hands. According to tradition, Ethan Allen on riding up was confronted by a freshet of abuse from the tongue of Phelps who loudly asserted his authority as the high sheriff of Cumberland County. He condemned the actions of the dashing Vermont leader and ordered Ethan and his men to disperse. When Phelps had finished, Ethan, astride his horse, reached over, knocked the Yorker's hat off and ordered his men to "take the damned rascal off."

With the most irritating of the New York partisans in the bag, Ethan and his force started for Brattleboro that night, only to run afoul of a company of Guilfordites who were lying in wait by the side of the road. They fired when the Vermont force approached and compelled Ethan to halt and consider. Convening in a war council, he and his lieutenants discussed every possibility including open warfare, with the sacrifice of one of the prisoners for every man killed by the ambushing Yorkers. Allen decided against a pitched battle. With his coat torn by a bullet, he hiked back to Guilford on foot. Here he gathered the people and in a deathly solemn manner announced: "I, Ethan Allen, do declare that I will give no quarter to the man, woman or child who shall oppose me, and unless the inhabitants of Guilford peacefully submit to the authority of Vermont, I swear I will lay it desolate as Sodom and Gomorrah, by God!"

The words of this already legendary figure undermined the sagging morale of the Yorkers, and while they fled in terror Ethan's men rounded up one hundred fifty cattle and many more sheep and hogs, which they herded out of town. They emptied the barns of grain and left behind them warrants for the arrest of any troublesome householders they couldn't find at the time of the raid. Ethan now resumed his march to Brattleboro, the rallying point for all the parties of militia. There the prisoners were sorted and sent to the Westminster jail under a guard to whom Ethan had given permission to fire if attacked.

Though Timothy Phelps was now on the wrong side of the bars, he informed his keepers of his right to command the jail; but his words attracted little attention. A swiftly convened Vermont court decided that the godless Yorkers were guilty of insurrection and ruled that their estates be sold and that the prisoners be escorted to the border, never to return under penalty of death. Meanwhile the condition of the jailed Yorkers was wretched—"a savage way to support a government," admitted Ethan, but it seemed the only way to maintain the authority of the state.

Unfortunately for the Vermont militia Timothy Phelps's pompous father, Charles, had thus far managed to escape Ethan's dragnet, though the state had entered his house and destroyed pamphlets and documents containing inflammatory propaganda. The rest of his valuable library, which included a large number of innocent volumes, was sold at auction. While his son was held at Westminster, Charles Phelps managed to slip out of the state and beyond the reach of the posse detailed for his capture. He went to Poughkeepsie and then, having received an appointment from Governor Clinton as Cumberland County's New York agent in Congress, he proceeded to Philadelphia, where he besieged the representatives "with missives supplicatory, missives memorial and missives remonstrative." He petitioned Congress for money and clothes, outlining how he had been pursued by a body of light infantry which had very nearly captured him; that he was now destitute and unable to return home. Congress dallied over the decision, for it did not wish to risk serious trouble between Vermont and New York. Sustained by funds from the latter state Phelps remained in Philadelphia for several months, a bee in the Congressional bonnet, doing certain damage to the New York cause in Cumberland County. At length, however, Congress decided that the Yorkers should be permitted to return to Cumberland and to regain control of their estates. Despite this act of Congress, Phelps had to petition the governor of Vermont for permission to return home. Hoping that the unruly Yorker was at last ready to quiet down, Chittenden issued orders that he be allowed to enter the state unmolested.

It became clear to Phelps, following his return, that Vermont intended to do nothing about Congress's resolution that the Yorkers' confiscated property be restored. He therefore confronted the Vermont authorities, brashly demanding the return of his lost property. They rejected this petition with disdain and reminded him that there was still a warrant out for his arrest. Even now, rather than subside, Phelps went to Guilford where the Yorker population was still comfortably large, and by mid-1783 he had begun to repeat all his old crimes against Vermont. On February 24th of that year the Vermont assembly had passed a law allowing the agitators in exile to return under certain conditions, chiefly that they would dwell in peace as Vermonters. Timothy Phelps returned to his farm but had not plowed many furrows before he could no longer endure the thought that the members of the court who tried, jailed and exiled him were still sitting in his home town. He put on his old uniform as New York high sheriff of the county, strode into the courthouse, and in a bellicose speech censured the judges as usurpers of authority, illegally holding court. He directed them to reimburse him for all the indignities which he had suffered and to restore every farthing of his property which the pretended republic of Vermont had seized. Drawing some papers from his pocket he started reading with great ceremony the recent resolves of Congress, when Judge Moses Robinson cut him off.

"What supercilious arrogance have we here?" the judge asked. "Sheriff, take that disorderly man into custody. We are not subject to the authority of Congress!"

Sheriff Elkanah Day, surprised if not confounded, failed to act before Phelps's booming voice was again filling the courtroom. "In the name and by the authority of the state of New York and of the Continental Congress, I command the unlawful assemblage before me to disperse!"

"Sheriff," proclaimed Judge Robinson after a momentary pause, "do your duty! Imprison the convicted traitor."

Realizing that his coup had failed and that the jig was up, for Day had drawn his sword, Phelps turned to the sheriff and said, "What is your will, sir?"

"You are my prisoner. Disarm yourself," commanded the sheriff.

Phelps now turned to the large audience; unbuckling his sword, he announced: "Fellow citizens of Cumberland County, your sheriff is deserted; his lawful authority is disobeyed; I yield to brute force." Adding a warning that terrible retribution from Congress would attend this act of the court, Phelps dramatically surrendered his sword to the sheriff, who led him away. The populace of Marlboro, almost entirely pro-Vermont in sympathy, followed the prisoner through the streets on the way to the guardhouse, hurling taunts and catcalls after him. Some thought that the noose would do him justice, for he had been ordered never to return to Vermont under penalty of death. He was conducted to the Bennington jail, where he took up the pen as the only weapon at his command, to inform the governor of New York of the "nasty, scandalous prison" and the "vile nest of detestable, seditious Vermonters . . . I meet with insult on insult. Vermont authorities have seized and sold all my goods, chattels and estate, and they keep me close confined in jail without any kind of support. My money is all gone and I live upon the charity of my friends. My family are put to the greatest straits. My health decays, and when hot weather comes I don't know what I shall do. The officers of Vermont tell me that I shall be in jail to all eternity unless I petition to their governor. I tell them I will see them all damned before I will [unless] Congress shall make them a state. It is to my own masters I stand or fall."

Ethan Allen occasionally dropped in at the prison to pay his sarcastic respects. He boasted that he could go to Albany and be head monarch in no time and that, furthermore, he had a good mind to do it. "Congress cannot release you," asserted the Vermont leader. "Congress can't break up states, much less this state. . . . You have called on your god Clinton till you are tired. Call now on your god Congress, and they will answer you as Clinton has done." Ethan advised him to appeal to Governor Chittenden. This Timothy with bitter reluctance was at last forced to do, as his prison rations were inferior and his health was rapidly deteriorating. At length, after promising allegiance to the Vermont Council at Arlington, he was permitted to leave the jail.

But Timothy Phelps was not yet ready to subside. Freedom presented him with tempting new projects of resistance, and with his father he soon resumed his old craft as New York agitator and pamphleteer. One January night in 1784, while he was visiting his brother Charles in Hadley, Massachusetts, a posse of Vermonters came across the border and forced the door to his brother's house. Mistaking Charles for Timothy, they pinned the former to the floor, but while they were binding him his wife appeared to identify Charles as an innocent victim. Timothy now appeared. They seized him with the intention of carrying him off to the jail in Bennington which he had so recently vacated. As soon as they had departed with Timothy in tow, Charles notified the Massachusetts sheriff in Hampshire County, who immediately put thirty armed men under Phelps's command. This force, overtaking the Vermonters at Bloody Brook in Deerfield, burst into the house where they were having breakfast and shouted: "Where are these damned Vermonters?" Thinking Yorkers were after them, the Vermont posse roughly resisted. After the fray was well started the Massachusetts sheriff identified himself and the Vermonters stopped fighting at once. They allowed themselves to be taken back to Hadley, where they were fined for riotous conduct. Meanwhile, however, the sheriff had learned all of the background and ended by promising the Vermonters help in any future action against their Yorker enemies.

While this was going on, the rising temper of the leaders of the Vermont republic found release in gathering the militia in numbers that threatened open warfare. Brattleboro on January 18 looked like a garrison. "The Sunday quiet was disturbed by the drum and fife and the church was deserted. . . . Bullets were moulded; guns prepared; belts burnished; buckles polished . . ." Early next morning when the assembled militiamen, three hundred strong, started on their march toward Guilford—that persistent carbuncle of Yorker sentiment—the snow, blown by a violent wind from the northwest, whitened their hair and the right side of their faces. The storm was still sweeping over the hills on the following day when the men reached Guilford. The sight of this grizzled force that had crossed the Alps of Vermont filled the Yorkers with fright. Though they had previously determined to fight to the last, they now ran while the Vermonters moved forward into the town, dislodging the last pockets of resistance in the various houses. The campaign halted for a day while the weary marchers warmed themselves at the fireplaces of their newly captured dwellings. On Wednesday morning they pushed forward to the home of Squire

Packard, one and a half miles from the Massachusetts line, where the Yorkers, concealed behind scattered hemlocks and maples, had rallied for a last-ditch defense. When the Vermonters moved up, Packard appeared in his doorway and advised Sergeant Silvanus Fisk, who was leading the attack, not to go beyond the near-by blacksmith shop or the Yorkers would shoot. Fisk ignored the warning and, as his men passed the shop, Yorker guns opened fire. Fisk fell with a ball through the stomach, and when a private near him asked if he was wounded, Fisk replied: "God bless you, don't ask any questions, but push on and kill some of the devils!" The Vermonters then surged forward and chased the Yorkers half a mile into Massachusetts.

When Ethan Allen arrived with reinforcements the Yorkers sent a flag from over the line, promising an end to their resistance and begging to be allowed to return to their homes. Allen wanted to enter Massachusetts and take them all prisoner, but he didn't quite dare. Thus the campaign ended.

"We are driven from our habitations, our houses are plundered. Our possessions taken from us. We are in a very miserable situation," complained the Yorkers to Governor Clinton, whose embarrassed administration now tried to extract from Congress an opinion on the disputed area. In February Timothy Phelps was once more in Philadelphia lobbying for a decision, but the responsible committee reported merely ". . . that upon the whole, it is the opinion of the committee that the most decided measures ought to be pursued, without loss of time, as well for the protection of our said suffering citizens, as for the peace and tranquillity of the said district."

Old Charles Phelps, again in jail at Bennington, petitioned the assembly for help, and when they let him out he at last took the oath of allegiance to the Republic of Vermont. A joint committee of the council and assembly reasoned that he had been a very troublesome character but that in early times when the country was being settled he had acted meritoriously. Thus they decided to return his estate to him. By 1785 it had become clear to the Yorkers in Cumberland County that Congress did not intend to decide about the disputed strip of land, but preferred to let nature take its course. Nature, in the form of the Allen party, had by then established a strong, well-regulated republic against which further resistance was the sheerest folly.

The advancing years mellowed Timothy Phelps who was now living on his Marlboro farm with a large family. Some of his colleagues in rebellion, however, moved within the borders of New York, whose officials, acknowledging these men as "sufferers," had granted them a special strip of land.

Charles Phelps, Esq., died in 1789 at the age of seventy-two, leaving behind him in the "meetinghouse" his beautiful and fine-mannered second wife—who later found a third husband. Though he had submitted to Vermont, Charles Phelps had never changed his mind. He dated his will at Marlboro "in the County of Cumberland in the state of New York."

V. The Case of the
Contrary Corpse

THERE was little about Manchester in 1788 to suggest the pristine white of today's Equinox House or the soft greens of lawn, garden and hedge. Manchester then was a raw and brawling frontier town in the land of Allen. It was a young village of farmers who had arrived to pit their backs against the stone-filled valley of the Battenkill, and their patience against the long winters in the shadow of Mount Equinox.

In 1788 four brothers named Boorn who had come from Massachusetts settled in the western part of the village. Of these Barney was a farmer and butcher. He built a garreted one-story house, married and raised a family of five children of whom three, Jesse, Stephen and Sally, were implicated in a murder mystery that rocked the whole state of Vermont. Sally married a mental incompetent named Russell Colvin, by whom she had two children. Colvin worked for his father-in-law, Barney Boorn, and lived with his family in Barney's house. Sally's brothers, Stephen and Jesse, resented the fact that she and Russell dwelt under the parental roof while they were obliged to go out and forage for a living as hired hands on neighboring farms. Relations between the Boorn brothers and Russell Colvin thus wavered between dislike and open hostility. From time to time hot words and even blows were exchanged, but in a hard-drinking town in a hard-drinking frontier state, no one paid much attention to this.

On May 10, 1812, Russell Colvin vanished. The community did not at first pay much attention, because Colvin was given to wandering off occasionally for no particular reason and returning quite as abruptly weeks or months later. But he usually took his son Lewis with him: this time he disappeared alone. Three years passed without a word from him. Even this might have been forgotten, or at least dismissed from the public mind, if Sally had not found that she was going to have a baby. A lawyer had advised her that while Russell was living she could not "swear" her unborn child on any other man for its support. For the purpose of maintaining the third addition to her family in her father's modest house (not, apparently, for covering up the indelicate matter of her promiscuity) she started to hunt for Russell.

Stephen and Jesse told Sally that she could proceed to swear the child on its natural father because they knew Russell was dead. Stephen remarked that Russell had gone to hell and that they had put him "where potatoes would not freeze." On one occasion Stephen had said that he wished both his brother-in-law and sister were dead. When a log pile burned up on the Boorn farm, and later when one of the barns went up in flames, townspeople speculated that the fires were set on purpose with the idea of destroying Colvin's hidden body. One of the neighborhood children had found Russell's hat in the field where he had last been seen working with Stephen and Jesse. Conjecture grew into suspicion and suspicion into certainty. The Boorns had murdered Russell Colvin.

Stephen, who had been the more outspoken about Colvin's going to hell and resting "where potatoes would not freeze," worried under the accusing eyes of his neighbors. If he had murdered Russell Colvin, he said, would he be likely to go around making such comments? What had really happened was that Colvin had been acting peculiarly that May day when they were taking stones out of the field. He had gone into the woods and that was the last they or anyone else had ever seen of him. This was one of the explanations advanced by the brothers. Another was that they were working on a different farm when Colvin disappeared. A third was that Stephen had killed a woodchuck which he had given to Colvin. Sally had cooked it for him, he had eaten it, and then had left the house never to be seen again. Actually, Sally had not even been in town when the woodchuck was killed, and the villagers well knew that the last time Colvin had been seen was when he had been working in the field with Jesse and Stephen. Meanwhile Jesse remained in town, but Stephen had moved to Denmark, New York, possibly to escape the cloud of suspicion that enveloped him in Manchester.

In the spring of 1819 Amos Boorn, uncle of Stephen and Jesse, had three visions one night—all of them the same. The following morning he related with astonishment that Colvin's ghost had appeared at his bedside three times, crying out each time that he had been murdered. The ghost had summoned Amos to follow him and, doing so, he had gone out into the field where Colvin had last been seen with Stephen and Jesse. Here the specter, before vanishing, had pointed out an old cellar hole about four feet square. Was this the place where potatoes wouldn't freeze? The pit was excavated at once. In the leaves and earth a button was found—also a jackknife, a penknife and some animal bones. The jackknife and button were brought to Sally Colvin. She described Russell's knife before she was allowed to examine this one, and proved beyond doubt that it was his. She said the buttons on his overcoat had a flower design on them, and when the dirt was rubbed away a similar design appeared. It was indeed a button from Colvin's overcoat.

This evidence strengthened the growing conviction that Colvin had been murdered by Stephen and Jesse Boorn. What apparently established the evil deed beyond doubt was the discovery made by a boy and his dog in a hollow stump not far from the cellar hole. After being attracted to the stump, the dog had begun to dig industriously at its base, and would pay no attention to the whistling and calling of his master. Finally he ran back and forth several times between his master and the stump. The boy, upon examination, found that the dog had scratched up some bones that looked as if they had been burned. The authorities were called, the rotted wood in the stump was carefully sifted and the bones taken away for examination. But the people needed no further proof that this was all that remained of Russell Colvin. The dream of Amos Boorn had been divinely inspired—the dog supernaturally directed to the stump. They were sure that the body had been burned when the barn was razed and that Stephen and Jesse had deposited the charred bones in the stump.

But the doctors, after exhuming a Mr. Sargent's amputated leg for comparison, finally agreed that the bones were not human. Only the toenails, also found in the stump, seemed to be human. An inquiry was overdue. Stephen Boorn was not called from New York, but Jesse was exhaustively questioned. Nothing additional suggestive of murder was revealed during the first four days of the inquiry, but on the fifth day, when Jesse saw the jackknife, he became highly excited and with trembling voice stated that he thought that Stephen had killed Russell Colvin. He said that there had been a quarrel in a field called the Glazier lot, and that Stephen had hit Russell on the back of the head with a club.

Jesse was locked in jail and Stephen was seized in Denmark, New York, and put in irons. On the way to Manchester he was advised that Jesse had informed against him and he was strongly urged to confess. Stephen protested his innocence. In Manchester Colvin's son said he saw Stephen strike his father in the field and that he had been scared and had run away. After talking with Stephen, Jesse retracted his entire statement. By now there was no doubt whatever that there had been a murder and that the Boorn brothers had committed it. They were imprisoned to await trial before the grand jury in September 1819. Also sweltering in jail was Barney Boorn, their father, who had been accused of being an accessory to the crime.

Sympathy for the hapless, if stupid, Colvin was acute, and the public was impatient for the time when the noose should tighten about the necks of Jesse and Stephen. Frequently visited by neighbors, members of the clergy and officials, they were advised that if they made a full confession things would go better with them. Their sentences might be commuted to life imprisonment. Lemuel Haynes, a Negro minister highly respected throughout the state, offered his sympathy, advising them to be meekly resigned to whatever fate awaited them. When he alluded to the forbearance of Christ in the hands of His persecutors, Haynes reported that Stephen said: "I am as innocent as Jesus Christ! I don't mean that I am as guiltless as He was, I know I am a great sinner, but I am as innocent of killing Colvin as He was."

But on August 27, shortly before the trial, Stephen suddenly asked for pen and paper because he wished to make a confession. On the morning of May 10, he wrote, he had been fishing down at David Glazier's bridge. Then he went over and talked with Colvin in the near-by field where he was working with his son. Colvin pointed out how much he had been worth to his father-in-law. Stephen called him a damned fool and a little Tory, whereupon Russell hit him over the shoulder with a stout beech limb. Snatching the club from Colvin, Stephen hit his brother-in-law on the back of the head. As Russell slumped down, Stephen told his son to get his uncle John. The boy asked if his father was dead. Stephen answered that he was not and that he should not tell anyone that they had been fighting. At this point young Colvin ran away. Stephen, realizing that Russell was now dead, called out to the boy that his father had gone away. Then he carried the body to the corner of the fence near the cellar hole and covered it with briars. After dark he got some boards out of the barn and dug a shallow grave. Placing Colvin in it with the loose boards around him in the form of a box, he took Russell's jackknife and cut some bushes which he placed over the body. Then he put some more boards on top of the bushes and earth over the boards. Several seasons later, while digging potatoes, he noticed that the grave had been disturbed, so he dug up the bones, put them in a basket and secreted them under the stable floor. When the barn was burned he gathered up the remaining bones, threw the largest of them in the river and dropped the rest into the hollow stump, covering them with rotted wood.

His confession confirmed the long-standing suspicions of the public to the last detail. There now remained only the formality of the trial before the grand jury to convict and condemn to death a man who did not have the fear of God in his heart but had been "moved and seduced by the instigation of the devil."

The trial, which began in September in a small and overcrowded courthouse, moved in October to the Congregational church. New testimony was presented by one Silas Merrill, a forger who had been doing time in the same jail where the Boorns were imprisoned. Merrill declared that one day in June, before Stephen had been brought to Manchester from New York, Barney Boorn had visited Jesse at the prison. After the old man had gone away Jesse appeared much disturbed, and later in the middle of the night he had awakened Merrill to tell him that something had come in the window and was on the bed behind him. Jesse was frightened, Merrill said, and felt a compulsion to tell him about the murder. The clubbing had been as Stephen later described it in his written confession, but Colvin had not died from these blows, Jesse had assured Merrill. As Colvin lay prostrate old man Boorn came up and inquired of his sons if Colvin was dead yet. They said no, and he went away. Shortly he returned and, finding Colvin still living, he went away again. When he returned a third time and found that Colvin was still alive, the old man said: "Damn him!" Then Jesse took hold of Colvin by the feet, Stephen raised him by the shoulders and, with the old man helping them, they carried him to the cellar hole. Here the eldest Boorn took a small penknife and cut Colvin's throat. Soon he was dead and they buried him in the cellar. Two or three days later Stephen was wearing Colvin's shoes. Jesse, according to Merrill's account, advised him to take them off, as Sal would know the shoes, and Stephen had done so.

When Stephen arrived in irons from New York State, Jesse acquainted him with the fact that he had told Merrill about the murder. Stephen then informed Merrill that what Jesse had said was true, but they had now agreed that Stephen would take responsibility for the whole business and make a written confession. Because Colvin had attacked him first, it was thought likely that he would get off with a charge of manslaughter. Merrill testified that the other details were as Stephen had described them in his confession.

The jury found Stephen guilty of murder, and Jesse an accessory to it. Both were condemned to be hanged. The large assemblage found the verdict satisfactory and impatiently awaited the appointed day, January 28, 1820, when Colvin's death would be avenged. The public thought Barney Boorn should also have been sentenced, but evidence against him had not been conclusive and he had been discharged. The members of the Baptist church took reprisal by dismissing his innocent and unhappy wife from their fellowship. Meanwhile the sentences against Stephen and Jesse were appealed to the state legislature. Reviewing the entire trial, that body sustained the death verdict against Stephen, but commuted Jesse's sentence to life imprisonment.

Stephen, weeping in his cell as the fatal day drew near, now steadfastly denied that he was guilty of murder. Beseeching the lawyers and judges to do something in his behalf, he suggested that an advertisement for news of Colvin be placed in the newspapers. If Colvin had been murdered, they pointed out, this would be fruitless; but so vehemently did he profess his innocence that the following notice was run in the Rutland *Herald* on November 30, 1819:

MURDER. Printers of newspapers throughout the United States are desired to publish that Stephen Boorn of Manchester, in Vermont, is sentenced to be executed for the murder of Russell Colvin, who has been absent about seven years. Any person who can give information of said Colvin may save the life of the innocent by making immediate communication. Colvin is about five feet, five inches high, light complexion, light colored hair, blue eyes, about forty years of age. Manchester, Vermont, Nov. 25, 1819.

On the day the notice was run the editor of the *Herald* commented that, while the facts of the trial pointed clearly to the guilt of the accused, "we readily give publicity to the notice and hope our brother editors throughout the United States will copy it into their respective papers, for really it would be a happy event if by these means one could be raised from the dead, another saved from the gallows and another from the gloomy abode of the State's Prison for life."

The murder had received attention in the northcountry press and by word of mouth. Both combined to produce the astonishing events of the next few weeks.

On November 26 the New York *Evening Post* printed an article discussing the discovery of the murder through Amos Boorn's dream. It so happened that in the lobby of a New York hotel there were gathered together, in interested conversation about the article, several men including James Whelpley of New York, a former Manchester storekeeper who had known Colvin, and Taber Chadwick of Shrewsbury, New Jersey. Chadwick was absorbed by the discussion. His brother-in-law, William Polhemus of Dover, New Jersey, had a hired hand who he thought matched the description of Colvin. Returning home and checking further, he at once wrote the editor of the *Evening Post* that several years previously a man answering to the name of Russell Colvin had come to work in Monmouth County, where he and his brother-in-law resided. Colvin was still living there—a short, fast-talking man, now almost completely deranged, who occasionally made statements that established his former residence as Manchester, Vermont. Chadwick suggested that someone who had known Colvin should come and identify the man, if it were indeed he, and thereby save the lives of innocent men.

Seeing Chadwick's letter in the *Post* and recalling their discussion in the hotel lobby, James Whelpley immediately went to New Jersey and visited Chadwick's brother-in-law, Polhemus. The latter informed him that his hired man, who had originally gone under the name of Colvin but had since changed it, was working in the field under the illusion that the farm belonged to him. Rather than confront Colvin there, Whelpley decided to wait until he returned from work and by various stratagems prove his identity both to himself and to Polhemus. When the deranged man came in from the fields he stared at Whelpley with blank unfamiliarity. Already quite sure that this was the man he remembered from his Manchester storekeeping days, Whelpley called Colvin by name. The laborer replied that although this had once been his name, it was no longer—that he was now another man. Queried about Manchester, Colvin said he knew nothing about the place. When he was asked how he got the scar on his forehead, he replied that he was hurt while cutting wood on the mountain for a Manchester neighbor of Boorn's, whom he called by name. By adroit questioning, Whelpley established beyond the remotest doubt that the murdered man was alive and standing before him.

The next task was to take Colvin to Manchester, for nothing short of a personal appearance there would convince the authorities or the townspeople that he was still alive. But Colvin refused to go. Whelpley at length succeeded in decoying him to New York City with the help of a young lady. From New York he finally managed to get him on a northbound stage by telling him that he was returning to New Jersey by a circuitous route. Meanwhile news reached Manchester that Colvin was alive. This was hard, if not impossible, to believe. When Stephen Boorn heard it he was greatly shocked and seemed to feel that if Colvin were to appear, he himself would die.

Whelpley and Colvin arrived in southern Vermont on December 22, only thirty-seven days before Boorn was to have been hanged. When they reached Bennington the county court ceased its deliberations and trading was suspended in the shops. As word sped from house to house that Colvin had been resurrected, the inhabitants crowded into the streets. When he called certain former acquaintances by name all doubt was dispelled, and as the stage pounded north from Bennington the roadside was wild with excitement. When it reached Black's Tavern in Manchester the cry "Colvin has come!" rallied every man, woman and child.

Perhaps because the jailer suspected foul play, he conducted Stephen Boorn to the tavern with the chains still fastened to his feet.

"Why are you in chains?" asked Russell Colvin.

"Because they say I murdered you."

"You never hurt me," said Colvin. "Jess struck me with briar once, but it did not hurt me much."

Joy filled Manchester. A cannon saluted fifty times and prayers were offered in a formal celebration. The townspeople, the lawyers, the judges and jury were only too glad to have been proved wrong. As for

Colvin—he was surprised to see his sons: he thought he had left them in New Jersey. Possibly because he had heard that his wife had been unfaithful, he did not care to remain with her, and soon returned to the Polhemus farm. As for Stephen and Jesse—they were soon liberated; and their mother was humbly invited to return to the fellowship of the Baptist church.

As for the legal profession—it solemnly resolved not to be caught again without a corpse.

VI. For One Pair of Stags

THE LYON OF VERMONT. Tomorrow morning at eleven o'clock will be exposed to view the Lyon of Vermont. This singular animal is said to have been caught in the bog of Hibernia, and when a whelp, transported to America; curiosity induced a New Yorker to buy him, and moving into the country, afterwards exchanged him for a yoke of young bulls with a Vermontese. He was petted in the neighborhood of Governor Chittenden and soon became so domesticated that a daughter of His Excellency would stroke and play with him as a monkey. He differs considerably from the African lion, is more clamorous, and less magnanimous. His pelt resembles more the wolf or tiger, and his gestures bear a remarkable affinity to the bear; this however may be ascribed to his having been in the habit of associating with that species of wild beast in the mountains; he is carnivorous, but not very ferocious—has never been detected in having attacked a *man*, but report says he will *beat women*. He was brought to this city in a wagon, and has several days exposed himself to the public . . .

—*Porcupine's Gazette*, January 6, 1797

MATTHEW LYON was fond of referring to the meager circumstances of his boyhood—particularly his debt to the pair of stags which replaced him in the yoke of indentured servitude. With scornful pride he would often exclaim "by the bulls that redeemed me!" His colleagues in the Congress of the United States knew what he meant.

Very little is known of his boyhood or his antecedents. Apparently he had saved enough to pay his passage from Ireland to America, although when the ship reached the colonies the captain, to whom he had entrusted his funds for safekeeping, indentured him to the wealthiest merchant in Connecticut. This man, Jabez Bacon, seems to have been a fair master but he was a Tory and Lyon a Whig, and he soon traded the young Irishman for the famous pair of bulls to one Hugh Hannah of Litchfield. If the privilege of choosing where he went had been Matthew's, he could not have gone to a more congenial spot: it was there that Ethan Allen, Remember Baker and other free-spirited adventurers like himself were then living.

By the time he was twenty-one Lyon had secured his freedom, a wife (the niece of Ethan Allen) and employment, probably at Ethan's ironworks in Salisbury. When Ethan forsook the iron business for land speculation, politics and border warfare in the hills and valleys of the New Hampshire Grants to the north, Lyon accompanied him, along with Thomas Chittenden, destined to be the first governor of the Republic of Vermont. At Hand's Cove early that May morning in 1775, Matthew was a lieutenant in Ethan's riotous company of Green Mountain Boys who were plotting against Ticonderoga, the British bastion that raised its stern face from the hills on the far shore of Lake Champlain. Strangely enough it was the Revolution now at hand that was to tarnish the luster of his future. The following year he was an officer in a company of enlisted men who mutinied one night because they were stationed at a northern Vermont outpost on the Onion River, far in front of the American lines.

"The soldiers," Lyon wrote many years later, "complained bitterly of the orders which bound them to the north side of Onion river, more than twenty poles wide, at that time not fordable, and but a single canoe to cross with. I endeavored to encourage them with assurances that we could withstand any number of Indians in our log house and a hovel or two which stood near; and, after a battle, if we should find the enemy too troublesome, we might retreat with honor. I urged them to their duty as soldiers and patriots. Every preparation was made to repel the attack which was expected from the enemy that night. Being fatigued and off duty, I had laid down to rest, with my fuzee in my arms. About nine o'clock in the evening I heard a violent bustle, with a cry of 'Turn out! Turn out!' I turned out and inquired where the enemy were discovered, and was answered, 'Nowhere.' The soldiers were paraded, and I found by what was said by the sergeants that they were about to march off and cross the river. I expostulated with them long and earnestly, pointing out the dishonor which such an action would reflect on their country. I urged them to stay the event of a battle, and I spoke the truth when I assured them that I preferred death in battle to the dishonor of quitting our post.

"All entreaties were ineffectual; they declared they had been abused —there was no chance for their lives there, and they marched off for the south side of the river. A sergeant returned with some soldiers, and called upon the officers to cross the river. As they were going to take the canoe to the other side, they insisted on our going, and threatened violence if we refused. The other officers, which were two captains and one lieutenant, seemed willing to go, and I did not think it my duty to resist alone."

Lyon was cashiered with the other officers. ". . . The mortification of being cashiered, and that very undeservedly, without any other aggravation, was, I believe, quite to the extent of my power to bear; had any indignant ceremony been performed, they would not have had my company at it, as the implements of death were in my power.

"The general sent for us to his own house and there, in a mild manner, communicated to us the sentence—no one present, I believe, but his aid; and we took our own time and manner of quitting Ticonderoga . . ."

Though he continued to serve the American army as a civilian, and serve it well, it was some time before the general command absolved him from blame and restored his rank. In the meantime he had suffered the blackest humiliation. Even as late as 1791, the year the Vermont republic became a state, it took courage—in the light of the damage the army had done him in the public eye—to announce his candidacy for representative in the United States Congress. He lost. He became a candidate again in 1792, and he lost again.

Had his energies been directed solely toward politics his second defeat might have destroyed his confidence. Instead he turned his attention toward the foremost object of his pride—Fair Haven. Not long after the death of his first wife in 1783, Lyon had married Governor Chittenden's daughter, Beulah. Taking her and four children by his first wife to the primitive township of Fair Haven (of which he was a grantee), he began his long labors to create a village where the Castleton and Poultney Rivers meet. He built a house and barn, then a dam and sawmill. He logged the four-acre park that he planned for the village green and on the streets that radiated from it he built houses of brick from his new brick kiln. From the iron military relics he had gathered at the Ticonderoga, Crown Point, Hubbardton and Bennington battlefields, he made spades and plows in the foundry he had constructed. He built a gristmill and a tannery so that he could make harnesses, saddles and shoes. He built an inn. He bought a printing press from Benjamin Franklin and hauled it home so that he might print the Fair Haven *Gazette*.

This was the man who, having twice suffered political defeat, ran a third time in 1796 for the office of Congressman from western Vermont—and this time won.

Sniffing the patrician air of Philadelphia, he at once sensed the unsavory "dynasty of Snobbium Gatherum," as a writer later described the administration of John Adams. Lyon had not even thoroughly warmed his chair in the House of Representatives before he arose to protest against his colleagues' custom of repairing as a body to the executive chambers to bow and scrape before the President. ". . . I have spent a great part of my life amongst people whose love of plainness of manners forbids all pageantry; I would be glad to see this custom done away. Were I acting in my own personal character, I perhaps might conform to this idle usage; but acting as I am for 80,000 people, every father of a family in my district would condemn me for such an act . . ." He requested that he be excused from the Presidential parade, and it was unanimously voted that he need not attend. The other representatives went, but they were observing the custom for the last time, as Jefferson abolished it when he entered the Presidency.

Meanwhile the Federalist hornets of aristocratic John Adams buzzed about Lyon in the House, and the Federalist newspapers such as the pro-English *Porcupine's Gazette* were fretting about the emergence of commoners such as Jefferson, Jackson and Lyon. "It will be seen in the proceedings of Congress," wrote the editor of the *Gazette,* a British pamphleteer who had come to America to help the Federalists, "that this beast asked leave to be excused from going with the rest of the members to wait on the President. Many gentlemen, who have seen him, do not hesitate to declare, they think him a most extraordinary beast." The *Gazette* announced a Gimcrack's Museum which would display the wooden sword of the hero of Onion River, together with "the musical notes accompanying that brave man in his triumphal exit from the camp at Ticonderoga." In the next room the Vermont Lion would be displayed—the greatest beast in the world. Attacked for being an alien and an immigrant, Lyon replied in Congress that he could not truly say that he was descended from the bastards of Oliver Cromwell, or from the Puritans who punished their horses for breaking the Sabbath, or from those who persecuted the Quakers or hanged the witches. He could, nevertheless, affirm that this was his country because he had no other and because he owned a share of it which he had obtained by honest industry. Conquest had led his country to independence; and, being independent, he called no man's blood in question.

Conversing with the Speaker outside the bar of the House late in January 1798, Lyon loudly castigated the representatives from Connecticut for their stand on a bill currently under consideration. He said the people of Connecticut had not been exposed to both sides of the matter and that they were being hoodwinked by their representatives. He further declared that if he went to Connecticut and edited a newspaper there for six months, the people would throw their present Congressmen out of office. Overhearing this, Mr. Griswold of Connecticut remarked that if Mr. Lyon went to Connecticut he ought to wear the wooden sword (which he had won at Onion River). Lyon ignored Griswold's remark although he had previously stated that there would be trouble if he ever heard the subject of the wooden sword mentioned again. Griswold now rose from his seat, approached Lyon and asked him if he usually fought his opponents with his wooden sword. Lyon turned to Griswold and spat in his face.

The House was in an uproar. When it finally came to order, Federalist Sewall from Massachusetts made a motion that Lyon be expelled from the House for "gross indecency." While the resolution was being considered by the Committee of Privileges the story of the fray swept through Philadelphia and along the entire seaboard. Many people found it amusing—far more so than President Adams and the Federalists in the House, who had been seeking a means to get rid of this thorn of a Democrat. The motion to expel Spitting Mat came up for consideration on February 2, but the Federalists failed to obtain the necessary two-thirds majority.

"Perhaps," Lyon wrote his Green Mountain constituents, "some will say I did not take the right method with him. We do not always possess the power of judging calmly what is the best mode of resenting an unpardonable insult. Had I borne it patiently I should have been bandied about in all the newspapers on the Continent which are supported by British money and Federal patronage, as a mean poltroon. The district which sent me would have been scandalized."

The fact that Lyon had retained his seat in the House exasperated Griswold, who had failed to achieve any measure of revenge. On February 15 before the House had been called to order and immediately after the prayer had been offered, Griswold rose; seizing a hickory stick he strode quickly to the desk of the Vermont representative, who was quietly studying his papers. With a vindictive expression on his face, Griswold raised the stick and brought it down on Lyon's head with all his force. Before Lyon could get up, Griswold, encouraged by the raucous shouts of the Federalists, hit him again. Lyon groped for his own cane, which apparently had slipped under his seat, and then, with Griswold after him, plunged forward among the other desks until he reached the open section in front of the Speaker. Here the gentleman from Vermont attempted to grapple with the gentleman from Connecticut, but finding this impossible, he rushed to the fireplace and grabbed the fire tongs. Before he could deliver a blow, however, Griswold seized the tongs by the other end. The weapons were shortly cast aside and the protagonists fell wrestling to the floor. As they did so the partisan Speaker, who had failed to call for order while Griswold clearly had the upper hand, protested vehemently. "What!" he shouted as other representatives tried to drag Griswold off by the legs. "Take hold of a man by the legs? That is no way to take hold of him!"

Restrained by the other representatives, Griswold and Lyon could no longer fight. Later, however, the two chanced to meet at the water table. This time Griswold was not armed and Lyon had a stick which he at once brought into play. With adroit footwork Griswold managed to avoid it until a Mr. Sitgreaves armed the Connecticut representative with a cane. At this point the Speaker called for order and the battle ended. The next day a southern Congressman made a motion to expel both Griswold and Lyon. This was presently modified to a resolution requiring both to pledge abstinence from fisticuffs in the future. They agreed—publicly.

"You will have seen the disgusting proceedings in the case of Lyon," Jefferson wrote James Madison. ". . . To get rid of his vote was the most material object. These proceedings . . . degrade the general government and lead the people to lean more on their state governments . . ."

It has been said that with the exception of John Jay, no man in the public prints was ever pelted with a heavier hail of second-rate humor, bad verse and puns than Matthew Lyon. This battery, however, was easier to withstand than the blows from Griswold's stick, and at the end of 1798 Lyon returned to Vermont in good spirits to feel the public pulse and assess his chances of re-election.

Immediately prior to adjournment the Federalist majority in Congress had squeezed through the notorious Alien and Sedition Laws, which President Adams had designed with the particular object of removing Lyon not only from Congress but from the country. Having thus been granted the power to fine, imprison or exile persons whom he judged inimical to the United States, the President and his Federalist auxiliaries now planned to trap Lyon under the provision of the law which made it a crime to publish material critical of the government or President.

Adams's minions were keeping tabs on everything that issued from Lyon's press at Fair Haven and all his communications to various people about the country. Lyon knew that the government was after him and as soon as the bill had passed he exercised particular care to remain in the clear. Three weeks before the bill had passed, however, he had written to a Windsor, Vermont, paper which had been attacking him. The letter defended his own conduct and portrayed the President as a lover of pomp and a seeker of adulation—a selfish man continually grasping for power. The Vermont journal held the letter until after the sedition statute had become law, and then published it. With this ammunition a Vermont grand jury, rigged by the Federalists (according to Lyon) with men unfriendly to him, met in Rutland on October 9 to judge the first victim of the new law. Lyon spoke two hours in his own defense, charging that the act violated the Constitution.

"The Judge," Lyon wrote subsequently, ". . . told the jury that my defense was merely an appeal to their feelings, calculated to excite their pity; but mercy, he said, did not belong to them. That was lodged in another place; they were to follow the law. . . . The jury retired about eight o'clock in the evening and in about an hour they returned with a verdict, *Guilty!* The Judge observed . . . that I had then an opportunity to show cause why judgment should not be pronounced against me, and to know what was my ability or inability to pay a fine, as a man of large property . . . ought to be obliged to pay a greater fine than one of smaller property. . . . The Judge, after an exordium on the nature of the offense, the malignity of it in me, particularly being a member of Congress, and the lenity of the Sedition Bill, which did not allow the judges to carry the punishment so far as common law did, pronounced sentence that I be imprisoned four calendar months [and] pay a fine of one thousand dollars.

"The marshall is a man who acted as clerk to some persons whom I had occasion to transact some business with about a dozen years since, when he first came into this country, in which he behaved so that I have ever since most heartily despised him; this he has no doubt seen and felt. The moment sentence was pronounced, he called 2 persons to give me in charge to. . . . I asked if they would go with me to my lodgings a few minutes, so that I might take care of my papers. I was answered in a surly manner, No; and commanded to sit down. I stood up . . ."

Instead of imprisoning him in Rutland, which would have been the logical place, the marshal chose the Vergennes jail. Here, after a long ride, the Vermont Congressman was incarcerated in a barren sixteen-by-twelve-foot cell "with a necessary in one corner, which afforded a stench about equal to the Philadelphia docks in the month of August." There was little light, no heat, and his sole communication with the outside world was a half-moon in the door through which he received food. Lyon said that there was always someone hammering on the exterior of the cell, or adding bolts or bars. He took pains to inform the jailer that since he did not wish to escape, a single thread would hold him, but had he planned to leave, nothing could prevent his departure. Access to writing materials was at first withheld but later granted in response to the vigorous protests of Lyon's friends. The marshal made it plain, however, that he would censor all papers leaving the cell.

Though the Federalists had managed to lodge one of their most powerful critics in jail, their victory was a Pyrrhic one. In the Democratic caucus for Congressman from western Vermont Lyon had very nearly drawn more votes than all of his adversaries put together. His subsequent imprisonment served only to increase his popularity among his constituents, who looked to the ballot box in the December elections as their answer to the machinations of President Adams. His enemies' worst fears were confirmed in December when the votes were counted and Lyon was found to have won by a large margin.

The Federalists faced his victory with more desperation and fear than surprise. Imprisonment had clearly made him a martyr. They suspected he might win and for some time had planned for this contingency. At first they had denied him use of pen and ink; then they realized that if he were allowed to write he would certainly violate the sedition law again. Thus there would be more evidence with which to extend his imprisonment, and it would make no difference whether or not he was elected. Lyon did not disappoint them. Shortly after receiving permission he had written a letter that was placed before another grand jury. The contents were found to be seditious. The jury indicted Lyon again and placed in the marshal's hands a warrant for his arrest as soon as the first sentence terminated in February 1799.

Meanwhile Lyon's friends were making sure that the moment he finished his term he would be released so that he might start at once for Congress. Since he had been unable to attend to his business enterprises, they doubted that he had enough money to pay his thousand-dollar fine. They consequently decided to raise the amount by holding a lottery.

Outside the jail early on the morning of February 9, 1779, the thumping of hoofs over the voices of many people could be heard along the riverbank. Looking through the window Lyon saw the forerunners of the cavalcade assembling to witness the liberation of their candidate. Sleighs arrived filled with Green Mountain Boys who had come to aid their officer of twenty years ago. At length, according to tradition, it was announced that in order to allow everyone present to have the privilege of contributing, each man could step forward and place twenty-five or fifty cents on the stump. The stump was mounting with silver when Beulah Lyon drove up. She declared that she and her husband were too proud to have someone else pay the fine, that some of their property in Fair Haven had been sold and that she had the money with her.*

In the jail Deputy Fitch was getting ready to release Lyon but warned him that he had in his pocket another warrant for his arrest which would be served as soon as his present sentence ended. When Fitch received the money he opened the door to the cell. The prisoner came out and, as Fitch prepared to serve the second warrant, Lyon plunged out of the jail, seized his wife, hoisted her into the sleigh and jumped up onto the seat next to her. He grabbed the reins and shouted to Fitch, "I'm on my way to Congress!" And there was noth-

---

* In *Mat The Democrat*, a recent study of Lyon, George L. Montagno disproves long-accepted accounts of the prisoner's release from jail. In one favorite version General Stevens T. Mason of Virginia was said to have collected a thousand dollars from colleagues in the government and to have set out through the winter with the bullion in his saddlebags. Montagno shows, however, that Senator Mason was in Congress for he is recorded as having voted in the Senate on February 8.

Other versions hold that Apollos Austin, uncle of the founder of the Texas city, appeared from Orwell with the thousand dollars. It appears that Lyon raised some of the money through his wife's efforts (though how much is a question), that part came from General Mason's solicitation and was delivered by someone else, and that the rest was raised through lottery.

There is also some confusion over the whereabouts of Marshal J. Fitch, for the fine was paid to his deputy, S. Fitch, apparently a relative. Be all this as it may, Lyon's release from jail was as triumphant as traditional accounts maintain.

ing Fitch could do about it, for Congress was in session and Lyon was a Congressman on his way to Philadelphia. The protective veil of Congressional immunity had fallen about him. "His journey was a triumphal march. A great concourse accompanied him on his way, with the American flag at the head of the procession; and as they passed along, the inhabitants of the towns on the line of march assembled numerously to greet him. Even children partook of the occasion. As he passed a school house in Tinmouth the children were paraded at the roadside, bearing a banner on which was inscribed: 'This day satisfied Federal vengeance . . . a detested understrapper . . . this day rises superior to despotism.' On his arrival in Bennington he was welcomed by a large assemblage who greeted him with cheers, original songs and a formal address, to which he briefly responded, and then pursued his journey."

As soon as Lyon took his seat in the House of Representatives a Delaware Federalist arose and moved that the Vermonter be expelled from Congress for having been convicted under the sedition law. The motion failed to pass.

In the Presidential campaign of 1800 Matthew Lyon had the satisfaction of witnessing the defeat of his archenemy, John Adams, and the Federalist party. When the contest between Jefferson and Burr was thrown into the House thirty-six ballots were taken. With a one-vote margin Jefferson acceded to the Presidency.

As soon as his friend took office Lyon wrote a long letter to John Adams, dated one minute after midnight on the fourth of March, 1801. Had the Alien and Sedition Laws still been in effect, the letter's contents would have given the former President enough evidence to imprison the Vermont Congressman for one hundred fifty years:

"Pitiful indeed must be your feeling in passing home through the now Democratic State, New Jersey, which formerly so copiously furnished you with piping hot addresses every morning for breakfast. . . . Should you stop at Philadelphia how melancholy must it seem to you; McPherson's band of Cockade boys are dispersed or grown up into Democrats, no Federal mobs there now to sing Hail Columbia and huzzar for John Adams, and terrify your opposers. Hopkinson's lyre is out of tune, Cobbet and Liston are gone, the Quakers are for the living President, and your old friend, Joe Thomas, I am told, can scarcely find duds to cover his nakedness; I am surprised you did not make him a judge. . . .

"You commenced your career . . . by professions . . . but they were mere professions; your mad zeal for monarchy and Britain, your love of pomp, your unhappy selection of favorites, your regardlessness of the public treasure . . . have divided the people . . . and fostered among them envy, malice and rancorous hatred. . . . Under your administration, sir, useless and expensive embassies have prevailed to an alarming degree. Offices and officers, almost without number, have been created and appointed, all out of the favored caste . . . capable, discerning and popular men have, by you and your minions, been discharged from the service of their country, without being vouchsafed a reason for their degradation . . .

"An Alien Law, sir, bears your signature . . . Perhaps in no one instance has our Constitution, our sacred bill of rights, been more shamefully, more barefacedly trampled on, than in the case of the passage of the bill called the Sedition Law. This, sir, was your darling hobbyhorse. By this law you expected to have all your follies, your absurdities, and your atrocities buried in oblivion. You thought by its terrors to shut the mouths of all but sycophants and flatterers, and to secure yourself in the Presidency . . . but how happily you have been disappointed—the truth has issued from many a patriot pen and press —and you have fallen . . ."

Soon after his 1799 term in Congress ended, Lyon returned to orderly Fair Haven, which had changed markedly from its rough appearance of a decade before. At the suggestion of Andrew Jackson, Lyon had made a trip to Kentucky, and having purchased a large new tract of land there, found his last days in Vermont filled with restlessness. His businesses in Fair Haven had failed to prosper during his absence in Congress and he had made many political enemies in Vermont. But most of all he longed for untouched terrain like the Green Mountain frontier of twenty-five years ago.

Assembling a number of his older children with their families, and the families of some Fair Haven artisans, he migrated south and west to the place he had chosen for a town on the banks of the Cumberland.

He called it Eddyville after the pioneer who was excavating the Erie Canal. Leaving his children to cultivate the colony there, he returned to Congress for the term of 1800-01, after which he came back to Vermont for his wife and other children whom he had left in Fair Haven until Eddyville could be established. He sold everything he owned except his printing press and left Fair Haven in April of 1801 in a caravan of covered wagons containing seventy other emigrants from the Green Mountains.

Passing four hundred miles through the forests of New York and Pennsylvania, they came to the junction of the Monongahela and the Allegheny at Pittsburgh, where they constructed flatboats. Drawing their wagons aboard they drifted down the Ohio until they reached the mouth of the Cumberland River. They poled and paddled up that stream and "one pleasant morning about the first of July, 1801," in the recollection of Matthew Lyon's youngest daughter, the colonel sighted Eddyville. "Madame Lyon," he said to his wife, "if you will come this way I will show you the first sign of our new house. Do you see those bluffs in the distance? Well, at the foot of those, in a beautiful bottom or valley, our Western home is situated. . . . There, there," the colonel said, "I see the large sycamore tree that stands on the bank just where we must land. Boys, we will give them a few guns to let them know we are coming!" From the muzzle of the small Revolutionary cannon, which was dragged out, a series of shots announced their arrival and brought all the inhabitants of Eddyville running to the shore.

With his family united once more, Lyon again started all the various industries he had developed at Fair Haven. In 1802 the people of western Kentucky selected him as their representative to Congress, and sent him back for seven consecutive terms. Continuing as the voice of the hinterlands and the frustrator of ambitious persons in the government, he blocked such schemes as that of Aaron Burr, who was attempting to detach the country's western lands and set up an empire. Throughout his many terms as Kentucky Congressman, Lyon acted with such independence, regardless of party affiliations or the consequences, that he made many enemies and did not always retain his friends. He thus found himself voting for the protective tariff with his old enemy in combat, Griswold from Connecticut, and against the

Embargo of 1812, championed by the Democratic party and Thomas Jefferson—from whom he found himself estranged.

In 1812 he built a fleet of gunboats in his shipyard on the Cumberland, with the plan of delivering them to New Orleans. A storm wrecked the boats—and Lyon's finances, since he had impetuously launched himself in the boat building business without waiting for a government contract. In 1820 James Monroe made him the United States factor to the Cherokee Nation and he set out again as an old man to make a new home on the Arkansas. This time he had no money and only his wife, his youngest daughter and a few faithful followers to help him carry out his plans. He settled a hundred miles above Little Rock at Spadra Bluff, cut down the forest and built a house of oak logs, split with broad axes. It had "2 rooms each 24' by 24' down stairs and half a dozen bed rooms upstairs with huge chimneys and open fireplaces built of limestone and with roof of white oak board and floors of clear white oak puncheons, hewn smooth as marble."

He ran for Congress from Arkansas but failed to be elected by the narrow margin of sixty-one votes. Lyon claimed his opponent stuffed the ballot box. It would have made little difference if he had won, for he died before he could have taken his seat.

His last journey was on a flatboat he had built at Spadra Bluff. He himself piloted the craft loaded with furs and Indian goods down the river to New Orleans, where he exchanged his cargo for products of every description, including machinery for a cotton gin he was building at Spadra Bluff. He fought his way back up the Mississippi in violent, sour weather and finally tied his boat near the mouth of the White River so that he might detour to Eddyville to see his family. Three months from the time he had started on his flatboat he returned to Spadra Bluff with all his bartered goods. At the age of seventy-three he had traveled three thousand miles, much of it upstream. The men with him said he was usually the first to jump off into the icy water when it was necessary to pull the flatboat across the shallows.

In Philadelphia and Fair Haven, in Eddyville, Washington and Spadra Bluff, the news of Matthew Lyon's death on August 1, 1822, must have saddened some people. There is not much doubt that there were others who were glad. And probably there were some who cared neither one way nor the other—for they knew the man merely through old Federalist jingles like this:

> 'Tis said that he brags
> How one pair of stags,
>   Erst paid for his passage from Europe;
> But the price of a score
> Would scarce send him o'er,
>   And pay for his hangman a new rope!
>
> O then ye are lucky,
>   Good men of Kentucky,
>   To choose spitting Matt for your idol;
> Come frolic and caper
> By the blaze of his taper,
>   And sing fol de rol, diddle di dol.

VII. The Pond that
Ran Away

JUST north of a height of land between the Barton and Lamoille Rivers, settlers had established a small community named Glover, a town that was not on a direct route to anywhere. With reluctance the hills of Glover yielded to the plow. The near-by mountain streams admitted at best a mere trickle of water to the saw- and gristmills. As in a hundred other Vermont hill towns winter came early and stayed late. Sometimes it rained all summer. Sometimes the ground cracked with the thirst of cloudless summer months, and the dwindling streams forced the trout down out of the hills to the lowland rivers.

In 1810 Glover was dry even in the spring. There was water in Mud Pond but the mills on the tiny stream which drained it were useless. Low water was expected during the summer months—in the spring it could not be tolerated. The people of Sutton, Wheelock, Sheffield and Glover therefore met to see how they might keep the water wheels turning. It seemed to one farmer that water might be diverted from Long Pond to Mud Pond and then to the mills below by digging a ditch through the height of land. Long Pond was one hundred fifty feet higher and ordinarily drained southward into the Lamoille, but the assembled farmers considered the northward ditch to Mud Pond feasible. Accordingly on June 6 they gathered with their picks and shovels on the bank of Long Pond, which curved for one and a half miles through a trough in the hills. Shortly the blows of their tools on the glacial till rang through the evergreen woodlands, and by noon they had cut a channel almost entirely through the height of land. The last few feet nearest the pond had been left so that the tired men could eat their lunch as they watched two volunteers open the channel.

To the spectators gathered from around the hills the removal of this last wall of soil and pebbles was as agreeable and important as the digging of a canal. It was the triumph of man over nature. The remaining ground narrowed to a thin wedge and a trickle of water from Long Pond, which for countless centuries had flowed south, oozed into the man-made opening to the north. Now, with a rush, the water flowed freely into the ditch. The marriage of Long and Mud Ponds had been achieved! As the minutes passed, however, the outflowing stream began to dwindle until there was no water at all in the ditch. Suddenly a deep rumbling was heard. The land in front of the astounded observers slowly began to sink. The trees started to shake. Before their eyes the ditch widened into a chasm. With a roar Long Pond lunged into the gap; as the men fled up the bank, the land dissolved in the torrent. Trees cracked and crashed into the widening abyss and catapulted forth in a fifty-foot wall of racing water. Within a few moments the banks of Mud Pond below collapsed under the assault and both ponds yielded their entire burden to the narrow valley.

Running before the flood with more than human speed, one villager snatched a Mrs. Wilson from the gristmill and carried her up the bank a scant second before the torrent seized the mill and kited it away from its moorings. Down roared the avalanche of water, earth and trees, cows, bridges, fences and barns, sending forth a rumble "like that of a mighty rushing wind with mutterings of distant thunder." Shortly after sundown the towering gray mass plunged into Lake Memphremagog twenty miles away, raising that expansive sheet of water a foot and chasing the fish up Black River. In a few hours the valley through which the unearthly wave had passed became a wasteland, heavily silted in or scoured to bedrock. "It ruined twenty acres of grass and ten of rye for me," reported one inhabitant. "The substance that is left on the land seems to be quicksand, fine as flour. It cleared all the timber on my lowlands. It floated up whole areas of cedar timber and carried them off again standing upright as they grew." At the point of its departure from Long Pond it sliced a gash through the hills three hundred feet wide and a hundred feet deep. At one place along its serpentine course it lifted and carried for half a mile a rock weighing one hundred tons.

Only the bed of Runaway Pond was left, and only the bed is left today. There was no one after June 6, 1810—at least in Sutton, Wheelock, Sheffield and Glover—who was not content to let the Lord regulate the water in the streams.

VIII. Heaven on Earth

IN Poultney, a small community secure in a fold of green-clad hills, there were two churches in 1805. Because her husband was a pillar of the Baptist church Mrs. Anna Wells also adhered to that faith, but with reluctance. The Congregationalists down the road worshiped more in accordance with her principles, yet it seemed she would end her life a Baptist, since Elder Kendrick, minister of the church, was a close friend of her husband and had for some time been a member of the Wells household.

One day Elder Kendrick borrowed a horse from Wells and rode to Fair Haven where he passed the night. In the morning it developed that the horse had kicked and crippled a horse owned by the landlord of the inn where Kendrick was staying. When the innkeeper was next in Poultney, Wells told him that he had warned the minister that his horse was a kicker and that unless the animal was by himself he would do mischief. He further said that Parson Kendrick on his return from Fair Haven declared that he had advised the landlord of the horse's ugly disposition. The Fair Haven hosteler replied that Elder Kendrick had said nothing of the sort. Called upon for an explanation, Kendrick denied that Wells had ever told him that the horse was mean. It was thus evident that either Kendrick or Wells was lying, and a dispute of large proportions arose.

A jury of Poultney Baptists was called to gather testimony. Anna Wells declared that she had heard her husband remind the parson of the horse's temper. Kendrick swore under oath that he had never been so advised. The jury promptly acquitted him; the stigma of guilt therefore fell upon Enos and Anna Wells, who were ostracized from the Baptist fellowship. Smarting under this assault upon their honor, Mrs. Wells turned to the Congregational church. After she had attended its services for a number of weeks she received a letter from the Baptists in which they asserted:

"You have told to several persons, at several times and places, concerning a horse, (about which Elder Kendrick and Mr. Wells had some disagreement) a story contrary to what you afterwards gave under solemn oath before a council. If what you told in the first place . . . was not as you affirmed it to be, then you are condemned by the word of God, in places too numerous to mention, and particularly, Eph. iv. 25: 'Wherefore putting away lying, speak every man truth with his neighbor,' and Rev. xxi. 8, we are solemnly warned that 'all liars shall have their part in the lake that burneth with fire and brimstone.' . . . We, therefore, are constrained to let you know, that we have no fellowship with you, nor can we have more till those things are removed . . ."

The letter was "Done in behalf and by the order of the church," and was signed "Clark Kendrick, Moderator."

Mrs. Wells replied that "in the presence of him who is the searcher of the hearts of men" she had never, either directly or indirectly, made any statement contrary to the solemn oath she had given. She considered the conduct of the church toward her "particularly in their *manner* of excluding me from their fellowship, to be arbitrary, unchristian, and devoid of that charity you are bound to exercise, so I am constrained in justice to myself, my family and the cause of my blessed Redeemer, to enter . . . solemn protest against your proceedings . . ." She charged that she had been unjustly judged and that when she had suggested her case be reviewed by an impartial council her motion had been refused. Therefore she had turned to the Congregationalists.

Although they thought Anna Wells innocent, the Congregationalists did not quite know whether or not to admit her to their fellowship, so they at length called upon the Congregationalists of Dorset, Pawlet, North Granville, Benson, Castleton, East and West Rutland, Middletown and Tinmouth for advice. Representatives from these various parishes met in Poultney on November 18, 1805, to re-examine the evidence and ascertain if possible whether or not Wells advised Elder Kendrick, before he started for Fair Haven, that his horse was a kicker. A committee of Congregationalists asked Elder Kendrick to repeat the evidence which the Baptist church had used in judging Anna Wells guilty. Kendrick not only refused to give it but prevented any Baptists from testifying. The Congregational council decided, however, that the facts weighed heavily against Kendrick and that the Baptists had passed judgment in a pagan fashion "contrary to the common maxims and usages of nations and societies, both civil and religious, either in ancient or modern times. . . ." A civil court also tried the case and, judging Kendrick guilty, directed him to reimburse the Fair Haven hosteler for the value of the horse he had lost.

In such a tenuous and painful manner did Anna Wells, whose secret desire had always been to become a Congregationalist, join the fellowship of her choice.

"At the time we promised the Baptist church that we would give information to the public of what we did in this matter," reported the Poultney Congregationalists, "we had not determined to have anything printed; but that we may not be chargeable of keeping any of our light under a bushel, but that it may shine and give light to all around us, we have thought proper to request a copy of the doings of the council, and commit the whole to the press."

Vermont was a seedbed in which freethinkers of the late eighteenth and early nineteenth centuries cultivated a curious variety of religions. Here in the forests and untilled valleys bloomed the oddest flowers of the Great Awakening, whose seeds, windblown from Connecticut, had first been planted by the missionaries Jonathan Edwards and George Whitefield. For nearly a century the prevailing winds of Puritanism had shown signs of shifting. The church had been the social, political and religious architect of Puritan life. Forces of liberty already hastening the Revolution were therefore arraigned quite as much against unbending religious doctrine as against Great Britain. With his "heart religion," which encouraged each individual to discover the presence of God with his own emotions and mind, Jonathan Edwards provided the theological vent through which one hundred years of pent-up free will escaped. The demagogue who carried these doctrines to the hinterlands of New England and galvanized legions of people was George Whitefield.

Nowhere in New England did the Great Awakening thrive as it did among the frontier rebels of Vermont. The stentorian voice of the Puritan church had scarcely been heard beyond the mountains. There was no one in the northcountry to dispute such revolutionary doctrines as those of Deist Ethan Allen who eschewed all formal religion in favor of his personal god, and who had expounded his views on religious matters in the first anti-Christian book published in America. The region abounded in potential converts. All that was wanting were the prophets.

In the 1790s a man named Dorril, who had hypnotized a group of people from Leyden, Massachusetts, migrated to Vermont; there, in the border town of Guilford, he enlarged his following. He believed that he was an agent of God and should exercise absolute spiritual and political control over his subjects. The Dorrilites shared all their property, ate vegetables exclusively and padded about in woolen slippers, for they did not believe in the slaughter of animals even for the purposes of clothing. Neighbors of the colony reported alcohol-

sodden revival meetings, and on this subject Joseph Lathrop, a prominent Massachusetts clergyman, asserted:

"In the northern part of this state, I am well informed, there has
lately appeared, and still exists, under a licentious leader, a company of
beings who discard the principles of religion and obligations of moral-
ity, trample on the bonds of civil society, spend the Sabbath in labor or
diversion, as fancy dictates, and the nights in riotous excess and pro-
miscuous concubinage as lust impels. Their number consists of about
40, some of whom are people of respectable abilities and once, of decent characters. A society of this description would disgrace the natives
of Caffraria."

Dorril's fragile kingdom disintegrated when he announced his immunity to pain at a meeting attended by a Captain Ezekiel Foster and
some other unbelievers. When Dorril announced, "No arm can hurt
my flesh!" Foster strode forth and planted a haymaker on the chin of
the revivalist, bringing him to the floor. As soon as his victim had
staggered to his feet, Foster hit him again and Dorril admitted he
could feel pain. The faithful followers dispersed, thus ending abruptly
the history of one of the earliest efforts to create a perfect society in
Vermont.

On a Middletown farm at the close of the eighteenth century there
lived a man named Winchell, who was said to have been a counter-
feiter before he turned to mysticism. It became known shortly that
Winchell was an expert with the divining rod, and several neighbors
financed his expeditions round about to unearth buried treasure. But
none was uncovered, owing to supernatural conditions which were
never quite right.

Winchell had a Middletown friend, a preacher by the name of Nathaniel Wood, whom the Congregational church had excommunicated
for "saying one thing and doing the contrary and persisting in con-
tention." Wood and Winchell joined forces to form a new sect, the
former donating experience and the latter investing his divining rod,
which had now become "St. John's rod" and capable of transmitting
divine revelations. Wood predicted that an earthquake would convulse
the world on January 14, 1801. He said that it would destroy the
wicked and all their possessions; but the frozen Vermont hills failed to

stir on that day, and the powers of the Divining Rod began to decline.

On June 1, 1801, less than four months after the world managed to survive Wood's earthquake, one Brigham Young was born, the ninth child of a basketmaker, who was the poorest man in Whitingham, Vermont. "We deem it of little consequence in what locality he was born," regretted the chronicler of Whitingham, unaware of the bright destiny of the Mormons, "it is sufficiently humiliating that Whitingham was his birthplace." Whitingham and the environment of upstate New York, to which the Youngs shortly moved, were sufficiently austere to make an unreconstructed rebel of Brigham Young. "It used to be a word and a blow with him," recalled his father, "but the blow came first." Later, when the elder Young urged him to take the Temperance Pledge, he reasoned, "I feel that I am bound, and I wish to do just right, without being bound to do it; I want my liberty."

On a remote hillside in the town of Sharon the illustrious architect of the Mormon church, Joseph Smith, was born into a family equally large and almost as poor. If the words of Judge Daniel Woodward of Windsor are to be believed, the elder Smith had sought Captain Kidd's treasure and "became implicated with one Jack Downing in counterfeiting money, but turned state's evidence and escaped the penalty." A Universalist turned Methodist, he had two visions while in Vermont and others after he moved to New York. Whether these revelations arose from the need for escape from the demanding soil of a Vermont hill farm, or whether they were inherent in the man, is of less consequence than the fact that his son later experienced them also. Young Joseph never doubted that he was a prophet of God, even in his early years when "he set up a comforting and comfortable system by which he combined faith in himself with faith in God, because he had convinced himself thoroughly that God had faith in him." Flights of fancy thus became truths, concrete and indisputable.

Such later tenets of Mormonism as plural marriage, dancing and theatricals, could never have withstood the public wrath if they had not been an integral part of the religious practice of Smith and Young. They believed themselves responsible only to God, and their legion of followers answerable solely to them.

Vermont, then New York and Missouri—

"I was born in Sharon, Vermont," declared the embattled Smith in his Missouri appeal to the Green Mountain Boys, "where the first quarter of my life grew with the growth and strengthened with the strength of that 'first born' State of the United Thirteen. With the revelations of Jesus Christ to guide me into all Truth I had good reason to enter into the blessings and privileges of an American citizen;—the rights of a Green Mountain Boy, unmolested and to enjoy life and religion according to the enlightened nineteenth century. To the disgrace of the United States this is not so. These rights and a large amount of property have been taken from me by executive authority. . . . We have sought redress in Missouri, in Congress and from the President. The only consolation received is that 'our cause is just, but the government has no power to redress us.'

"The Missouri marauders took our arms and still retain them and the United States militia still compels us to do military duty and for lack of arms the law forces us to pay our fines . . .

"Having failed in every attempt to obtain satisfaction I am compelled to appeal to the honor and patriotism of my native State; to the clemency and valor of the 'Green Mountain Boys' . . .

"And in this appeal let me say: raise your towers; pile your monuments to the skies; build your steam frigates; spread yourself far and wide and open the iron eyes of your bulwarks by sea and land; and let the towering church steeples marshal the country like the 'dreadful splendor' of an army with bayonets; but remember the flood of Noah; remember the fate of Sodom and Gomorrah; remember the dispersion and confusion at the Tower of Babel; remember the destruction of Pharaoh and his hosts; remember the handwriting upon the wall, mene, mene, tekel upharsin; remember the visit to Sennacherib and the 185,000 Assyrians; and remember the Lord Almighty will avenge the blood of his saints that now crimson the skirts of Missouri. Shall wisdom cry aloud and not her speech be heard? . . ."

And then Salt Lake.

Of the other sects which sprang from Vermont during the Great Awakening, none prospered like the Mormons, nor did any permanently influence the culture of a state or region as did the followers of Smith and Young in their desert garden. Like roman candles, most of the Vermont cults flared briefly in the late eighteenth and early nineteenth centuries and flickered out. Such was the fate of a strange company called the Pilgrims, who drifted down from Canada on a search for the promised land which led them to Woodstock, Vermont. The leader of the Pilgrims was a red-bearded giant named Bullard, who in the usual fashion of these cults directed his followers' every activity. Though the members of other sects often owned property in common, it was state socialism with the Pilgrims—Bullard owned it.

In their effort to return to the fundamentals of Biblical life the men shaved their upper lips but not their chins, and dressed in bearskins and leather girdles. Since they did not believe in bathing and rolled in camp-meeting frenzy on the Vermont roads, it was with considerable relief that the citizens of Woodstock witnessed their departure, one hundred strong, in the fall of 1817. Seeking a permanent haven they wandered west to Troy and other New York towns. On one occasion a Baptist elder and his friend reported that when they requested Bullard to outline the principles of his religion "he and some of the others poured forth upon both of us a torrent of abuse such as surpassed all that may be heard in a grog shop from the lowest of the profane rabble, when ministers of the gospel are made the theme of derision." Moving on to Essex, New Jersey, and to Cincinnati, the Pilgrims at length reached New Madrid, Missouri, where Bullard's magnetism ebbed and the disciples wandered away.

By 1830 flames of revival were scorching the Vermont terrain. Hardwick was the birthplace in 1837 of an odd clan called the New Lights. Jonathan Edwards would have been aghast had he known that this sect had adopted the name of the larger, and at first respectable, movement which he had started. Indeed, horror would have struck any of the New Light divines, such as Eleazar Wheelock of Dartmouth, had he witnessed the bizarre activities of many of the Vermont sects that had inherited the New Light banner. Gone was the intellectual quality of the movement, to be replaced by an emotional power of great force.

The Hardwick group was actually a part of the second great revival which swept across New England after a twenty- or thirty-year decline in religion and morals following the Revolutionary War. The postwar revival, however, seemed to have many of the traits of the prewar revival, plus some of the elements of moral and religious decline of the war period itself. The Hardwick New Lights first identified themselves by screaming in church and by rendering passages of the Scripture in a shrill, sudden chant that disrupted regular worship. Attracting large numbers of converts from the neighboring towns, they moved from a school building to the south meetinghouse where, in zoological frenzy, they passed Sabbath mornings "barking in imitation of dogs, foxes and cuckoos, jumping, swinging their arms and rolling on the floor." In accordance with divine ordinance the men grew beards until one of their number revealed a heaven-sent message to the contrary, whereupon the beards were sacrificed. Composed chiefly of ignorant ne'er-do-wells the sect lasted a year and then disintegrated under the cross-fire of orthodox ministers.

William Miller, born just over the Vermont border in New York, startled the people of the Green Mountain state, to say nothing of the rest of the country, with a prediction that the world would end sometime between 1843 and 1844. Though Judgment Day failed to materialize and they were forced into a hasty revision of their estimated span of life, the Miller disciples did not abandon their prophet; they presently created the Seventh Day Adventist church.

The Deists and the Dorrilites, the Mormons and the Pilgrims, the New Lights and the Millerites, were not the only contenders for the souls of errant and freethinking Vermonters during the Great Awakening. Mary Baker Eddy, mother of Christian Science, was born in near-by New Hampshire, where she first evolved the principles of her system of mental healing. Although Shaker colonies were not original products of the hill country, they also flourished there. And nowhere was Spiritualism destined to prosper as in the Vermont of the late 1800s.

During the 1830s and 1840s tremors of revival shook even the conservative, the skeptical and the orthodox. Russel Streeter, reporting the activities of the Reverend Jedediah Burchard during a Woodstock revival meeting, revealed what a hellfire preacher could do to a respectable Vermont community in 1835:

"To give any description of the multifarious concern of offering up requests for prayers—getting people into the anxious seats, and the inquiry room, and the little children into Mrs. Burchard's department or school, so that people who never witnessed the scheme of operations can have any adequate conceptions of it, will be impossible. It puts description at total defiance. . . . Mr. Burchard told his hearers on Thursday P.M. that in order to have a revival they must bring in their *requests* for prayers, and pile them right up before God Almighty, and in due time he would look them over and answer them. . . . God looked over their *requests,* and sent his Holy Spirit right into the heart of the unconverted, as quick as *that;* (slapping his hands together.)

"And you must put up requests for all the different professions in this place; and for the merchants, mechanics, and clerks; for the young men in particular who are led astray by the devil and his servants, and are going down to hell, and for apprentices, and young children. And for all the towns round about; Windsor, and Hartland, and Pomfret, and Bridgewater, and Perkinsville, and Springfield. Don't be afraid of putting up too many requests. Pile them up—table them up before God Almighty, and he will look them all over, just as a merchant does a bundle of orders, and answer them, one after another. . . .

"Then came in requests of all forms and sizes, from different parts of the house, many of them from persons whom Mr. B. claimed as his converts, from the towns he had recently visited; and some of them were given off in such a vain and tossing manner, that I forbear to call names. They were stationed about the house in such a manner as to produce the greatest effect, having come here on purpose to help the preacher set fires to the mass of combustible materials. . . . And so it went on, request after request, for the conversion of a 'wife,' 'a son,' 'a daughter,' 'a brother in the state of Maine,'—'a son-in-law and three grandchildren in the Western part of New York,'—'an uncle, aunt and two cousins, in Boston,' or Baltimore, or New Orleans, or Ohio. . . . Sometimes three or four would be up at a time, and Mr. B. would catch and drive on equal to any auctioneer, when bids came in rapidly.

"Preparatory to getting the people into what are called *anxious* seats, in the meeting house, Mr. B. entraps them in the following manner. He asks 'every man, woman and child,' to rise, 'who believes that there is a God, that they may be prayed for.' The audience, generally, rise immediately. But instead of praying the manager compliments them, and says, 'Take your seats, if you please.' They do it. He then makes some curious remarks, and invites 'every man, woman and child to rise up at once, who desires salvation through Jesus Christ,' and flatteringly adds, 'You *all wish* to be saved. Rise up, *rise up.*' As before, those who do not understand the plot, rise; and even though a considerable number keep their seats, Mr. B. says 'All have risen; take your seats—sit down.' . . . . Mr. B. then artfully says that all who rose who are not converted, *pledged* themselves to come forward after the usual exercises are over and be prayed for. . . . The lads and others are invited from the gallery to come down, and corporals are stationed in suitable places to hurry them onward. Without reflection they come rushing down by scores; tittering and skipping along, as though on the road to muster. Mr. B. orders the people in the aisles to make way for those lads and young men and women. If more room is needed, he says, 'Get out of the way, old Christians, and let those young sinners have a chance to be saved' . . . Such a rushing, scrambling, and hauling as takes place, cannot be conceived.

"Mr. Burchard comes out of the desk, with the light tread of a cat and the cunning of a fox; races about the house, through the aisles, over the pews, and the *tops* of the pews, crying, 'Come every man, woman and child, and be prayed for; come forward, come right forward, young friends, don't be afraid. There, do step aside, brother, and let that daughter go out,—lead her up,—come, come, there yet is room —the door of salvation is open—sing, sing there—"Come holy Spirit heavenly Dove,"—Sir,—do go forward, it won't hurt you at all. What are you doing here, brethren, why don't you exert yourselves,—the Holy Ghost is in our midst—God knows it,—O poor sinners, do escape from hell, now the spirit is moving.' . . . I stood at the outer door several times, and could hardly believe that any creature that had not a 'familiar spirit,' could be all over the house in half a minute, and speak with several voices, as at the same time. As I approached and saw *how* and *who* it was, the stories of my grandmother in regard to witches and wizards came upon me with thrilling effect, and had I 'left my reason and philosophy at home,' I should have been a *convert* to the

doctrines of witchcraft, ghosts and hobgoblins, I should seriously have
believed a *ghost* was in the 'white house.' . . .

"Having coaxed, and frightened, and dragged his company into the
forward pews, he would have some intervening exercises, some dolor-
ous ode or something else, to give himself time to breathe, and eat
'rock candy,' (or as some say, a preparation of opium). . . . 'Now, will
you give your heart to God, and receive, therefor, the eternal joys of
heaven? God Almighty has *promised,* that if you will give him your
heart, he will crown you with immortal glory.—Answer my question,
then; will you give your heart to God? "I don't know." Why! I am
astonished that a man of your standing—the son of one of the first
lawyers in Vermont—a man of college education, and the cashier of
the Bank of Woodstock—I am astonished that you *don't*. Well, Sir, are
you *willing* to give your heart to God? Yes, Sir, I am *willing* to do it.
What, *willing* to do it, and yet *don't know* whether you will or not.
Here, Sir, I come to you, in great want of money; and ask you if you
have fifty dollars that you can spare for a few days. You answer, yes.
Well, Mr. Marsh, are you *willing* to lend it to me? Yes. Well, will
you do it? . . .'

"When he had received an answer in the *affirmative,* he would order
the recording angel to register the name on high, and tell Gabriel to go
to heaven and report the conversion of another sinner, that the celestial
arches might reverberate with louder shouts of praise. But, if the answer was in the *negative* he would generally reply, 'Then you will be
damned,' or 'Go to hell,' or something similar . . . and then after
others had prayed, drop upon his knees before them in the broad aisle,
and scream just as loud as he could for his life—leaning at least half
way back to his heels—telling God what the scriptures say about agon-
izing and groaning in prayer, and in what book and chapter he could
find it! . . . Never did I hear a crazy New-Light blunder together
such a blustering, disconnected compound of words and phrases; for
they could not be called sentences. . . . Judges, and lawyers, and doctors, and generals, and all subordinates to four corporals; and squires,
and merchants, and mechanics; mothers, maidens, and misses, were
upon the alert, 'hunting for souls,' as it was said of the false prophetesses of old. . . . It was really humiliating to see 'the ermined judge'

chasing about the village, and seizing almost every unBurchardized heretic he met, from 'Sambo, to his illustrious master'; and driving into every barroom, work-shop, kitchen and corner, to induce man or maiden to go to the inquiry room. . . . Judges and prophetesses converting people 'by force and arms.' But they labored not alone; for every zealot became a leader, and, as is said of Lacedemonian soldiers, 'Every private was a captain.'"

Because teaching bored John Noyes he abandoned Dartmouth and in 1799 crossed the river to hire out as a clerk in a Brattleboro store. By the time he was forty he had a prosperous trading post of his own but he had been far less successful in love. With his brothers he shared what was known in his mother's family as the Atkinson Difficulty—a shyness in the presence of ladies so painful that his brothers had found it easier to woo and marry their own cousins. John blushed his bachelor way through youth to early middle age before he summoned enough courage to ask Polly Hayes, the aunt of a future President, to marry him. Since she was not a cousin, John had triumphed, though tardily, over his brothers—and the Atkinson Difficulty.

The first child, John Humphrey Noyes, Jr., arrived in 1811. Fifteen years later, when the Great Revival was dominating the countryside, young Noyes started off to Dartmouth. As the son of Tutor Noyes he was introduced to the college's most distinguished alumnus, when the latter was visiting Hanover. "I wish," said Daniel Webster, "I could do you as much good as your father did me." This was perhaps John Noyes's most memorable experience at Dartmouth, but it meant nothing to his future as compared with the recurrence of that old family difficulty.

"I swear by Jove," the long-necked, freckled youth promised himself, "I will be impudent! So unreasonable and excessive is my bashfulness that I fully believe I could face a battery of cannon with less trepidation than I could a room full of ladies with whom I was unacquainted." To bolster his self-esteem he bought a pair of square-toed boots, some bell-bottomed pantaloons and a pyramid hat, and soon found himself facing the post-graduate world full of optimism. As an apprentice he entered the law office of his brother-in-law, Larkin G.

Mead (father of the sculptor and architect), but a revival experience changed the course of his life.

The town of Putney, to which the Noyes family had moved, was seething with the excitement of a series of revivals filling young and old with the desire to save the world from slavery, alcohol and ignorance of the will of God. In September of 1831 at the end of his first year's practice of law, John Humphrey promised his mother that he would attend a four-day revival meeting at Putney, but that no one need worry about his being converted, as he loved the world and its pleasures too much. Exhausted at the end of the meeting he came down with a cold, took to his bed and began to pray and to brood about the uncertainty of life. In a perspiration of fever he turned to the New Testament whose well-read scriptures brought him a sudden new concept of life—eternal life without which all earthly existence was meaningless. As soon as he recovered he put the law behind him and started out for the theological seminary at Andover. He was dissatisfied there, for it seemed to him that the business of preparing for the ministry was too prosaic.

"What would the churches, with their glowing zeal and their glorious revivals think," he asked himself in his journal, "if they could look in upon us and see how lifeless we are?" He rebelled against this orthodoxy. In spite of the repeated warnings of his father and brother-in-law to keep away from the heretical fringe, John Humphrey began to meet with a group of radicals who called themselves The Brethren. "Never," he promised his father, "will I be compelled by ministers or anyone else to accept any doctrine that does not commend itself to my mind and conscience."

Proceeding to Yale, where he was guided by no less an evangelist than "Pope" Timothy Dwight, Noyes eagerly funneled his energies into welfare work among New Haven Negroes and into the New Haven Anti-Slavery Society. A brief tour as minister in North Salem, New York, followed his graduation, but he shortly returned to New Haven again as a member of the Free Church. By this time he had become an uncompromising rebel who no longer believed that only clerics and monastics could walk with God. There was something wrong, he thought, with the religious creeds and moral codes under whose tenets great masses of people lived in sin. Why must mankind have to wait until the Hereafter for salvation? Before increasingly large congregations the zealots of the Free Church voiced their grievances and sought the equation for a perfect earthly life. Noyes shared the belief, commonly held at that time, that the second coming of Christ had already occurred. If this was true, then he was already living not in an era of promise but in one of fulfillment. Contrary to the thinking of the Calvinists, and in accordance with the teachings of such prophets as John Wesley, the world was thus free from sin.

One New Haven night when he was lying sleepless in bed Noyes had a profound experience that inspired all that came later. "Three times in quick succession," he reported, "a stream of eternal love gushed through my heart and rolled back again to its source. Joy unspeakable and full of glory filled my soul. All fear and doubt and condemnation passed away. I knew that my heart was clean, and that the Father and Son had come and made it their abode." The conviction that he had achieved absolute purity of heart and freedom from sin made easier his task of abandoning such orthodoxy as praying three or four times daily, observing Sunday as a holy day, and adhering to the Ten Commandments. By the time he met Miss Abigail Merwin he was a confirmed convert to his own new version of Perfectionism. Although eight years younger than Abigail, and though he described his affection for her mostly in spiritual terms, it was real love, and she soon became Perfectionist number two. Psychiatrists might have linked Noyes, the Atkinson Difficulty, Perfectionism and Abigail with what occurred some time later when he suffered a "dark night" of three weeks' duration following the removal of his license to preach by the New Haven association. It was apparently a period of deep melancholy during which he suffered pressure about his heart and lungs. He prepared for death—but awoke instead with a new joy in his heart. Interpreting this as rebirth or "resurrection," he wandered the streets of New York at night, dispelling the last dark shadows from his spirit. There his friends found him in a state of exhaustion and took him back to New Haven.

Apparently the Atkinson Difficulty was still bothering him in 1837, for Abigail was betrothed that year to a man named Platt. John

Humphrey was greatly distraught. He still considered that she belonged to him, and in the so-called Battle-Ax letter, written to a friend and destined to become a turning point in his career, he announced his views concerning marriage.

"When the will of God is done on earth, as it is in heaven," he declared, "there will be no marriage. The marriage supper of the Lamb is a feast at which every dish is free to every guest. Exclusiveness, jealousy, quarreling, have no place there, for the same reason as that which forbids the guests at a thanksgiving dinner to claim each his separate dish and quarrel with the rest for his rights. In a holy community there is no more reason why sexual intercourse should be restrained by law, than why eating and drinking should be—and there is as little occasion for shame in the one case as the other. God has placed a wall of partition between the male and female during the apostasy for good reasons. But woe to him who abolishes the law of the apostasy before he stands in the holiness of the resurrection. . . . I call a certain woman my wife—she is yours, she is Christ's, and in him she is the bride of all saints . . ."

Widely known within a few months, the letter's contents raised a hornet's nest of conflicting opinions, but the strength of his convictions rendered the prophet immune to the public sting. In Boston he discussed the abolition of slavery with William Lloyd Garrison (who had begun his notorious Abolitionist career in Vermont). Noyes declared that the government was not only infidel and reprobate, but villainous, oppressive and "antagonistic to the spiritual forces which are working for the introduction of holiness, peace and human brotherhood." He wanted the North to withdraw at once from the Union. Later he announced that he, at least, was renouncing his allegiance to it and "asserting the title of Jesus Christ to the throne of the world . . ."

Noyes had meanwhile turned his attention to the scene of his youth —Putney. There in 1838 he married Harriet Holton, whom he had converted to Perfectionism. On their wedding trip the happy couple journeyed to Albany to buy a printing press, which they set up at Putney to enlighten the world about the teachings of Perfectionism. Enlisting the aid of his young brother and Harriet's two sisters in the setting of type, Noyes soon had his printed torchbearer, *The Witness,* in regular production. Since 1834 he had planned to use Putney as a proving ground for Perfectionism and as a means of escape from the strife between the libertine New York adherents and the intellectual ones in New Haven. He wrote that in 1836 he had returned to Putney "and remained at my father's house during the following winter. At this time I commenced in earnest the enterprise of repairing the disasters of Perfectionism and establishing it on a permanent foundation; not by preaching and stirring up excitement over a large field, as we had done at the beginning, nor by laboring to . . . discipline broken and corrupted regiments . . . but by devoting myself to the patient instruction of a few simple minded, unpretending believers chiefly belonging to my father's family. . . ."

Old, respectable Squire Noyes regarded John's experiment with a mixture of pride and aloofness, while his wife was alternately hostile and submissive. The villagers, particularly as the years passed, considered John a blot on the fair escutcheon of Putney. But the converts who arrived to join the colony during the latter 1830s held him in unquestioning reverence and believed that he was everything he believed he was. Conducting the "home talks" of the early Perfectionist family, he has been described as an impressive figure, tall and well formed, with a large head and prominent features, blue-gray eyes and sandy hair. Not even his enemies could dismiss him as a charlatan or crackpot. His son Pierrepont Noyes later wrote that "his intensity of thought, common sense, argumentative power, eloquence, sympathy, originality, earnestness and self-sacrificing abandonment to principle all combined to give him an ascendancy over the minds of his hearers like that of the Hebrew prophets." He was likely to be intolerant, however, of the occasional member of his flock who questioned his judgment. If this occurred the unhappy subaltern found himself either ostracized or humbly penitent for having challenged the word of God.

The Putney day began at five in the morning and progressed on a regular schedule which included Bible study, education, printing and cultivation of the soil. Dwelling in three houses owned by Noyes, the colonists shared all the various tasks necessary to sustain their store and two farms which the Noyes children had inherited upon the death of their father in 1841. Freely spending a rather large additional patri-

mony on a society which was drifting rapidly towards communism, John Humphrey got into a great deal of trouble with his mother. She looked aghast upon the curious collection of people, now numbering over three dozen, who had arrived to eat up the family savings. In family affairs she no longer had any say whatever. John was even selecting husbands for her daughters from the Perfectionist ranks. She pleaded and protested, but on each occasion her small old voice was silenced by the loud Perfectionist chorus of her children. Whenever she criticized John he would rebuke her and ultimately he "convinced me that my feelings were under the delusion of Satan; advised me to pray much to be delivered from this accusing spirit and licentious tongue. . . ."

The determination to allow neither family nor fortune to interfere with the dictates of his conscience now brought the prophet to the threshhold of a dangerous series of experiments. As early as 1838, shortly after his arival in Putney, he had begun to ply the art of mental healing. Elsewhere in the country even orthodox ministers were reporting astounding physical cures through "magnetism" or "mesmerism." In 1840 Noyes administered "large doses of faith with moderate doses of brandy and wine" to David Harrison, a friend who was running a high fever and who had been under the fruitless care of a doctor. Harrison's recovery within twenty-four hours signaled a new and broader program of "animal magnetism," which was presumably a combination of mental and physical therapy.

The prophet's star patient was Harriet A. Hall, who had been sick since 1839 with dropsy and other ailments, including liver trouble, a bad cough, pressure on the brain, "a serious affection of the spine" and suspected consumption. Bedridden for several years she had lain almost blind in a darkened room. By what Noyes's Putney periodical, *The Spiritual Magazine,* called "the laying on of hands," Mrs. Hall was so far cured as to be able to "walk, to face the sun, to ride miles without inconvenience and with excessive pleasure." During Noyes's early visits he had talked with her and read portions of the Perfectionist creed. After a few weeks her eyesight improved so markedly that she was able to read books he had brought, and soon she was writing and walking. At this point Noyes turned her over to the care of another colonist,

Alexander Wilder, under whose treatment her health soon turned for the worse again.

Wilder, meanwhile, was becoming as mentally and physically sick as his patient. For some time he had served as perhaps the foremost guinea pig for experiments in animal magnetism. He later reported that in 1843 he had submitted to a series of treatments and "by reason of their continuation for some weeks and being operated upon by several of his [Noyes's] family, a diseased state of mind and body was produced. For many months I suffered a very great depression of spirits. I felt myself in connection and rapport with influences which caused the keenest mental anguish and knew not how to free myself. A nameless fear, despondency, gloom and despair paralyzed my strength of mind. A morbid attachment for individuals was induced, and the whole corporeal system partook of the disorder. The intervals of pleasure, like the exhilarations of intoxicating drugs, gave relief for a little season but only to plunge me into a deeper gloom. To heighten my misery Noyes began to berate me, charging my sufferings to various causes and even to the influence of the Devil. This devil, or evil genius, I now know, emanated directly from him."

Until Noyes persuaded him to assist in the magnetizing of Mrs. Hall, Wilder had begun to feel more cheerful. However his despondency soon returned and he had to abandon a practice which he said was "more corrupting and enervating than beneficial to the persons engaged in it."

Shaken and demoralized, Wilder left the Perfectionist Community, and Mrs. Hall, distraught over the rift between Noyes and Wilder, slipped quickly back into her former hopeless state. Ministered to by at least ten doctors, she hovered at death's door for three and a half years before Noyes once more visited her, this time accompanied by Mary Cragin, the wife of one of his stanch colonists. Mrs. Hall was currently suffering from ulceration of the kidneys and her eyes could not bear the light. Noyes, however, commanded her to get out of bed. Mrs. Hall promptly responded by rising and seating herself by the window. The prophet now raised the curtain and Mrs. Hall's eyes were curiously unaffected by the light. Soon she had left first the sickroom and next her house and, giving at least the illusion of health, was seen riding through the streets in the prophet's carriage with John Humphrey, proud and exalted, seated beside her.

At this moment Noyes had reached the peak of his popularity, which is to say that he was not being loudly damned by the people of Putney. Soon, however, he undertook to treat a Miss Mary A. Knight, who unfortunately died in the final stages of her cure. This not only caused a few disturbances in the magnetic field of Noyes's own faith but raised a tempest of public reproach. Yet he would neither abandon animal magnetism nor disavow it, since he could not forget how he had miraculously cured himself of a long-standing throat ailment in 1845. Moreover his other patients had nearly all responded favorably. The Putney colony was only as strong as the minds and bodies of its disciples: it needed all of their physical and mental resources to reach the lofty goal of Perfection.

In 1846 the Putney colonists after much thought adopted a perilous program of what they called Complex Marriage. Noyes believed Perfectionism could not attain perfection without plural marriage, an idea which he had been advocating in principle, at least, ever since he had lost Abigail Merwin. There is a reasonable doubt whether the chicken or the egg came first—now, as before, it seemed to be Noyes's own emotional problem that gave rise to the principle of Complex Marriage, not the reverse.

The loss of Abigail was a blow from which he had never quite recovered, since God had ordained that she should be his. When he heard that she had separated from her husband he had sent for her, but she had not come. Then he had written to her that unless she came another woman would take her place. Still she did not come; and he had then married Harriet Holton. Still his affection for Abigail remained and when her husband died he again hoped in vain that she would return. His first disappointment had led to his marriage to Harriet; the final one to an affair with Mary Cragin, the wife of one of the colonists.

He often walked about the Putney countryside with Mary, deep in the bonds of spiritual love. One soft summer evening, after strolling far from town, the two sat down to rest and suddenly found themselves almost overcome with physical desire. "After a moment we arose and went toward home. On the way we stopped once and took some liberty of embracing, and Mrs. Cragin distinctly gave me to understand that she was ready for the full consummation. I said 'No, I am going home to report what we have done.' On reaching Mr. Cragin's house, I called a meeting of the four, related our doings, and offered the transaction for criticism. My wife promptly and entirely sanctioned our proceeding. The upshot of the conference was, that we gave each other full liberty all round, and so entered into complex marriage in the quartette form. The last part of the interview was as amicable and happy as a wedding and full consummation soon followed."

In 1847 Noyes announced that the Kingdom of God had come to Putney, and henceforth the colonists could not attain Perfection without embracing the Complex Marriage covenant. He was careful to distinguish between free love—in which he did not believe—and Complex Marriage. The former was irresponsible flirtation; the latter obligated every colonist to communal care of the children. Noyes felt certain that the self-seeking quality of the traditional marriage would disappear in the new system. "Men and women," he announced, "will mingle like boys and girls in their employment and labor will become sport." In the upstanding village of Putney, however, he soon found that Complex Marriage was a bear whose tail he could scarcely hold on to. Although the colonists were sworn to secrecy, rumors of wild parties rocked the town. Renegade Perfectionists were anxious to cleanse their souls by telling what they knew. The parents of neighborhood maidens, whom the Perfectionists had tried to convert, publicly divulged each infamous detail of their encounters with the prophet.

One of the village girls whose near loss to Perfectionism aroused the wrath of Putney was pretty, fifteen-year-old Lucinda J. Lamb. According to Hubbard Eastman, a village preacher who wrote a book exposing the Perfectionists, Noyes took a fancy to Lucinda and engaged several female colonists to try to attract the girl to the Community. At first Lucinda's parents did not object to her presence at meetings and even allowed her to board at the Community House, but they later became alarmed. When they took steps to remove her they found themselves in difficulty with Noyes. "God is the father of her spirit," he warned them. "You have the legal right and the physical power to dispose of her body—to send her where you will. God has the absolute

right and the irresistible power to direct the movements of her spirit
and fix her heart on the Kingdom and followers of his Son . . ."

Undaunted by the damage that might be done to her spirit, Lamb
placed Lucinda under the protection of his son and some friends in
Fayetteville, New York. But mere distance could not sever the bonds
of Perfectionist affection. John's brother, George Noyes, and John
Miller, another colonist, appeared in Fayetteville the morning after
Lucinda's arrival there and asked to see her. When her guardians refused, George declared his intention of marrying her and arranged a
personal interview. George did not, however, succeed either in marrying her or in bringing her back to Putney.

Meanwhile John Miller decided to try his luck by mail:

"We shall all be delighted to see you once more at our house, and we
expect to have the privilege next Saturday evening. . . . We have very
happy times at our house, more so than ever, all that is wanting is your
presence to make it completely so. Though you are absent you have
been the subject of conversation several evenings . . . Mr. Noyes said
he wished to express his entire approbation of your conduct, and that
he was very pleased with you."

A second and more ardent letter from Miller expressed "our friendship for you and our connexion with you is nearer and dearer than
anything this world knows anything about, and we shall prove it to
you in every possible way." Lucinda managed to return to Putney.
When her parents appeared at the Community to remove her again
John Humphrey was reported to have shaken his fist at Mrs. Lamb,
told her that she had done enough to sink to the lowest depths of hell,
and that she could not have her daughter. But the Lambs were able to
rescue Lucinda once again and to ship her seventy-five miles away—far
enough to discourage any further contact with the wolves.

By 1847 ten years of hearsay had aroused the people of Vermont to
an awareness of the monstrous design of the Community's life. As if
struck by an adder, Harriet Hall's husband, who had himself been
drifting toward Perfectionism, recoiled from his investigation of the
movement and hurried to Brattleboro to lodge with the state's attorney
the charge of adultery against John Humphrey Noyes. When the
grand jury found a bill against the prophet on June 10, hot invective

blistered the leader and his followers. The public demanded that the state authorities immediately cut this carcinoma out of the body politic.

The blue of the late fall sky bathed Putney in a serenity it had not known for nearly a decade. Facing a jail sentence and the attachment of his property, John Humphrey had fled, leaving his Community in a weakened and leaderless condition. It was a hounded but not a haggard man who now looked toward New York State as the new home of the Perfectionists. Persecution as malignant as that of the Roman emperors had been committed by the state of Vermont, but the prophet accepted his exile with calm. The bourgeois and the magistrates of Vermont with their archaic customs and laws were, of course, wrong. Noyes had not sinned because he knew that in the eyes of God it was not possible for him to sin. " 'Whatsoever is not of faith is sin'; and to him that believeth, 'all things are lawful.' God tells me that He does not care so much *what* I do, as *how* I do it and by this word I walk in all things. I never inquire whether it is *right* to do this, or *wrong* to do that, but whether God *leads* me to do it or not. I look not at the thing to be done but at the influence by which it is done. These principles I apply to the use of women, ardent spirits, money . . ."

There had been no licentiousness in Putney. On the contrary, during this time in the early 1840s when the country was pockmarked with all kinds of irresponsible societies, Noyes believed that the members of his Putney Community had lived in strict discipline—even in their sexual life. Putney Perfectionists had been completely responsible to one another and to their Community. Putney was no free-love colony; it was an honest experiment to cure some of the ills of a turbulent and changing society. To him the Community "instead of causing the flood, built the ark, and . . . set about the work not a moment too soon."

If mankind was to move toward a more perfect society something had to be done to elevate the sexual impulse and to make it part of the life of the spirit. It was not enough that a bodily instinct should draw one man and one woman together. If it could not bind a whole society together, then eternal conflict and hatred would be the lot of the human race. It had been a promising and noble experiment. His Vermont enemies might have stalemated it, but they could not obliterate it; of this he was certain.

For a few years Noyes labored at Willow Place, the Perfectionist colony in Brooklyn; but Brooklyn was not the promised land of the Perfectionists. The new Heavenly Association soon migrated to a site near the Oneida Indian "castle" in the wilds of upstate New York. Here, just prior to the Civil War, the willing hands of the colonists began to build, brick by brick, the walls of an immense Community House, destined to be the nerve center of Perfectionism. To house about fifty men, women and children, the solid three-an-a-half story structure contained a dining room, schoolroom, parlor, reception room and separate sleeping quarters for the men, women and married couples. The years of poverty had passed by this time. A man named Newhouse, the designer of a fine steel trap, had brought his invention with him into the Perfectionist family and Noyes soon had every man, woman and child engaged in the production of traps. They were widely sold throughout the United States and Canada and laid the foundation for the gigantic enterprise in Community Plate which would one day make Oneida a name of world renown.

At ten o'clock each morning a clanging bell would announce recess and all the trapmakers, cooks and community farmers would drop their tools and repair to the printing office for a midmorning lunch, which was followed by a brief interval of dancing in the garret. The rest of the day was composed of work and relaxation—of music and education and discussion groups engaging in Mutual Criticism, which was Noyes's favorite device for removing friction. Every Perfectionist, including the prophet himself, periodically underwent a searching vocal scrutiny by his fellow members. This, according to John Humphrey, made for a pervading sense of humility and tolerance.

Now, at long last, the prophet had created a fine laboratory where he could test all the theories he had previously evolved in Putney. The colony's property was owned by all its members and the fruits of their labor were distributed to all alike. Into the system of Complex Marriage Noyes had introduced a program of "male continence," which achieved birth control by allowing intercourse without consummation. He had also introduced Stirpiculture, a Darwinian program of scientific breeding in which the best of the colony's physical and mental specimens were united to produce offspring. Noyes considered himself an ideal candidate for this program and even after he was in his sixties he became the father of nine of the fifty-eight children born in the stirpicultural period.

As the years passed the prophet became more and more the father-confessor of the entire Perfectionist family—a counsellor and arbiter to whom all the colonists looked for guidance. Yet he was not a dictator, and for thirty years Oneida continued to be the purest experiment in communism (or "religious socialism" as the colonists termed it) that the country had ever known. Noyes had thoroughly examined the merits and pitfalls of all the other isms, such as Mormonism, Spiritualism, Fourierism, Kabylism and Swedenborgianism. He had dismissed most of them as being nonreligious or semireligious or purely social, as failing to be based on love and religion which to Noyes were the two deepest experiences of man. Except for their denial of love and their separation of the sexes, he deeply admired the social and religious life, the faith, steadiness and prosperity of the Shakers. Perfectionism owed much to the Shakers. Indeed, his Community had borrowed at least something from most of the other societies.

During its twenty-year reign at Oneida, Perfectionism was as roundly damned as it had been in Putney. It was also admired. "I am bound to say as an honest reporter," declared a correspondent in the *Woman's Journal,* "that I looked in vain for the visible signs of either the suffering or the sin. The community makes an impression entirely unlike that left by the pallid joylessness of the Shakers, or the stupid sensualism which impressed me in the few Mormon households I have seen. The fact that the children of the community hardly ever wish to leave it; that the young men whom they send to Yale College, and the young women whom they send for musical instruction to New York, always return eagerly and devote their lives to the community—this proves a good deal. There is no coercion to keep them, as in Mormonism, and there are no monastic vows, as in the Roman Catholic Church. This invariable return, therefore, shows that it is of a kind which wins the respect of the young and generous. A body must have great confidence in itself when it thus voluntarily sends its sheep into the midst of the world's wolves, and fearlessly expects their return."

Long after it was all over, Pierrepont Noyes, one of the sons of John Humphrey, recalled:

"There has survived in my memory an impression that the relation between our grown folks had a quality intimate and personal, a quality that made life romantic. Unquestionably the sexual relations of the members under the Community inspired a lively interest in each other, but I believe that the opportunity for romantic friendships also played a part in rendering life more colorful than elsewhere. Even elderly people whose physical passions had burned low preserved the fine essence of earlier associations. Child as I was, I sensed a spirit of high romance surrounding them, a vivid youthful interest in life that looked from the eyes and spoke in their voices and manners."

But the prophet's brave new world did not endure. After Noyes grew old and willed the destiny of Oneida to one of his sons, dissension divided the colonists into bitter groups. The condemnation of the outside world that John Humphrey had so well succeeded in rebuffing now shredded the delicate fabric of his social structure. By 1880 the Perfectionists had abandoned Complex Marriage and Stirpiculture. Private ambition had succeeded community welfare. A corporation making Community Plate replaced the large family which had thrived so long on the manufactures of the spirit. When it was all over John Humphrey could at least tell the self-seeking world that "we made a raid into an unknown country, charted it, and returned without the loss of a man, woman or child."

With his wife and a few faithful followers the Putney prophet retired to the Canadian side of the Niagara River—an infirm old man living out his last days within hearing of the roar of the falls.

IX. Laborers in Learning

O NE way in which schoolmasters could show their disapproval of Samuel Hart for being a Universalist was by treating his children unfairly. As a small girl Emma Hart sensed this prejudice and held her teachers in quiet disrespect. Though girls were not expected to be educated in 1800, or even to be capable of learning very much, Emma pursued such masculine subjects as geometry and at fifteen entered an academy in Berlin, Connecticut. Since no college in the world accepted women, her formal education ended when she received her academy diploma.

But even if she could not be taught further, she could teach. In 1807 at the age of twenty she became preceptress of an academy for girls in

Middlebury, Vermont. The boys' grammar school occupied the first floor of the academy building there, and Emma, with thirty-seven girls from Vermont and New York, held her classes in a large room upstairs. The task of teaching several different subjects simultaneously to girls of different ages was less distressing in the fall and spring than in the winter, when a single small fireplace lent the frigid room no more than an appearance of warmth. On zero mornings, as soon as the minds and bodies of her students began to congeal, she would form them into a long double line and start them around the room in a country dance. Because she discarded many of the archaic rules, the girls, "a remarkable band of maidens ranging from about 12 to 16," liked Miss Hart and she was pleased with them.

At the end of the first year she found that community prejudice was threatening to destroy the school by magnifying religious differences among her pupils. Of the Vermonters who stoutly upheld Emma and her seminary at this time, none was more faithful than a Middlebury gentleman, twice a widower, named Dr. John Willard. This respected man not only won her gratitude but her heart. She became Emma Willard. Marriage and expectant motherhood forced her to abandon the school for a time, and it was not until 1814, when her husband suffered financial reverses, that her thoughts returned actively to the frontier of female education.

Her husband's nephew, John, had boarded in her household while attending Middlebury College, and through him she had gained an intimate familiarity with the interior of a men's college. By studying John's texts and his examinations she was able to accompany him from day to day and semester to semester. There was nothing in the curriculum, she decided, that was either superior or forbidding to a woman's intellect; her sex had been subjected to gross discrimination. Possibly a woman's place was in the home, but marriage would be a far richer experience if it could also be an intellectual partnership.

To relieve her husband's financial burden Emma opened a school for girls in her own home, and with signal success offered them the same subjects that were being taught in Middlebury. She asked the college authorities to let her students sit in on the men's classes, but they would not permit this. She asked if she might go to the boys' examinations to learn college methods, but they would not permit that. Thus she was forced to lift her school into the realm of higher education by her own bootstraps. She called it her Female Seminary, as all others established in the same pattern were afterwards termed. Meanwhile over a period of years she quietly evolved a Plan for Improving Female Education, sharing her secret only with her husband, because "I knew that I should be regarded as visionary almost to insanity, should I utter the expectations which I secretly entertained in connection with it. But it was not merely on the strengh of my arguments that I relied. I determined to inform myself and increase my personal influence and fame as a teacher, calculating that in this way I might be sought for in other places, where influential men would carry my project before some legislature for the sake of obtaining a good school."

Governor Van Ness invited Emma Willard to take charge of a female seminary to be opened in connection with the University of Vermont at Burlington, but these plans went awry, and Emma was forced to look to the state of New York for the future of her girls. She succeeded in presenting her views before members of the Albany legislature, and ultimately they voted her a charter for the Waterford Academy for Young Ladies, a school which later bore her name. This public measure granted the entrance of women to higher learning.

Some say he was put in a basket and placed on a Brownington doorstep, and that because they found him early in the morning they named him Twilight—Alexander L. Twilight. But the facts seem to be that he was born in Corinth, that his father died when he was very young, and that he was indentured to a neighboring farmer for the rest of his youth. It is known that at seventeen he was not only a devout Christian but an insatiable reader, and that after buying the final year of his apprenticeship from the farmer he started off across the hills for the Randolph academy of the Reverend Rufus Nutting. Extracurricular labor also enabled him to attend Middlebury College, from whence he graduated in 1823. He hired out as a schoolmaster in Peru, New York, and in 1827 received from the Champlain Presbytery at Plattsburg a license to preach. Soon he was back again on the Vermont shore of Lake Champlain, now as a preacher-teacher in the town of Vergennes.

But the verdant upland hills of home drew him north. By 1829 he had settled down as principal of the Orleans County grammar school in Brownington. In this high township of two hundred inhabitants, a church, inn and a cluster of houses, he resolved to spend his life.

However Alexander Twilight was not long satisfied with the grammar school. In his imagination he saw on top of the hill a large academy, through whose doors boys would enter from the hill farms, and, after several seasons, they would leave with qualities of mind and spirit which would help them become leaders in their towns and counties. Possibly this phantom school of his mind's eye would one day draw students from other states. Perhaps it would become a great academy.

If such a school were to be built, he decided in the mid-1830s, his own hands and those of a few neighbors would have to raise the walls, as his resources were meager and his inclination toward an academy in Brownington was not widely shared. But there were no obstacles greater than his desire to build the structure. Salvaging what energy and time were available beyond his duties at the grammar school and church, he harnessed an ox to a stoneboat and started hauling great chunks of granite from a neighboring farm to the plateau above the road where the stages passed. This task was no more enormous than squaring the chunks with hand tools and hoisting them into position, but there are many days in two years and Twilight worked every spare moment—mornings and evenings, Saturdays and holidays. He built an ascending earthen ramp around the building and the hard-laboring white ox would trudge up the incline dragging a block of stone after him. Eventually the academy began to take on the massive proportions of the structure that had long dwelt in Twilight's imagination.

When the great rectangle of earth was drawn away from the masonry the minister could sense the rare satisfaction of those who reach the summit of their ambitions. The building was four stories high and as solid as the rocky pinnacles which dominate Lake Willoughby to the southeast. It was, in its own rugged simplicity, as eloquent as the ancient temples of the Acropolis. Indeed, Twilight named it Athenian Hall. The lofty sixty-by-forty-five-foot structure could be seen from every hill within three miles. It had thirty rooms and sixty windows, a large kitchen, dining room and recitation rooms of ample size. Fifty students could live and study here.

From the counties of northern Vermont they came to Alexander Twilight's granite academy to learn English and chemistry and Latin, philosophy and botany, history and geology, spoken French and music. They say that a settler who was building a log house some miles away heard a bell ringing and hastened across the hills to learn where it came from. It was Alexander Twilight summoning his students to morning class. When the settler saw the great building he could scarcely believe it possible.

The force of Twilight's character as a temporal and spiritual leader became apparent at once. Of the fifty-seven students under his guidance in 1839, five graduated from college, five became preachers, five or more became lawyers, two became judges and others became legislators and merchants. It is said that Twilight taught better than he preached, that he was a peculiarly gifted instructor. His discipline consisted chiefly in appealing to his students' honor, but failing in this he could, by satire and ridicule, cut a rebellious student down to size. The task of managing fifty boys of high-school age for four terms of twelve weeks each was one which could not have been discharged, even in an era of sunup to sundown labor, by one with less will than Twilight. His wife Mercy, whom he had married in 1826, was a strong woman devoted to his work. She supervised the kitchen with its stone floor, its large fireplace and its hand-wrought cooking implements and managed the countless daily details of housekeeping.

Athenian Hall became the best-known academy in northern Vermont, but when Alexander Twilight died in 1857 the school died with him. There remained only the silent testimony of the worn front step, the initials notched in the sixty window sills—and the more eloquent testimony of the living who had been taught there. Mrs. Twilight closed the heavy front door and retreated with her memories into the vast recesses of the building. With the coming of the railroad the four-horse stages no longer clattered up the hill, and the village of Brownington drowsed. Yet time could not easily disturb the massive granite blocks of Athenian Hall for, as the people of Brownington remark, "They built heavy in those days."

X. Steamboats in the
Ground Swell

WHILE the neighbors were in church Mr. Fix-It tried out his
steamboat. There was barely room for him and his assistant
and the boiler and the homemade machinery and the pile of kindling,
but Fix-It was presently thumping along the clear Connecticut at
four miles an hour.

George Washington was President at this time, Thomas Jefferson
was Secretary of State and Robert Fulton was a young man who
would not even begin to think about the *Clermont* for a decade.

Samuel Morey had been experimenting with steamboats for at least
three years before he embarked in his teakettle that summer Sunday.
As early as 1790 he had crossed Fairlee Pond in a tiny steam-driven
craft. He had tried paddle wheels in the bow, paddle wheels amidships
and paddle wheels in the stern. He was quite satisfied that the rigging
of sailing ships sang with twilight winds—James Watt's steam engine,

it was clear, had seafaring qualities. Others, such as Fitch and Rumsey, agreed, but none was earlier than Mr. Fix-It to put the engines and paddle wheels to work successfully. In 1795 a patent signed by George Washington recognized Morey's "new and useful improvement in the mode of applying the force of steam," but the public paid scant attention, even when the inventor fired the boiler at Hartford and steamed down to New York City. Of those present on that occasion there were a few who considered the boat more than a curiosity, among them Chancellor Robert Livingston, who later joined with Robert Fulton to build the *Clermont*. There was none who saw the fragile craft for what it really was—a forerunner of the age of steam on the rivers, lakes and oceans of the world.

His efforts to interest New Yorkers in his invention were unavailing and Morey returned embittered to Fairlee Pond. Yet he did not long restrain the wheels that were turning in his head. He produced a model that Charles Duryea called the first internal combustion engine. Its principles found their way, two generations later, into the automobile and the airplane.

In his Orford workshop Mr. Fix-It tinkered practically to the end of his long life. "It only remains," he wrote in later years, "for me to have the engine applied to a carriage on a railroad, and when that is done, I shall think I have done my part."

In 1807 the paddle wheels of the *Clermont* thrashed the Hudson all the way from New York to Albany, and proved to the many what Samuel Morey's diminutive craft has suggested to the few. Steamboats would transport people from the Atlantic seaboard down the broad rivers which threaded the fastnesses of the Mississippi basin. Fleet side-wheelers would range the length and breadth of eastern waters, shortening the distances between their ports of call.

The keel for the *Vermont*, the first steamboat after the *Clermont*, went down under the oak tree in back of Isaac Nye's Burlington store. One day late in 1808 the clatter of sledge hammers against the wedges that held her on the ways announced the vessel's baptism. Amidst the catcalls of wind-and-canvas diehards who had gathered for the launching the *Vermont* creaked sideways into the water of Lake Champlain—to settle into the mud like a fat old woman into an overstuffed chair.

Her builders, James and John Winans, who had helped Fulton with the *Clermont,* presently extracted her, installed her ornery engine and anounced in June 1809 that they were able to "pass Lake Champlain with safety and dispatch." The one-hundred-twenty-foot boat left St. Johns, Quebec, at nine o'clock in the morning and arrived at White-hall, New York, twenty-four hours later, having averaged five miles an hour when the wind wasn't blowing. For six years she lurched from one end of the lake to the other. One day in 1815 her connecting rod broke. Torpedoed from within, as it were, the *Vermont* sank at once in the Richelieu River three miles north of the American-Cana-dian border. Nevertheless she had proved her worth, to the extent that at least three companies and two wildcat operators were shortly run-ning steamboats on Lake Champlain.

A fourth, the Champlain Transportation Company, received its charter in 1826, two years after Daniel Webster argued the Fulton-Livingston monopoly to extinction before the Supreme Court and opened the waterways of the nation to free steamboating. However free steamboating was not the object of the directors of the Champlain Transportation Company. They achieved a monopoly of a strategic waterway simply by scuttling or buying out their competitors. Travel-ers between Montreal and New York preferred water transport to the corduroy or dirt roads over which the stages bumped. Shippers found the steamers swifter, and filled their holds with quantities of merchan-dise destined for New York, Montreal, or the communities around the lake. The Champlain Transportation Company waxed prosperous, then affluent.

In the early 1830s it determined to build a ship of unparalleled ele-gance, one which could steam through the waves at fifteen miles an hour. The *Burlington,* launched in 1837 at the company's Shelburne Harbor shipyard, exceeded specifications. She had a paddlebox twenty-four feet high with an elegant female painted on it. The paneled ma-hogany doors to the staterooms had plated handles and pilasters with Doric capitals. Brass belaying pins encased the engine. "The decks," declared Charles Dickens in his *American Notes,* "are drawing rooms, the cabins are boudoirs, choicely furnished and every nook and corner of the vessel is a perfect curiosity of graceful comfort and beautiful contrivance . . . a perfectly exquisite achievement of neatness, elegance and order; superior," Dickens was sure, "to any other in the world."

The captain, no less than the boat, exceeded specifications. On a lake busy with workaday canalboat skippers and tugboatmen hauling lumber tows, Richard Sherman was a polished, priggish gentleman of whom President Martin Van Buren remarked, "He thinks the world is a steamboat and he is the captain." Sherman refused to take aboard the *Burlington* "a quantity of slaughter hides belonging to Lyman Brainerd, on account of the offensive smell, and for which the said Brainerd [has] commenced his suit against this company."

With characteristic perseverance and acumen a Peter Comstock of Whitehall, New York, whose steamboats had been purchased by the Champlain Transportation Company in 1826, started building a ship at Whitehall which was designed to equal the *Burlington* in every respect. The directors of the Vermont company met this threat by buying Mr. Comstock's unfinished steamer for twenty thousand dollars. They further agreed to pay him a thousand dollars a year for eight years as their company's "agent" at Whitehall, providing he wouldn't start any new steamboat projects. They then completed his steamer, named it the *Whitehall* and added it to their line with another new vessel, the *Saranac,* which had been constructed at Shelburne Bay.

The deal with Comstock had hardly been consummated before a group of New Yorkers rolled more black clouds of competition over the Adirondacks and onto the lake by announcing their plans for a fine new steamer. The directors of the Champlain Transportation Company solved the problem in the usual manner—they bought out the directors of the new corporation and elected three of them to their own board.

Hardly had this taken place before the eight-year agreement with Comstock ran out. He resigned as agent at Whitehall, organized a new company and started building another steamboat. Deciding that it was too expensive to maintain their monopoly in the traditional manner, the directors of the Champlain Transportation Company resolved to fight. Comstock was no more prepared for this than were his backers, who were reported to have been some directors of the Vermont company who chose this method to leaven its fat surplus. Now there was nothing for the New Yorker to do but finish his boat and enter the races.

Enter the races Comstock did. His new steamer *Francis Saltus* was not as large as the *Burlington*, but was slim and slick as a pickerel, designed to equal the *Burlington's* rating of fifteen miles an hour. Slashing its rates, the Champlain Transportation Company placed the *Burlington* on the same schedule as the *Saltus* in order that the public might ride the lake's most luxurious boat at the same price. It didn't work out that way, however. Captain Chamberlin, master of the *Saltus*, was popular, while Richard Sherman's pandering to the elect and the fashionable alienated great numbers of travelers. Sherman had also incurred public disfavor by carrying British troops on the *Burlington* during the Canadian rebellion, when no other American vessel was available to them.

The two steamers would line up at the opposite sides of the same dock at Whitehall with "runners" shouting their solicitations for both companies. Whenever there were crowds on hand at sailing time, Captain Chamberlin would lean out of his pilothouse and, to the tune of *Little Brown Jug,* rend the air with these verses:

> Dick Sherman is so very slick
> The fops all swarm around him thick,
> As humbugs 'round a pot of honey;
> So Dick's cologne brings him the money.
>   Ha, Ha, Ha. That's the fun
>   For Dandy Dick of the *Burlington.*

> His decks are scrubbed with so much care
> That Cowhide boots can't come in there;
> If you can't make your money rattle
> You must go forward with the cattle.
>   Ha, Ha, Ha. That's the fun
>   For Dandy Dick of the *Burlington.*

> Oh! Dicky is a gallant lad,
> He makes the ladies very glad;

He smiles and flirts with great parade,
And then makes love to the cabin maid.
Ha, Ha, Ha. That's the fun
For Dandy Dick of the *Burlington*.

The *Saltus* and the *Montreal*
Will drive him from the Lake this fall.
Ha, Ha, Ha. That's the fun
For Dandy Dick of the *Burlington*.

The public responded favorably to this propaganda, and when it became obvious that the decks of the *Saltus* were consistently more populated than those of Sherman's boat, the Champlain Transportation Company had to act. It put the *Burlington* on night run and placed the *Saranac,* commanded by the popular P. T. Davis, opposite the *Saltus*.

Since there was now little to choose between the vessels, the struggle shifted to racing. Thick smoke poured from the two steamers' stacks as they churned up the lake at excessive speeds made possible by plying the boilers with a barrel of tar, resinous wood or inflammable freight. To gain the advantage, one or the other vessel frequently skipped a landing or two. The ships' bars plied the passengers with spirits, which dulled their suspicion that the boilers were straining at pressures beyond those for which they were designed. At the climax of the excitement travelers lined the decks hooting and placing bets. Fearing a disaster, the Champlain Transportation Company curtailed the sale of liquor and issued orders against racing and leaving landing places ahead of time. These rules were presently rescinded, though. The company was more interested in the outcome than the wildest rooter on deck.

Fortunately for the passengers the contest between the *Saltus* and the *Saranac* ended in an economic, rather than a boiler, explosion. With a larger reservoir of cash, the Champlain Transportation Company was better able to survive the low-rate war. Comstock eventually capitulated and the *Saltus* was taken over by three Troy receivers, from whom the monopoly immediately tried to purchase the boat.

Failing in this and faced with the continued competition of the Troy receivers, who were running the *Saltus,* the directors of the Champlain Transportation Company laid down a two-hundred-forty-foot keel at the Shelburne Bay shipyards.

Early one morning in the spring of 1847 citizens of Burlington saw a bright new steamer in their harbor opposite the *Saltus,* her milk-white sides accenting the proud letters of her name: *United States.* A crowd gathered. As sailing time neared, billows of smoke rose from the lofty stacks. Suddenly, before anyone was ready, the water began churning white under the paddle wheels of the *Saltus.* She burst away from the dock, putting yards of water between herself and the still dormant *United States,* from whose pilothouse window there peered the determined, bewhiskered face of Captain William Anderson. He studied the fleet *Saltus* as she widened the breach between herself and the dock. The face in the pilothouse window turned aside. Down in the shiny engine room of the *United States* sounded the clang of a brass bell. With the sure hand of experience, the engineer admitted steam to the stoutest engine on the lake. Then he took hold of the throttle and pulled it down as far as it would go. The *United States* came to life. Above the vessel the walking beam worked violently. Below, the paddles beat the water to a foam. Pandemonium reigned on shore and on the decks of the steamers. The breach between the *Saltus* and the *States* continued to widen at first; then stayed the same; then grew smaller. Steadily the *United States* crept along the *Saltus's* stern until she was broadside. As whistles blew and voices grew hoarse the *United States* forged by, leaving the *Saltus* to thump shamefacedly along in her wake.

The superior speed of the *United States* wilted the Troy receivers of the opposition boat. The following year the *Francis Saltus,* with another small vessel which the opposition had been building, came, as did all things, under the control of the Champlain Transportation Company. There was rejoicing among the directors, but if the hearty laughers could have read in a crystal ball the future of the *Saltus,* despair would have replaced their jubilation.

From the time of its establishment in 1826 Vermonters had controlled the Champlain Transportation Company. During the year

1849, however, a number of directors were destined to arise one morning and find that they'd truly been "sold down the river." Some of their colleagues had quietly disposed of their stock to a syndicate headed by the charlatan of Hudson River transportation, Daniel Drew, who for some time had plotted to engorge the juicy plum that was the Champlain Transportation Company. Drew maintained the fiction of Vermont control by securing a St. Albans man, Oscar A. Burton, for president of the company. This manipulator had hardly taken office before he declared a dividend of fifteen dollars a share, voted himself a ten-thousand-dollar compensation and acquired a house at Burlington famous for the great stone lions guarding the paths. The public regarded him with disdain and it was not long before reports began to circulate of a new opposition ship on the ways at Whitehall designed to replace the old *Saltus,* recently taken over by the company.

Newspapers expended a springtide of editorial ink on behalf of the new ship, which received the name *R. W. Sherman*—possibly because Dandy Dick had parted company with the monopoly. "Captain Chapman has issued circulars to the public notifying the community that the R. W. Sherman will be ready to commence making her regular trips. . . . He states positively that O. A. Burton or any other old line director cannot have the directing of her business, and that she will sail as an opposition boat—opposition to the old line, opposition to his prices and slow sailing steamers. We certainly like the tone and spirit of his manifesto and the news falls among the old line conductors with the effect of a 24-pound shot, as if they have been expecting to place her in their line to sail in connection with the 'States' and had supposed, until Chapman's Coup d'Etat, that the bargain and sale was definitely settled, and that a captain of their own selection was to step on board and politely bow Mr. Chapman off."

Failing to scuttle the opposition by injunctions and other devices he "had the impertinence," asserted Captain Chapman, "to circulate a report that he had purchased the *R. W. Sherman* . . . What Mr. Burton intended to accomplish by issuing such a base and contemptible falsehood is best known to himself. . . ." Chapman charged that Burton had let it be known that he (Burton) had bought the *Sherman* so that the public would think it was owned by the monopoly and not patronize it. The independent owners of the boat would accordingly suffer. "Anyone who is acquainted with O. A. Burton knows that 'truth to him is stranger than fiction.' Mr. Burton does not own the *Sherman,* he has not bought me . . ."

". . . It may be gratifying to the public," declared a Burlington newspaper, "to know that the new steamer, *R. W. Sherman,* is now in the quiet and peaceable possession of her lawful owner, Captain T. D. Chapman. . . . The people want an independent boat . . . an independent boat they shall have . . . the money of an unscrupulous monopoly in the hands of 'pliant tools' who have accidentally acquired the confidence of honest and unsuspecting stockholders, will not prevent it."

At last dawned the day of the *Sherman's* maiden voyage.

"In due time the gallant *Sherman* took us aboard, and as the superb and graceful boat moved from the wharf, hearty cheers arose from the animated crowd assembled to greet her, while the *Saltus,* crowding steam, was creeping along the eastern short of the Lake, some three miles ahead of the *Sherman,* like a suspected codfish, and in vain hope of reaching Burlington first, by virtue of having made but one landing since leaving Whitehall, while the *Sherman* had made all. But the *Sherman* swept into her course, and gallantly passed the *Saltus* . . . and who can measure the hearty cheers that greeted the noble steamer and her popular commander as she approached and left our wharves—all the while 'sonorous blowing martial sounds' under the management of the Whitehall and Burlington bands."

The Burlington *Free Press* was transported: "She passed the *Saltus* this morning . . . as easy as though that boat were going the other way—and if any responsible man has a seedy sort of hat . . . we are prepared to wager one of Barnum's 'ne plus ultras' that she will make mincemeat of the *United States* on the first opportunity."

Alas, the blow that shattered the independents apparently came from within their own ranks. "A few days ago it became a matter of public note that certain persons, composing a majority of the board of directors . . . in express violation of the articles of association, and without consultation with the stock holders, leased the [*Sherman*] to the aforesaid monopoly, commonly called the Champlain Transportation Company for a sum not sufficient to pay expenses . . . thereby making the stockholders liable for the balance of the expenses; hoping in a short time (after playing this diabolic and treacherous game) to compel the stockholders in the new company to sell their interest at a price to suit the convenience of the above-mentioned directors of the new company . . ."

Perhaps Burton's most remarkable feat during his series of manipulations in the 1850s was selling the Champlain Transportation Company, with the exception of its charter, to the Rutland and Burlington Railroad—shipyard, steamboats and all. It is clear that the railroad wanted the steamers to facilitate their connections with the northern part of the lake. The reasons Burton wanted to sell are more obscure. He was not, of course, a sentimental man, and he realized a quick profit from the transaction. Having acquired the public-sponsored concern which had just built the *R. W. Sherman* and another large steamer, the *Canada,* he at once put them both into service to compete with the railroad to whom he had just sold his old company's shipyard and steamboats.

After two years of operating the boats (with Burton and his two new steamers as opposition), the railroad surrendered. At a sacrifice it sold back its steamboat properties to the Champlain Transportation Company. Something now occurred, however, for which Burton hadn't bargained. The railroad did not sell back to the old company the steamer *Francis Saltus.* It drifted on to other interests. Burton assembled his directors in another strategy conclave to devise a plan to repurchase the *Saltus,* but try as they would they couldn't regain control of the perennial troublemaker. When Burton had exhausted legal and semi-legal means he launched a program of simple piracy. The Supreme Court might have untangled the legal implications that accompanied the action that followed, but what it all boiled down to was that posession was nine points of the law.

The Rutland and Burlington Railroad had sold the *Saltus* to the Plattsburg and Montreal Railroad, and they in turn had sold it to a Mr. Price of New York—one of the directors of the road. All this time the steamer was operating in competition with the transportation company. Burton at length succeeded in striking up an agreement with the opposition whereby Price would receive twenty-five thousand dollars if he'd lay up the *Saltus*, allowing the company to handle the lake traffic for the Montreal and Plattsburg Railroad. Price agreed, took the cash and laid up the *Saltus* according to the bargain.

About six weeks later—on June 10, 1856—one of Burton's own men, Captain Chamberlin, former master of the *Saltus*, crossed the lake at night with a prize crew. They boarded the steamer, bound up the watchman and set him ashore. Starting fires in the boilers they steamed out of Plattsburg harbor into the broad lake. Captain Chamberlin's excuse, fabricated by Burton without question, was that he had a claim on the *Saltus* for repairs he had once made on her.

At this point it was logical to expect that Price as owner of the *Saltus* would raise a commotion. Apparently, however, he had been amply remunerated by the company. But Price, in turn, had a backer, a Mr. Cook, who hastily filed suit against Captain Chamberlin and the Champlain Transportation Company. After much bickering and agitation the court awarded the custody of the *Saltus* to Mr. Cook, and the old company had to surrender it. But Burton and Chamberlin were just warming up. A little later, while the *Saltus* was docked at St. Johns, Quebec, Captain Chamberlin took another prize crew, seized her again (on the same technicality of a claim for repairs, but this time under Canadian jurisprudence) and sailed her up the Richelieu River into Lake Champlain. They steamed to Shelburne Harbor where they beached the vessel and took out part of the machinery which they hid in the bushes. Finally they opened the seacocks on the steamer *Whitehall* and sank her directly astern of the *Saltus*.

It was on a June day that the sloop *Hercules* from Plattsburg sailed into Shelburne Bay, her deck crowded with one hundred seamen. The sun was hot on the water and the invaders, who had come to take back the *Saltus*, were quiet with resolution. As they rounded the point their eyes met a sight that at once depressed them. The *Saltus* was lying near the shore with the steamer *Whitehall* sunk directly outside her. Completing the semicircle about the *Saltus* were the vessels *United States* and *Canada*, each with a full head of steam, their crews standing by. As the hundred men drifted closer it seemed more hopeless than ever, for the *Saltus* was chained with heavy links to a tree on shore, while "Henry Campbell sat on the chain, a revolver in his hand and dared anyone to remove the cable." When it seemed as though there must be an explosion of some kind, Sheriff Flanagan of the invading forces drew a revolver on Judge Smalley of the defenders, but the judge didn't scare a bit. At last the frustrated crew of the sloop *Hercules* turned about and sailed bitterly back to Plattsburg without its quarry—and with a gloomy report for Mr. Cook.

Once more resorting to the law, Cook started a final suit against the company. The litigation turtled through the courts, the result being a familiar one in the annals of the Champlain Transportation Company. It again purchased the *Saltus,* together with a release for all claims and damages.

The *Francis Saltus* had caused too many sleepless nights over a period of years—for it was now 1859—so it was with grim satisfaction that the directors ordered her dismantled and sunk. Soon after this edict the old steamer settled into the waters of Shelburne Bay. She has never been heard from since.

XI. Do Not Follow but Lead

IF disagreement is the fertilizer of free society, then nineteenth-century Vermont was a catalyst for the growth of democracy.

In the American Revolution there were Tories in Vermont and they were outspoken. But there were more Democrats than there were Tories. At the time the republic became a state there lived east of the mountains large numbers of confirmed Federalists, devoted to the principles of Washington and Hamilton. West of the mountains near the shores of Lake Champlain dwelt radical Jeffersonian Democrats like Matthew Lyon. There was disagreement in Vermont about the War of 1812 and the only reason Vermonters fought in it was that the Union was committed to fight. The state was embroiled in religious dissension all during the early 1800s. Then came the revivals, which thoroughly burned over the Vermont hillsides and marshaled the people in a moral phalanx against the excesses of frontier life. The author of *The Green Mountain Boys,* Daniel P. Thompson, recalled that in his youth "taverns became common and constant resorts, inviting to idleness, money spending and all sorts of dissipation. Rum drinking rapidly increased, and brought along with it the usual train of street broils, acrimonious quarrels and keen litigations. Gambling was a common practice, libertinism found too many victims in the unsophisticated, unsuspecting and therefore unguarded female community. All those stained the records of the week days, while the sabbaths were desecrated by horse racing, match shooting, street games, holly day amusements, visiting and pleasure parties."

In the midst of the religious revivals the great war against booze gripped the people of Vermont. By 1832 the two hundred twenty clubs of the Vermont Temperance Society had boarded up hundreds of distilleries and stigmatized saloon proprietors and tavern operators. *The Inebriate's Lament,* sung to the tune of *Long, Long Ago,* indicates the thoroughness with which the temperance society had carried out one of the most fervent of Vermont's political, social and religious nineteenth-century crusades:

> Where are the friends that to me were so dear,
>   Long, long ago—long, long ago.
> Where are the hopes that my heart used to cheer?
>   Long, long ago—long ago.
> Friends that I loved in the grave are laid low—
> Hopes that I cherished have fled from me now—
> I am degraded, for rum was my foe—
>   Long, long ago—long ago.
>
> Sadly my wife bow'd her beautiful head—
>   Long, long ago—long, long ago.
> Oh, how I wept when I knew she was dead—
>   Long, long ago—long ago.
> She was an angel—my love and my guide—
> Vainly to save me from ruin she tried;
> Poor broken heart! it was well that she died—
>   Long, long ago—long ago.

When some of the Masons of the Batavia, New York, chapter black-balled William Morgan in 1826, he wrote a tract exposing their activities. Shortly thereafter he disappeared, which led the public to believe that the Masons had spirited him away and murdered him. The indignation of the northcountry arose in political reprisal. As might be expected, the New England spearhead of this movement was Vermont—the only state to deliver its votes in 1832 to William Wirt, the anti-Masonic Presidential candidate. This party so completely controlled the state for four years that by 1834 virtually every Masonic lodge had given up its charter, and only then did the movement against secret societies begin to lose its force.

Colonel Jonathan P. Miller of Randolph, whom the Greeks had honored with the title of The American Dare Devil in recognition of his aid in their effort to thrust off Turkish control, had returned to Vermont and joined the Montpelier lodge of the Masons. But he withdrew at the height of the anti-Masonic upheaval. When this movement had lost its fire he was one of the leaders who gathered under the Whig banner despondent refugees from various political parties. Sheep-growing Vermont was now effervescing with fervor for Daniel Webster and high tariffs. In 1840 ten thousand people poured out of the hinterlands and covered the side of Stratton Mountain to hear the magnetic orator.

There was one issue that dwarfed all the others, and that was abolition of slavery—a cause in which Vermont was the prime mover.

Together with a guarantee of religious freedom and free manhood suffrage, the abolition of slavery had been written into the Constitution of Vermont—the first among the states to deny human enslavement. In the Revolution during a raid near Ticonderoga, a Negro woman named Dinah Mattis and her child Nancy fell into the hands of Vermonters, together with other British prisoners. Ebenezer Allen freed these two, certifying that according to the resolves of Congress prizes of war were the property of the "captivators" but that it was "not right in the sight of God to keep slaves." Therefore Allen granted Dinah and her child the right to pass and repass freely anywhere in the United States. In 1793 Judge Theophilus Harrington of Middlebury, trying the case of two fugitive slaves, ruled that only "a bill of sale from God Almighty" would make him recognize slavery. He let them go.

Lemuel Haynes of West Hartford, Connecticut, the illegitimate son of a white hired maid and a Negro slave, joined the Minute Men during the Revolution and fought under Benedict Arnold at Ticonderoga. Later he became an eminent Vermont minister and friend of the chief justice of Vermont and of the governor. He preached 5,500 times in Rutland over a period of thirty-three years and delivered countless other sermons about the state.

In 1786 the legislature of Vermont passed an act fining persons guilty of selling or removing Negroes from the state, and requiring that the fine be paid to the Negroes in question. By 1805 the slave trade was being severely censured in the state senate, and the following year bills were introduced not only to prohibit this traffic but also to punish slave traders with death. As early as 1819 Vermont was strongly protesting the extension of slavery to western territories. At the same time interest arose in transplanting slaves from the American continent to Liberia. To accomplish this, the first State Colonization Society in America was shortly formed at Montpelier. Two decades later eighty-nine antislavery societies had sprung up within the state. In 1838 the Vermont legislature resolved to prevent entrance into the Union of any state tolerating slavery. Tabled in the United States Senate, this measure was cited by Calhoun as "the first move from a State," and "a new and bold step . . . from a higher quarter." Meanwhile in the House of Representatives, Vermont Congressman William Slade went so far as to advocate ending slavery in the District of Columbia. Amidst angry protests from the southern representatives Slade quoted the Declaration of Independence and the constitutions of several states, and would have gone on with quotations from Benjamin Franklin and James Madison if a southern Congressman had not cut him off.

"He has discussed the whole abstract question of slavery," Mr. Wise of Virginia declared heatedly, "of slavery in Virginia, of slavery in my own district, and I now ask my colleagues to retire with me from this hall." A great deal of confusion followed and the next day Congressman Patton of Virginia moved that "all petitions, memorials and papers referring to abolition of slavery or buying, selling or transferring slaves in the United States be laid on the table without being debated, printed, read or referred and that no action whatever shall be had thereon." Passed by a vote of 122-74 this resolution, the notorious "gag rule," was condemned by the Vermont legislature as "a daring infringement of the right of the people to petition, and a flagrant violation of the Constitution of the United States." When Senator Prentiss of Vermont tried to introduce a subsequent resolution of the Montpelier legislature—that the annexation of Texas be prohibited, and that slavery be abolished—Senator King of Alabama, president pro-tem of the Senate, declared: "The honorable Senator who presented them knew full well that if Congress, by any possibility, could be induced to act upon them, at that moment the Union would be at an end."

Despite the fact that Vermont seemed to show the country a wall of inflexible opposition to slavery during the 1830s, there was within the state nothing like agreement on the subject. In 1835 when the state legislature granted the Reverend Samuel J. May, a vehement Unitarian spokesman of the Massachusetts Anti-Slavery Society, permission to address the citizens of Montpelier in Representatives' Hall, hecklers hurled stones and eggs through the windows. The meeting proceeded in disorder and May might have been mobbed if a Quaker woman had not taken his arm and escorted him safely through the crowd outside the building. Nevertheless he accepted an invitation to speak the following evening in the old brick church. The next day he was warned against speaking by a group of prominent men who claimed that they represented great numbers of their fellow townsmen, and even members of the legislature. Posters appeared cautioning the public, especially the ladies, against attending the meeting, as force would be used if necessary to prevent him from reaching the rostrum. In the evening, while the people of Montpelier were gathering at the appointed hour, May entered the church and sat down on the platform. When he arose to speak, Timothy Hubbard, a local banker known to be in favor of slavery, stood up and ordered May to cease this "ungospel and anti-union harangue." May replied that he would stop if Hubbard or anyone else could offer a good reason why, in a land of free speech, he should forgo the talk he had been invited to give.

May proceeded with his address but his words were muffled by cries of "Down with him! Throw him over! Choke him." A Mr. Knapp arose and exhorted the proslavery men to desist. He said that they were disgracing not only themselves but the town and the state. As May commenced to speak for the third time, however, they advanced in a body toward the pulpit. At this point Colonel Jonathan Miller, the American daredevil famed for his part in the Greco-Turkish War, sprang between May and his attackers. "Mr. Hubbard," boomed Miller, "if you do not stop this outrage now I will knock you down!" The proslavery men hesitated, then abandoned their attack. But the audience now began to disperse and May was therefore deprived of his second opportunity to be heard in the state capital.

Proslavery sentiment was not confined to Montpelier. At Rutland May had been mobbed on five occasions, and at various times and places others of his radical stripe had spoken in an atmosphere charged with hostility. There were those in Vermont who were against the extension of slavery to new territories annexed by the United States, but who were willing to allow it to continue in states where it already existed. Some Vermonters favored the recolonization plan of returning the Negroes to Africa. Others did not believe in any form of Abolition. They felt that slavery was none of Vermont's business and that the Negro question could be resolved far more satisfactorily in the southern states where slavery existed. As a recent Vermont historian has remarked, "It is much easier to condemn an evil a long way from home than it is to view with broad-minded toleration affairs that disturb one's own political household." It is true that Vermont had no commercial connections with the South, or with the slave trade.

The first Episcopal Bishop of Vermont, the Reverend John Henry Hopkins, in many respects a man of imagination and liberal impulses, was one of the most outspoken defenders of slavery. He agreed that it was evil but thought that Abolition ought not to be forced upon the South unless the North was willing to purchase the slaves and gradually remove them to Africa.

The voices of those who advocated less than the eradication of slavery trailed away as the years passed. Public sentiment, fostered by inflammatory editorials and by fiery agents of liberation, grew firmly

Abolitionist. In 1844 the state legislature condemned slavery as "a monstrous anomaly in a free government." In his annual message four years later, the governor affirmed that ". . . Vermont has taken the ground of irreconcilable hostility, and she must and will continue to maintain it." In 1850 the legislature announced that ". . . the brave and patriotic people of Hungary are entitled to our warmest sympathy in their unsuccessful struggle for the liberty against the despots of Austria and Russia." To balance the entrance of Texas into the Union as a slave state, Green Mountain legislators proposed that Canada be peacefully annexed by the United States, upon just and honest terms with the British government.

The Fugitive Slave Law, an act of Congress that inflamed the north-country even more than the Missouri Compromise, drew this memorial from the Vermont legislature:

"Resolved, that the Fugitive Slave Law of 1850 is a violation of the Constitution, an insult to the Free States, an outrage on the rights of man and a disgrace to the statutes of the Nation; and the people of Vermont will indignantly rebuke any Senator or Representative of theirs in the National Congress who does not use his influence to bring about its entire repeal. . . ."

Copies of the various resolves went to Congress, and often to the governors of several southern states. In Georgia the assembly lawmakers resolved that the governor of that state transmit to the governor of Vermont a proslavery resolution enclosed in a leaden bullet, together with a coil of rope and some gunpowder. "Resolved, by the General Assembly of the State of Georgia, that His Excellency, the Governor, be and is hereby requested to transmit the Vermont resolutions to the deep, dank and fetid sink of social and political iniquity from whence they emanated, with the following unequivocal declaration inscribed thereon:

"'Resolved, that Georgia, standing on her constitutional palladium, needs not the maniac ravings of hell-born fanaticism, nor stoops from her lofty position to hold terms with perjured traitors.'" Georgia further resolved that His Excellency, President Pierce, be requested to employ a sufficient number of able-bodied Irishmen to proceed to the

State of Vermont, and to dig a ditch around the limits of the same, and float "the thing" into the Atlantic.

When William Lloyd Garrison was editing his slight country weekly, *Journal of the Times,* Horace Greeley, a journalist in the next county, called it "about the ablest and most interesting newspaper ever issued in Vermont." A great editor and reformer was paying tribute to a great reformer and editor.

Garrison was only twenty-one when he edited the *Journal,* and even before that he had published the *Free Press* in Newburyport, Massachusetts, his birthplace, and *The National Philanthropist,* a temperance periodical, in Boston. Garrison went to Vermont from Massachusetts in 1828 seeking a radical environment sympathetic with his urge to reform the country. Very early he announced that only death would stop him from denouncing slavery as a crime which had "no parallel in human depravity." Freeing the slaves, he pledged, would be uppermost in his pursuits. "The question is now what can New England do to remove the evils of slavery. . . . What can she do! She can enter the halls of Congress with two millions of voices. She can raise a note of remonstrance, like the roar of the ocean when awakened by the tempests of heaven. . . . Citizens of Vermont! Let not your sympathies harden, nor your strength lie dormant. Do not follow but lead . . ."

These were among his first pronouncements against slavery. Thus dedicating his life, the sensitive, self-centered youth left the Green Mountains and with the dogged will of a fanatic shocked all New England with his outcries. In Baltimore he was lodged behind bars for a time. Returning to Boston he hired the hall of an infidel society—the only one available to him—and flamingly denounced slavery to a small and fireproof audience. In his room he printed a newspaper, *The Liberator,* which at the end of the first year amassed a circulation of five hundred.

By 1834 the number of subscribers had jumped four times and Garrison was receiving notoriety from the District of Columbia, which fined or imprisoned Negro readers of his weekly, and from the state of Georgia, which had placed a bounty of $5,000 on his head. Garrison pursued his goal with such passion that he antagonized even groups of northerners inclined toward antislavery. But he was not sorry for his excesses. "An immense iceberg, larger and more impenetrable than any which floats in the Arctic Ocean," he explained, "is to be dissolved, and a little *extra heat* is not only pardonable, but absolutely necessary."

The ranting of his editorials and his voice produced unexpected results. The New England Anti-Slavery Society, which he established in 1832, had 1,350 local branches by 1837. Four years later New England was electric with the spirit of liberation. By this time, however, there was a deep cleavage between the "gradualists"—such as clergymen and members of the colonization societies—and the radicals who favored "immediatism." Because he was arrogant and would not compromise, Garrison was largely responsible for this schism. He lost many of his old comrades in rebellion. Among them was Orson S. Murray, a Vermonter whom he had once called "one of the most successful advocates of emancipation in New England."

The indignation of those northerners who did not wish to have the issue of slavery agitated in any form boiled up in a Boston street outside the rooms where *The Liberator* was printed. An irate band of citizens scattered the members of the Female Anti-Slavery Society meeting inside, tied Garrison up and dragged him through the streets to the city hall, where the mayor and some of his aides succeeded in protecting him from further violence by putting him in jail. This diminished neither his resolve nor his intense activity to accomplish it. In 1843 the masthead of *The Liberator* contained the words, "Resolved, that the compact which now exists between the North and the South is 'a covenant with death and an agreement with Hell'—involving both parties in atrocious criminality and should be immediately annulled."

Strangely enough, Garrison was a pacifist who expected that slavery could be eliminated by agitation, pressure and persuasion. When, in response to the deepening sentiment for Abolition in the 1850s, the Republican party came into being, Garrison supposed the fight was over. He regarded violence with but little less hatred than he did slavery. He could not countenance such acts as the insurrection of John Brown.

When war came Garrison subsided. Even as *The Liberator* ceased publication at the crux of the fighting, the North found itself in unanimous sympathy with Garrison's principles, and he became a national hero. He was invited to address Congress on April 15, 1865. He was among the notables at the Fort Sumter flag-raising. Then, since he had spent all his money in his work, Congress presented him and his wife with a bank draft for thirty-one thousand dollars.

During the War of 1812 a farmer named Jason Jones allowed his cows to graze on the campus of the University of Vermont. The college had ruled that cows would not be permitted there for the time being, as the janitor was cleaning up the green for commencement. But the cows were accustomed to eat the lush campus grass and Jones was determined not to interfere with them, chiefly because the students had tried to get rid of them by painting their tails and dressing them up in old trousers.

One night Thaddeus Stevens and another student killed one of the cows with an ax that they had stolen from a "pious" student. The two conspirators returned the blood-stained implement and retired to await developments. Early next morning the students and townspeople of Burlington gathered around the carcass while the infuriated Jones went to the president of the college to obtain redress. The president launched an investigation, in the course of which the bloody ax was discovered on the premises of the pious student. Despite his pleas of innocence, he received the blame for the crime. It looked as though he would be expelled from college although he was to have been graduated with high honors on the following day.

Stevens and his friend had not realized that the penalty would be as heavy and they were now sorry—but if they admitted their guilt they would surely receive the penalty of the convicted student. They at length decided to confess to Jones, who "wasn't a bad fellow after all and might be prevailed upon to help them out of their difficulty." When he understood the details of his cow's death and the plight of the worried students, Jones promised to help them out—if they would pay him twice the value of the cow as soon as they were able. They hastily agreed and Jones went at once to the college authorities. He told them he had learned that the cow had been killed by soldiers who were going down the Onion River in a boat from their encampment, and that they had not had time to dress and remove the meat. Jones sounded so sincere that the president exonerated the pious student, and the consciences of Thaddeus Stevens and his friend were clear. Some years later, when he was rising in the political councils of the country, Stevens sent Jones a draft for the highest-priced cow on the market, together with a watch and gold chain.

Because the government took over the building for the use of troops, forcing the college to close, Stevens did not graduate from the University of Vermont. He received his diploma instead from Dartmouth, climaxing the hard-won years of education that had begun in Danville, the town of his birth.

What happened to his father is not clear. To his mother had fallen the task of raising Thaddeus, whose congenital lameness precluded the rigors of life on a farm. "I really think the greatest pleasure of my life resulted from my ability to give my mother a farm of 250 acres and a dairy of 14 cows, and an occasional bright gold piece which she loved to deposit in the contributors' box of the Baptist church which she attended. This gave her much pleasure and me much satisfaction. My mother was a very extraordinary woman. I have met few women like her. She worked day and night to educate me. I tried to repay her afterwards, but the debt of a child to his mother, you know, is one of the debts we can never pay."

He attended a Vermont academy prior to entering the University of Vermont and Dartmouth. Following his graduation at Hanover he recrossed the Connecticut to teach school at Peacham while he pored over law books in the evenings. After a year he went to York, Pennsylvania, to teach and to conclude his preparation for a legal career. Following admittance to the bar he went, prophetically in the light of what would come, to Gettysburg. Grubbing about for the paltry fees that must sustain any young lawyer he slowly moved to the forefront of his profession in that section of Pennsylvania. By 1830 he had won nine out of the ten cases he had tried before the Supreme Court, six of the decisions having reversed those of the lower court.

Three years later he was in politics as representative in the state legislature from Adams City and was in the thick of the anti-Masonic movement, for which he was a crusading spokesman. "The oaths of

Free Masons are inconsistent with pure morals, true religion and the permanent existence of liberty. . . . They swear to promote one another's political preferment. This is not a dead letter. It is acted on throughout the Union. Twenty of the twenty-four states are governed by Masons. They hold two-thirds of the offices. None but a Mason can be President. Henry Clay is Grand Master of Kentucky. All this monopoly of power is brought about by a band of men constituting less than one-twentieth of our voters. Surely there is a magic influence in Free Masonry. It corrupts the fountains of justice; stays the arm of the law; stops the regular action of government; binds the mind in darkness."

In 1838 Stevens was the nucleus of a disturbance known in Pennsylvania as the Buckshot War, a fight between Stevens's Whig party and the Democrats for control of the state government. The struggle became focused upon one section in which Stevens claimed there was fraud in the vote-counting, and he announced that the Whigs had won by one thousand votes. The judges ruled that the district should be disqualified. This decision threw the election over to the Democrats. Refusing to accept the verdict of the judges, Stevens proceeded with plans to organize the legislature as if the Whigs had won.

At legislature time voters filled the streets of Harrisburg and milled about as the situation at the capitol came to a head. Stevens's seat in the house, according to his own words, was guarded by "8 or 10 of the most desperate brawlers . . . armed with double-barreled pistols, bowie knives and dirks." Although the situation within the hall presaged chaos and even violence, there was no compromising between the leaders of the two parties. The Democrats chose their own speaker, while Stevens nominated one for the Whigs and led him to the platform. Two sets of tellers were appointed and two committees to inform the governor that the respective houses were ready for business. The decision as to which body—the Hopkins House or the Stevens Rump—was the legal one, devolved upon the senate. Nothing further could be done until that decision was made.

Suddenly, while the senators were being sworn in, rioting snapped the tension. Stevens and other legislators were advised to escape through a back window. Scarcely had they done so when the mob surged into the hall. Anarchy now prevailed throughout the city, forcing the governor to call out the militia. Upon the arrival of the soldiers the rioting ceased. At this point three of Stevens's Whigs went over to the Democrats, giving the latter a clear majority, which broke the parliamentary stalemate and ended the so-called Buckshot War.

Stevens gave vent to his indignation by vacating his seat and returning to Adams County where he continued to snipe at the Democrats. The next term Adams County re-elected its irascible, mulish, hard-drinking bachelor representative with an overwhelming plurality. The voters considered him not just a political seeker after power but a man of principle, an opposer of special privilege, a friend of republican government and of small people. During the years that immediately followed he proved that he was such a man, winning even the respect of his political enemies. He was the standard-bearer for free education in Pennsylvania. When it seemed that he had lost his thorny struggle for free schools owing to the opposition of the childless rich, he reversed the tide of voting in a dramatic address before both houses of the legislature. He was a champion of thrifty government and of tariffs to protect American manufactures against the invasion of foreign products.

And he was an austere foe of slavery. It had long been a tradition that no fugitive slave tried in a court within the neighborhood of his practice was ever returned to bondage. Scarcely had he begun to direct his efforts toward emancipation, however, when his Gettysburg partner failed, involving him in heavy debt. In 1842 he moved to Lancaster and for eight years prospered in a private practice which enabled him to discharge his debts. Then in 1848 he won a seat in the House of Representatives. The mounting struggle for emancipation at once absorbed him. Like other Vermont denouncers of slavery, Stevens would brook no halfway measures. Conciliation formed no part of his speeches:

"He can hold no property. His very wife and children are not his. His labor is another's. He and all that pertains to him are the absolute property of his rulers. He is governed, bought, sold, punished, executed by laws to which he never gave his assent, and by rulers whom he never chose. He is not a serf, merely, with half the rights of men, like the subjects of despotic Russia; but a naked slave, stripped of every right which God and nature gave him. . . ."

A Kentucky Congressman observed that because of Stevens's reputation for slander and vilification, no respectable Negro would associate with him were he to come to the South to live.

"Well, if this be so," Stevens replied, "let us give all a chance to enjoy this blessing. Let the slaves who choose, go free; and the free who choose, become slaves. If these gentlemen believe there is a word of truth in what they preach, the slaveholders need be under no apprehension that they will ever lack bondsmen."

After his second term ended Stevens returned to his law practice and remained out of politics in Pennsylvania until the Republican party was established in June 1856. As a delegate to the first convention of the new party he foresaw the gathering political strength which would make possible Congressional decisions that were hitherto impossible. Therefore in 1858, at an advanced age, he returned to Washington as a Republican to begin his final exhausting but climactic decade of Congressional duty. The guns of Fort Sumter would soon speak. The House of Representatives was a shambles of broken political segments, but it was Stevens who joined at least the northern ones together.

"I almost tremble for the South," chided one of his opponents, "when I recollect that the opposing forces will be led by the distinguished hero of the Buckshot War. However gloomy the catastrophe his saltatory accomplishments will enable him to leap out of any difficulties in which he may be involved. I understand [referring to Stevens' withdrawal through the window] that he gave in a conspicuous way a practical illustration of peaceable secession."

Stevens was one of the few men in Congress who thwarted last-minute northern compromises, for if slavery were continued in any form it was not worth it to him to save the Union. When war came Stevens, as chairman of the House committee on ways, means and appropriations, was burdened with the crushing task of financing the armies of the North. In 1865 he became chairman of the House committee on reconstruction. As a vengeful advocate of the scorched-earth policy he favored confiscating southern estates and preventing southern leaders from holding high national offices. Thousands of northerners had been killed; his own estate, representing his life savings, had been destroyed by southern armies, and therefore along with masses of northern people he favored retaliation. The Civil Rights Bill, which he and other radical leaders of both houses espoused in an effort to redistribute political power among the states, was vetoed by the President, an enemy of the scorched-earth policy. Johnson thus earned the bitter and undying enmity of Stevens.

"I would ask you," the President shouted to the crowd below the balcony of a Cleveland hotel, "why not hang Thaddeus Stevens? . . . I tell you, my countrymen, I have been fighting the South, and they have been whipped and crushed and they acknowledge their defeat and accept the terms of the Constitution; and now as I go round the circle, having fought traitors in the South, I am prepared to fight traitors at the North . . . though the powers of hell and Thaddeus Stevens and his gang were by, they could not turn me from my purpose. . . ."

"I know not what record of sin awaits me in the other world," declared the old ornery Congressman, "but this I know—that I have never been guilty of despising a man because he was poor, because he was ignorant, or because he was black."

"Simon," Stevens announced to his cousin on August 11, 1868, the day he died, "the great questions of the day are reconstruction, the finances, and the railway system of the country." That evening before he died two Negro ministers came into his room and asked if they might pray with him. They told him he had the prayers of all the colored people in the country.

To the Town of Peacham, Vermont, he bequeathed "$1,000 at 6% in aid of the Library Association which was founded at the Caledonia County Academy—if the same is still in existence.

"To the Trustees of the graveyard in which my mother and brother are buried in the town of Peacham, Vermont, $500, the interest to be annually paid to the sexton on condition that he keep the graves in good order and plant roses and other cheerful flowers at each of the four corners of said graves every spring. . . ."

When Abraham Lincoln first saw five-foot, one-hundred-forty-pound Stephen Douglas he called him "the least man I ever saw"; and so he was, except for his head which was notably oversize for his small frame. The Illinois railsplitter was referring to the physical Douglas, not Douglas the orator or politician. Douglas on the platform, Lincoln appreciated, was indeed The Little Giant.

Because his father died young, the Brandon, Vermont, youth set out on foot for Middlebury, fourteen miles away, to become apprenticed to a cabinetmaker. Two years later, his mind already awakened to the great political issues of the day, he entered the Brandon Academy. His schooling was completed in Canandaigua, New York, where his mother had moved following her remarriage. From this place he started west in search of a career, arriving in Jacksonville, Illinois, at the age of twenty with thirty-seven cents in his pocket. After a few months of teaching he opened a law office in 1834, and from that time on he rose in politics with startling swiftness. Before he reached his majority he was leader of the Jacksonian Democrats in his district, and within another year the state legislature had named him district attorney for the first judicial circuit. Almost at once he gained a seat in the Illinois legislature and accepted a Springfield office as registrar of public lands. He ran for Congress against Lincoln's law partner, John T. Stuart, and lost by five votes. This was no setback—he became secretary of state. Before he had held that office three months he was appointed to the supreme court of Illinois at the age of twenty-seven. Scarcely a year later he lost a race for the United States Senate by a narrow margin, yet he also turned this defeat into victory by winning a seat in the House in 1843.

Congress now vibrated to the voice of this combustible young Vermonter, who, during a speech, was likely to throw away his tie and unbutton his waistcoat to allow his vocal cords and gesticulating arms more freedom. He became chairman of the committee on territories at the beginning of his second term in the House and fought for internal improvements in the West. He did not like the Anglo-American agreement for mutual occupation of the Oregon Territory and suggested that settlers going west should "squat out" the British fur traders. "If war comes, let it come. We may regret the necessity which produced it, but when it does come, I will administer to our own citizens Hannibal's oath of eternal enmity. I would blot out the lines on the map which now mark our territorial boundaries on this continent, and make the area of liberty as broad as the continent itself."

In 1846 Illinois sent him to the Senate, where he also became that body's chairman of the committee on territories and continued his earnest task of opening the rich and endless West. During a trip to Europe he refused to wear before various potentates any special clothes that an American would not wear when visiting the President. "Europe is antiquated, decrepit, tottering on the verge of dissolution. When you visit her, the objects which excite your admiration are the relics of past greatness: the broken columns erected to departed power. Here everything is fresh, blooming, expanding, and advancing. We wish a wise, practical policy adapted to our condition and position."

That policy, he felt, should be one of buoyant, unfettered expansion, perhaps not even limited by the west coast. Eventually America might want to blanket the islands of the Pacific with her sovereignty.

In 1847 he married the daughter of a wealthy North Carolina slaveholder, who presented him with a Mississippi plantation. Douglas returned it, not because there were slaves on it, but because he did not know how to run a plantation. His wife, however, eventually inherited the estates and Douglas therefore acquired the onus of being married to a slaveholder.

On the question of slavery he was, with Clay, one of the Senate's prime compromisers who thought the extremists were rushing the country toward war. He felt that the Negroes were an inferior race and apparently he did not think slavery morally wrong—at least he never said it was. On the other hand he never condoned it. He felt that it was a matter that could best be handled by the people of the respective territories then being settled in the West. He was sure, in any event, that this problem was not important enough to cause a rift in the Union.

Carrying forward his plan of letting the people decide about slavery, he introduced and succeeded singlehandedly in passing the Kansas-Nebraska Bill of 1854 which replaced the Missouri Compromise. This enraged the North, for it resulted in permitting slavery in northern areas where it had hitherto been prohibited. Douglas remarked that he might travel all the way from Boston to Chicago in the light of his own burning effigies, but he nevertheless considered that his bill would ultimately solve the slavery question. He did not think that it was worth sacrificing the Union for all the Negroes in the world.

Of course he also had his eye on the Presidential nomination. In 1852 some states seriously considered him, but he had not been strong in the South. The repeal of the compromise would make him stronger there in 1856; and if, as he calculated, the only candidate who would have a chance would be a Democrat with southern support, he would be the logical man. Thousands of northern Democrats turned against Douglas's noncommittal policy, and the largest city in his own state lowered its flags to half-mast and tolled its church bells when he elected to speak there on September 1, 1854. For four hours from eight until midnight Chicagoans hissed and booed as he repeatedly attempted to talk, and later mobbed his carriage on the way home. The narrow victory of Buchanan for the Democratic nomination of 1854 did not, however, greatly disturb Douglas: he was only forty-three and if he watched his political fences he could look forward with optimism to 1860.

But in his 1858 contest for re-election to the Senate from Illinois the politically agile Vermonter faced Abraham Lincoln. To match the homespun humor, the melancholy, the integrity and the logic of this gaunt figure, Douglas summoned up all of his adeptness and every gesture of his polished forensic skill. On the crossroads about the state the towering Lincoln and the pint-sized Douglas met seven times in a series of debates that have become legendary. From every point of the compass thousands of people streamed to the assembly places by water, rail and horseback, until there was a sea of faces and banners and canvas signs in front of the wooden platform. Douglas liked to travel in the elaborate directors' car of the Illinois Central Railroad, which he had helped to found. A series of shots from a brass cannon on the rear platform would announce his arrival. Then the baritone voice of the dynamic Douglas would roll smoothly out over the crowd. The audience would bend before The Little Giant's nimble, forceful arguments like willows in the wind.

And yet, as Lincoln pointed out, his "specious and fantastic arrangement of words" enabled him to prove "a horse chestnut to be a chestnut horse." "His fluency covered many rocks and quicksands," wrote an auditor of the debates. "He was gifted with the faculty of gliding deftly from one thing to another turning the hearers' attention away from the real subject of debate so adroitly that the break would not be noticed, and presently the audience would be swimming in a new channel in company with him, not having missed the connection with the main theme."

Then the uneasy, high, and halting voice of Lincoln penetrated the air, at first seemingly a dissonance, but his thoughts came in order and in earnest simplicity and went to the hearts and heads of his listeners with the deep force of great music. "He may say he don't care whether an indifferent thing is voted up or down, but he must logically have a choice between a right thing and a wrong thing. He contends that whatever community wants slaves has a right to them. So they have if it is not a wrong. But if it is a wrong, he cannot say people have a right to do wrong. . . .

"That is the real issue. That is the issue that will continue in this country when these poor tongues of Judge Douglas and myself shall be silent. They are the true principles that have stood face to face from the beginning of time; and will ever continue to struggle. The one is the common right of humanity and the other the divine right of Kings. . . ."

Even as Douglas returned to the Senate he could not have helped sensing the greatness of this man whom he had vanquished—as great as the momentous issue which he, Douglas, had so artfully dodged. He had never made a moral decision about slavery and now it was too late. The campaign of 1860 brought home to him his errors of judgment. The southern Democrats would not have him and most of the northern states, including his native Vermont, were for Abraham Lincoln and the Republican party.

When the ungainly railsplitter stood ready to give his inaugural address and could not find a place to put his hat, Stephen Douglas came forward and held it.

His ancestors had settled in the rebellious Scotch-Irish town of Londonderry, New Hampshire. His father was a day laborer in West Haven, Vermont, having moved there in midwinter from Amherst, New Hampshire, one hundred miles away, bringing his wife and five children and a few odd pieces of furniture stacked in a homemade sleigh. When he had owned his own farm in New Hampshire, his father had been somewhat better off; but since he had been a poor manager he had gradually been forced to sell even his personal effects until there was practically nothing left but the bare walls of his farm-house. In West Haven he had hired out as a woodchopper for $3.50 a week and as a day laborer in the fields. The five children spent much of their youth in a two-room cabin which their father rented for $1.50 a month. At mealtime they gathered around a porridge bowl into which they all dipped their wooden spoons.

His father wished him to become a farmer or a blacksmith, but he was continually looking in the country newspapers for an opening in a printing office—a search that was finally rewarded in 1826 when he was fifteen. A printer's assistant was needed on the *Northern Spectator*, published in East Poultney twelve miles away, so he promptly started off to that place on foot. He found the editor, Amos Bliss, who was also the Baptist minister of East Poultney, working in his garden. When Bliss heard a polite, uncertain voice inquire if he was the editor of the *Northern Spectator*, he looked up and saw a pale, threadbare youth with a rather large head on which sat a small-brimmed felt hat.

"Don't you want a boy to learn the trade?"

The minister's surprise and doubt were, after a few moments, re-solved in the question "Do *you* want to learn?"

"I've had some notion of it."

Bliss said that it took education to become a printer and inquired if the young stranger had been to school.

"No. I haven't had much chance at school, but I have read some history and a little of most everything."

"Where do you live?"

"West Haven, sir."

"How did you get here?"

"I walked over."

"What's your name?"

"Horace Greeley, sir."

Bliss did not feel that a green youth like this could fill the job but sent him over to see the foreman of the printing office. The foreman returned the odd boy with a slip of paper on which was scribbled "Guess we'd better try him."

When, shortly thereafter, his parents decided to move from Vermont to Pennsylvania, Greeley nearly gave up his newspaper job. They left and he stayed on, burying his loneliness in work—in setting type, cranking the press, reading proof and the exchange papers. He joined the local debating society and in odd hours walked about the countryside. Soon he was welcome and his shabby figure, slight stoop and hurried gait were familiar in the vicinity of East Poultney. But if anyone had told the neighborhood people that Greeley would become the founder of the New York *Tribune* (forerunner of today's *Herald Tribune*) or that his friend, Poultney-born George Jones, would found another of the world's great newspapers, the New York *Times,* the community would have been amused. At this early juncture Horace and George probably would have joined in the laughter.

During his four-year apprenticeship at the *Spectator* East Poultney was the scene of a hunt for a fugitive slave who had reportedly crossed the New York line into Vermont. The Poultney villagers did not seize the Negro, but rather his white pursuer, whom they hustled out of town. "I never saw so large a gathering of men," Greeley recalled. "Everything on our side was impromptu and instinctive. Our people hated oppression and injustice and acted as if they couldn't help it."

Greeley's *Spectator* job, which had been paying him his board and $40 a year, ended in 1830 when the paper ceased publication. Now nineteen, he tied up his possessions in a red cotton handkerchief and left Vermont. After spending a week on an Erie Canal barge he struck off on foot across western New York to Pennsylvania to join his family. For fourteen months he worked on his father's Erie farm, then trudged to New York to hunt up another newspaper job. He found one and then another, and did good work at low wages but he was not retained, chiefly because he was so eccentric. Returning briefly to East Poultney to renew old friendships and get his bearings he found it a "blissful dream." He wrote that in the hours shared with friends from whom one has been separated one lives the essence of years past and to come.

Back in New York at twenty-two with a partner and capital of $200, he launched a printing firm as a means of publishing the *Morning Post,* a two-cent daily. This folded after two weeks. His partner was drowned in the East River and the firm might have collapsed if his partner's brother-in-law had not stepped in to help salvage at least the accounts for which they were doing job printing. The health of the concern gradually improved, but it had no sooner done so than Greeley brought out another journal, the *New Yorker*. In this literary and scientific weekly he published a story by Charles Dickens, a writer than unknown even in England, and stories by Edgar Allen Poe, whose genius Greeley was quick to recognize. Although the paper lost money and had to be supported by the printing business it attained a respectable circulation, and Greeley was soon known in New York newspaper and political circles as a resourceful editorial writer.

On July 29, 1835, he wrote, "I paid off everyone tonight. Have $10 left and have to raise $350 on Monday. Borrowing places all sucked dry. I shall raise it, however." Despite these ominous financial problems the *New Yorker* soon had five thousand readers, many of them youths whom Greeley was advising to go West. By this time he was more than merely well known; he was conspicuous. Leaders of the state Whig committee called on him while he was in the composing room setting type and asked him to edit their party newspaper in Albany. Greeley agreed to this because he was an ardent Whig, and so for three years he shuttled back and forth on Hudson River steamboats between Albany and New York, trying to excite his growing public in both cities with log cabins, hard cider and Tippecanoe and Tyler too. It is traditional that Greeley made up many of the log-cabin campaign songs himself, printing the music and words on the back page of his Whig journal. It was a colorful campaign and it was the young editor more than anyone else who put the breath of life into it.

Harrison's victory raised Greeley to state and party eminence as great as that of any Whig chieftain, but he did not take advantage of his position. It was his editorial page, the conscience of the public, on which he continued to concentrate his energies, making certain that those whom he had helped to place in power carried out their campaign promises.

Except as a means of publishing better newspapers money meant no more to Greeley than political power. Because he habitually put every extra dollar back into his paper or printing business, he was chronically short of cash. He was hard up in 1841, but he brought out a new daily, the *Tribune*, with offices located in the rear of the second floor and in the attic of 30 Ann Street. He begged and borrowed the type to set it up and the forms had to be wheeled to a press blocks away, but this little journal was the forebear of the immense and celebrated newspaper of later years. It was Greeley's eager crusading voice that made the *Tribune* catch on. In the years that followed he was for moral reform, for abolition of slavery, for the rights of workingmen and for profit sharing. As capitalists knitted their brows he organized his own employees into the first printers' union and shared the *Tribune* stock. He sent a reporter to cover the first woman suffrage convention—and printed one of the few fair stories about it. He was interested in attempts to improve the structure of society and saw to it that the *Tribune* kept abreast of the various movements. John Humphrey Noyes and the Putney Community attracted his attention, as did Brook Farm, and he entered actively into Fourierism. He persuaded transcendentalist Margaret Fuller to write in the *Tribune*, and also New Hampshire-born Charles A. Dana, whom Greeley thought a promising young journalist. Thus by the middle 1840s the Vermont printer's devil of a little more than a decade before had begun to evolve a radical, critical, contrary, crusading newspaper that was, like its editor, already becoming a national institution.

In 1836 Greeley had married Mary Cheny of Cornwall, Connecticut. It was a partnership that was to prove most unsatisfactory, if not tragic. Mary was dour and introverted and, as the years passed, she became a hypochondriac whose perversity reached every corner of the barren East River house into which they had moved with their young son. To the detriment of home life she frequently burdened the Greeley house with intellectuals from Boston, spiritualists and practitioners of mesmerism. She kept her child away from other children and in baby clothes until the age of five, refusing to cut his long golden hair and submitting him to rigorous scrubbings twice a day. Although she whipped him frequently she doted on him, as did her husband, who, however, passed far too much of his time at the *Tribune*

to be of much help in bringing up the child. Greeley had originally selected the large, shabby house because of its extensive wooded grounds
where he could chop trees as a relief from his mental labors. It was
also designed to provide their son, Pickie, with a safe place to play as
soon as he was old enough. Mrs. Greeley not only disliked the place
but would never do anything to make the interior homelike. There
were no rugs, curtains or pictures, and only a few necessary pieces of
furniture. But it was home to Greeley, who had never known anything
better and he, at least, was happy there until 1849 when five-year-old
Pickie died.

"Ah Margaret! The World grows dark with us," he wrote Margaret Fuller in Italy. "You grieve for Rome has fallen; I mourn for
Pickie is dead! The one sunburst of joy that has gladdened my rugged
pathway has departed, and henceforth life must be heavy and rayless. I
have never had an intimate friend—my life has been too intensely
busy and my aims not entirely common; but this one dear being already promised to be my friend in every trial, my solace in every care.
To him my form and features were the standard of beauty, and even
my singing was music. He was my one auditor who never tired—my
companion on whom my leisure hour was ever spent and never wasted.
I had no hope, no dream of personal good or distinction of which his
delight, his advantage, was not the better part; and now he is dead . . ."

The sickening events of his home life could not, however, infect the
outlook of one who believed that there were many things to be
watched in the country and who also felt a moral obligation to watch
them. He practically lived in the *Tribune* rooms—the days were not
long enough. Arriving at the office with his ill-fitting coat bulging
with newspapers and notes, he would hastily remove his low-crowned
hat, from which various other memos would flutter to the floor. In his
barren office he entertained an endless stream of visitors, many of
them unimportant, and attended to a myriad of details in addition to
his editorial writing and general editing. Various meetings of groups
or movements in which he was interested further encroached on his
working day so that he was frequently unable to leave the office before
eleven o'clock at night. In 1848 he went to Congress to fill an un-

expired term and in the short period of three months he clipped the wings of his colleagues by ending the "mileage racket," the practice of padding their travel expenses.

As time went on politics loomed ever larger in his large sphere of interests. Like most other emigrés from the northcountry he was fiercely democratic. After seeing Queen Victoria at the Crystal Palace Exposition on a trip to Europe, he took a characteristic potshot at the institution of royalty. "The Queen was here by Divine right of Womanhood, by Universal Suffrage, or anyhow you please; but what have her Gentlemen Ushers of Sword and State, Ladies in Waiting, Master of the Horse, Groom of the Stole and such uncouth fossils to do with an exhibition of the fruits of industry? What in their capacities have they ever had to do with industry except to burden it? The Mistress of the Robes would be in place if she ever fashioned any robes."

At home Greeley was disillusioned with the Whig party because of its do-nothing attitude concerning the most important question of the day—slavery. ". . . Neither Mr. Clay's plan nor Pres. Fillmore's plan nor any plan can stop slavery agitation so long as slavery shall not merely exist but insist on extending its domain. . . . The slave-catching fugitive slave bill will make a hundred Abolitionists oftener than it catches one slave. Doesn't the South understand that they cannot get their escaped slaves no matter how many laws are crowded upon the statute book? For the North does not and will not return them. They hide them and send them to Canada."

In 1853 the now celebrated editor of the *Tribune* tried to improve his dreary home life by moving thirty miles out of New York to Chappaqua. As a part-time farmer he strove to revive the memories of his youth by working in the fields, chopping wood and performing other such outdoor tasks. Here, however, his second son died, plunging Greeley into new grief. The disposition of his wife, to whom he was always charitable, was even more wretched than before. An editorial colleague reported the following scene after an overnight visit at the Greeley's Chappaqua home:

" 'Things have gone pretty well on the farm, Mother, while I have been away,' remarked Greeley.

" 'They haven't gone well in the house, Mr. Greeley,' shot back the wife. 'The roof has leaked and everything is being ruined.'

"'No, Mother, I don't think everything will be ruined,' replied Greeley. 'You know you will not allow anyone but Mr. C. to repair the roof and he is away.'

"It was dark when supper was over—if a meal composed of bread, butter, milk, apple-sauce, custard and cocoa can be called a supper. My efforts to see the time from my watch resulted finally in the light of about two inches of candle.

"'Could Mother not furnish a better light?' asked Greeley.

"'That one is good enough,' came the reply like an electrical discharge.

"Greeley happened to say it was difficult to find help that would have a deep interest in the work. 'If I had charge of affairs,' spoke up Mrs. Greeley, 'I would give my directions and they would be obeyed.'

"'Why, Mother,' said Greeley, 'you have charge here—in my absence.'

"'Damn it, I haven't!' was the quick response. 'I'm a cipher here— a mere slave! I've no rights; no respect is shown me.' But the real disclosure of temper came when Greeley took the cover off a big willow market basket containing things he had bought in the city to please the family. He was plainly proud of his purchases. First he produced a fine calf-skin. She held it to her nose and threw it under the table.

"'Horrid!' she exclaimed. 'It smells like a beast.'

"Then came a pair of shoes. 'These will never do,' said Mrs. Greeley. 'They are too large.'

"'How do you know, Mother? You haven't tried them on.'

"'I don't want to try them on! Haven't I got eyes to tell whether a shoe is a rod too long for me? You can carry them straight back!'

"'Well, Mother, here is a pair of rubbers for Ida,' said Greeley, handing them over for inspection.

"'What horrible things!' exclaimed Mrs. Greeley. 'They are too heavy; they would kill the child! She will never, never wear them! You don't seem to exercise the least judgment in what you buy. If you had any sense you wouldn't bring anything of this kind into the house.'"

When Stephen Douglas introduced his Kansas-Nebraska Bill in January 1854 to organize the new territory and permit slavery, Greeley burst forth in an editorial battle cry to rally the North. The *Tribune* at once became the flag-bearer of emancipation and the Abolitionists quickly fell in behind it.

But a voice was not enough. A new antislavery party was necessary —a party that would well up from the farms and villages of the North with sufficient strength to flood Congress with an overwhelming number of candidates. Long before the public knew about it this party was in the making, and one of the founders was Horace Greeley. Its inventor was rural-New York-born Alvan Earl Bovay, a graduate of Norwich University in Vermont, a lawyer, teacher, radical agitator, surveyor and unsuccessful politician. Bovay migrated west to Wisconsin on the advice of Greeley. Later he professed that his political activities there were the result of experience gained in Vermont. In 1852 he visited New York and went to lunch at Lovejoy's Hotel with the editor of the *Tribune*.

"A new party will come from the Whigs joining with all the scattered elements that have dropped away from the Whigs and Democrats," Bovay said earnestly. "This party will divide the country; it will take to itself all the North . . . Its banner will be the exclusion of slavery. This party will embrace within its ample folds all those elements now fighting in scattered battalions."

"What would you call this party you see looming so clearly?" asked Greeley, with the skepticism of a seasoned politician.

"I have a name," said Bovay. "It is a name that will attract and not repel; that has a reason behind it. The name is Republican."

Two years later in 1854 Bovay wrote Greeley from Wisconsin that the *Tribune* was now a power in the land. "Advocate calling together, in every church and schoolhouse in the free states, all the opponents of the Kansas-Nebraska bill, no matter what their party affiliations," he counseled. "Urge them to forget previous political names and organizations and band together under the name I suggested to you at Lovejoy's Hotel in 1852. I mean Republican."

The Kansas-Nebraska Bill passed the Senate. A few days later a group of disgruntled Whigs, Free-Soilers and Democrats, led by Bovay, filed into a white Kansas schoolhouse and came out Republicans. The Kansas-Nebraska Bill now passed the House; the *Tribune* took up the cudgel and the Republican party was launched.

Even while Greeley vigorously trumpeted the Republican party he was for a time strangely interested in Stephen Douglas. He apparently felt that he might bring the only man he thought could win a Presidential election to a firm declaration against slavery, if not into the fold of Republicanism. The reporter for the Chicago *Daily Times* said he saw Greeley in Washington "scrabbling down Pennsylvania Avenue looking like a Methodist exhorter, with his flapping white coat, broadbrimmed white hat and fringe of white hair, hurrying to give counsel to Douglas."

"I think Greeley is not doing me right," Lincoln justly complained. "His conduct savors of injustice. I am a true Republican and have been tried already in the hottest part of the fight, yet I find him taking up Douglas—a veritable dodger—once a tool of the South, now its enemy —and pushing him to the front . . ."

But at the Republican national convention of 1860 it was the unpredictable Greeley who sleeplessly engineered delegates so that Abraham Lincoln won the nomination. The editor of the *Tribune* emerged a hero not only of the convention but of the party. It was now the unpredictable Greeley, however, who thought that the South would have remained in the Union if it had not been pushed into secession by the North. Yet it was also the tempestuous Greeley who stanchly defended Lincoln in his struggles with a hostile cabinet and Congress, and who prodded the President to emancipate the slaves. "Forward to Richmond!" blazed the *Tribune,* rushing the Union Army into the ill-fated battle of Bull Run.

Following the assassination of Lincoln and the end of the war it was the same Greeley who outraged the North by helping bail Jefferson Davis out of jail. "Magnanimity in triumph!" he preached to the disgust of the North and the disinterest of the South. William Lloyd Garrison thought Davis should be hanged. The noncommittal Vermont Democrat, Stephen Douglas, called Vermont's Thaddeus Stevens a "black Republican." "Rebels have no rights," Stevens had sniped before his cheering colleagues. "They are at the will of their conquerors."

The erratic *Tribune* editor did not think so—and he was willing to sacrifice his career to the dictates of his conscience. As he wrote later, "Of course I threw away the senatorship in 1866—knowing that I did so—and did myself great pecuniary harm in 1867 by bailing Jeff Davis; but suppose I hadn't done either? Either God rules this world or does not. I believe he does."

Greeley continued to follow his conscience and his heart in the years after the war. He invested in preposterous business schemes and vague projects and lost money to inventors, ne'er-do-wells and designing culprits. He could not find all of his ideals in the Republican party nor in any party, so his politics were hopelessly mixed. The key to his thinking may have been in a letter written in 1860 to young men in political life. "The moral I would inculcate . . . is summed up in the Scriptural injunction—'Put not your trust in princes.' Men, even the best, are frail and mutable, while principle is sure and eternal. Be no man's man but Truth's and your country's. You will be sorely tempted at times to take this or that great man for your oracle and guide—it is easy and tempting to learn, to follow, and to trust—but it is safer and wiser to look ever through your own eyes to tread your own path, to trust implicitly in God alone . . ."

Because he thought the Republicans were not doing right by the South he abandoned his party and his friends to run on the Liberal Republican and Democratic ticket against Ulysses S. Grant. He fought a spirited campaign but went down in pitiable defeat. Within a few weeks the Vermont printer's devil was dead—of a broken heart, they say.

Twenty years before bayonets impaled the issue of slavery, the north-country was dotted with stations on an invisible railroad which hustled Negro refugees to freedom in Canada. They entered Vermont from the lower Connecticut valley, from Albany and Troy (at a point five miles west of Bennington), from Lyme and Littleton in New Hampshire and from the Hudson River via the canal to Lake Champlain. They were hidden in carriages, in wagons, in canalboats and steamboats and, when the railroads came through in 1849, in baggage and freight cars. Negroes could identify the houses at which they were welcome along the Albany-Troy-Bennington route by a row of white-painted chimney bricks. As they progressed along all of the various trunk lines, station agents informed them where they would find their friends in the journey ahead.

Stephen Boardman of Norwich, on the Vermont side of the Connecticut River, aided more than six hundred slaves to freedom, some of whom narrowly escaped capture by their former owners assisted by the United States authorities. On one occasion Boardman assumed the responsibility of keeping a slave and his wife and child from the hands of their owner, who was accompanied by the United States marshal with his deputies and three bloodhounds. Boardman soaked his charges' shoes in spirits of camphor and, with little time to spare, hid them in a cornfield cellar hole. Shortly the slaveowner appeared with the federal authorities and demanded the right to search the farm. Boardman refused because they had no warrant. After many harsh words and threats they departed to get it, while Boardman made hasty arrangements with his son to remove the slaves. At twilight the younger Boardman escorted them through the orchard and woods to a back road where his father was waiting with a wagon. From here Boardman drove them twenty-five miles, probably to Randolph, where he put them in charge of an underground agent on the crew of a Vermont Central freight train leaving the next morning for Canada.

Owing to its central location Montpelier flourished in the underground traffic. Stagecoach drivers deposited the fugitives at the house of Colonel Jonathan P. Miller, one of several industrious agents. The American Dare Devil fed them, clothed them if necessary and arranged their passage to the next station. Joseph Poland, who also lived in the capital, secreted the Negroes in a closet of his printing office until further transportation could be arranged. In western Vermont at Ferrisburg, Rowland T. Robinson, father of the Vermont folklorist, had started one of the state's earliest antislavery societies, which he served as secretary. On the second floor of his home the Quaker hid the dark fugitives in a compartment to which entrance was inconspicuously gained by way of a bedroom. Up the back stairs to the forbidden room young Rowland Robinson's Aunt Anne carried trays of food. In the night hushed whispers and the quiet tread of feet signaled the mysterious guests' departure for Charlotte or Burlington toward the north, or their arrival from the south.

The underground lines from the east and south joined at Burlington, where great numbers of slaves were forwarded to the border by rail or stagecoach, or by water to St. Johns, Quebec, on the steamboats *Franklin, Phoenix, Saranac, Whitehall, Francis Saltus* and *United States*. Lawrence Brainerd, a prosperous St. Albans merchant and railroad and steamboat official, placed the rail and water facilities in the service of the black traffic. The principal agents on the underground line at Burlington were Joshua Young, minister of the Unitarian church; Lucius Bigelow, one of his parishioners, and an insurance man named Salmon P. Wires. Young hid the slaves in his barn, Wires frequently concealed them in his insurance office and Bigelow secreted them in an ell of his three-story colonial house next to the Burlington Female Seminary, immediately above a deep ravine through which the trains passed to Canada. The slaves had been instructed to leave the train on the outskirts of Burlington, from which point they followed the tracks at night to Bigelow's, where they climbed the steep bank to the refuge of his house.

Wires and Bigelow were under frequent surveillance by the federal authorities, but operated boldly and without being caught. On one occasion when the master of the concealed slaves arrived in town they simply put their charges in their carriages and drove off. Late one Saturday night Bigelow aroused the minister, Joshua Young, and took him to Salmon Wires's office, where sleeping on the floor were six tattered and hungry Negroes, three of them from the same Virginia plantation. Young procured food, then he and Wires entered Edward Peck's store and appropriated clothing for which they later paid the merchant. The next night Wires and Bigelow drove the slaves to St. Albans and put them on the train for Montreal.

Arriving in Burlington and determining to stay, one fugitive procured employment as a waiter at the Lake House, a hotel on the waterfront. He and his wife bought a home and proceeded to raise a family. He was terror-stricken one day by the sight of his master, who had seated himself in the dining room of the Lake House. He ran to Lucius Bigelow, who took him out of town and put him on a train. Returning to Burlington Bigelow explained to the waiter's wife what had happened and arranged to have her and the children join him. Then

Bigelow sold their house and forwarded the proceeds.

Wires and Bigelow were men of means who accounted to none for their actions. It was not so with Joshua Young. He had come to the pulpit of the stately Burlington church from Boston, where he had succeeded Francis Parkman as pastor of the New North Unitarian Church on Hanover Street. A burning Abolitionist, Young found his more heated antislavery sermons rather coolly received by some of the wealthy Burlington conservatives in his congregation. But he would not retrench. He was greatly distraught over the hanging of John Brown, whom he had admired as the most courageous and self-sacrificing of the Abolitionists, and when he learned that the body would be brought for burial from Virginia to North Elba, New York, on the opposite shore of the lake, he resolved to attend the funeral services. When his wife inquired if he thought it wise to go, Young said that it might not be wise but he was going just the same. John Brown's body passed northward through Vermont in the gray of December 1859 to a point near Vergennes on the lake shore, whence it was ferried to the New York shore and conveyed to North Elba. Young and Bigelow set out for Vergennes with the intention of meeting the train carrying Brown's body; failing in this, they proceeded through a furious blizzard to North Elba, where they arrived after spending twenty-four hours en route with nothing to eat. Although he had come to the funeral purely in sympathy, it happened that Young was the only minister there and he was accordingly asked to conduct the ceremony.

While they were carrying John Brown to the grave on the white mountainside, the martyr's wife broke down. Joshua Young whispered to her the text from St. Paul: "I have fought the good fight, I have finished my course, I have kept the faith: henceforth there is laid up for me a crown of righteousness which the Lord, the righteous judge, shall give me at that day."

A Burlington newspaper took Joshua Young severely to task for preaching the funeral sermon of one whom it considered a felon and a traitor. Six of the most prominent families left the fellowship of his church and many others in the congregation treated him and his wife with the contempt of silence. Joshua Young resigned his pastorate. There was no other way out.

XII. Disorder on the Border

STRANGE men had been in town for several days but the citizens of St. Albans, only fifty-five miles south of Montreal, were accustomed to travelers. In the life of a northcountry town hundreds of miles removed from the din of the battlefield, the morning of October 19, 1864, was quite like any other.

A few minutes after three o'clock in the afternoon, while Cyrus N. Bishop, teller of the St. Albans Bank, was working at the counter, two men entered the lobby, proceeded to Bishop's window and drew two large revolvers. Bishop jumped into the directors' room in which another clerk was working and tried to close the door, but the two men reached it before he could snap the lock. Forcing it open they seized the frightened teller and, pointing two revolvers at his head, advised him that if he attempted further resistance they would blow his brains out. Bishop asked them what they were going to do. They said they were Confederate soldiers detailed to come north to rob and plunder, as the Union soldiers were doing in the Shenandoah valley. In the meantime they had pulled out three bags of silver, too heavy to lug away. As they opened the bags and started stuffing their pockets and satchels with coins, three of their confrères who had just entered the bank joined them to share in the loot. The safe in the banking room was relieved of about seventy-five thousand dollars in greenbacks, and several citizens of St. Albans were also seized and robbed as they stepped into the bank.

Martin Seymour, the clerk who had been in the directors' room when the raid began, suggested that if the bank was being robbed as an act of war, the soldiers ought to allow the employees time to make an inventory of what they were taking so that the bank might lodge a claim with the government for indemnification.

"God damn your government!" snapped one of the Confederates. "Hold up your hands!" After forcing the occupants of the room to swear that they would not report the robbery until two hours after the raiders had left town, the soldiers withdrew.

The Franklin County Bank was the next target. When the first rebel entered it there were only two employees on duty, one of whom, the cashier, Marcus Beardsley, was seated near the stove talking with a St. Albans man. The raider asked Beardsley the price of gold. The cashier replied that the bank did not deal in it and referred him to a customer just entering with a deposit. With this man the rebel exchanged greenbacks for two gold pieces. The two townspeople now departed, leaving the employees and the raider, who was shortly joined by four of his accomplices. Presently one of them advanced from the corner and drew his gun. The others immediately followed suit.

"We are Confederate soldiers," announced the leader. "There are one hundred of us. We have come to rob your banks and burn your town." Beardsley was transfixed. The other employee, Clark, made a run for the door but was halted by the threat of death. The raiders now went through the drawers and the vault, removing a great many packages of bills. As they were doing so Clark again tried unsuccessfully to escape and this time was locked into the vault. Beardsley protested this inhuman act, saying that it was airtight and that only a few minutes of life was possible inside. Ignoring this plea, the Confederates, now ready to leave, also closed Beardsley in the vault. By hollering and pounding on the walls for twenty minutes the two were heard and saved by shouting the combination of the lock to their rescuer.

In the meantime the raiders were assaulting a third bank, The First National. Here the only occupants were Albert Sowles, the cashier, and deaf, ninety-year-old General John Nason, who was seated reading a newspaper. The first Confederate to approach Sowles drew two revolvers and announced, "You are my prisoners. If you offer any resistance I will shoot you dead." Another raider drew a third revolver, a foot and a half long, so that Sowles was adequately covered while two other Confederates searched the cashboxes and the vault. They found five bags of coins which Sowles told them contained pennies. To make sure, they opened one and scattered the contents on the floor. They left the bags without discovering that one of them was filled with gold. Stuffing their pockets and valises with bank bills, treasury notes and bonds, the raiders withdrew. They had just gone out the door when William Blaisdell entered and inquired what these men had been doing. Upon learning that the bank had been held up he seized one of the Confederates who had come up the steps after him with a drawn revolver, threw him to the ground and landed on top of him.

"Shoot him! Shoot him!" the other raiders shouted to the prostrate Confederate; but with the Vermonter on top of him this was not so easy. The muzzles of two revolvers were now pressed against Blaisdell's head. He was presented with the alternative of either releasing his hold on the raider or having his brains blown out. At this point old General Nason abandoned his newspaper, creaked forward and suggested that "two upon one was not fair play." Blaisdell capitulated and was pushed at the point of a gun across the street to the village green where the Confederates were gathering all the witnesses. General Nason, who could hear nothing and who had seen little because he had been reading his newspaper during the robbery, inquired of Sowles, "What gentlemen were those?"

Thirteen Confederates out of a total of twenty-two had been engaged in robbing the banks. The others occupied themselves with preventing pedestrians on the main street from seeking help at the near-by railroad shops where hundreds of men were employed. All passers-by, together with observers on the veranda of the American House, were assembled on the green and kept quiet with threats of annihilation. As an old jeweler, C. H. Huntington, was passing along the street oblivious of what was happening, a man stepped out of a carriageway, tapped him on the shoulder and told him to cross to the green or he would be shot. Thinking the man was drunk, Huntington said, "Oh no, I guess you won't shoot me." The robber fired. The bullet was deflected by one of Huntington's apparently indestructible ribs and left only a flesh wound—which did not prevent him from passing over to the green under his own power.

Some of the Confederates now hastened to Field's and Fuller's livery stables for horses on which to make their getaway. When Field objected he received a bullet through his hat. Fuller was just returning to his stable as Lieutenant Young, commander of the raid, was making the foreman lead seven horses into the street. When Fuller ordered him to take them back the foreman warned him to keep still or he would be shot. Lieutenant Young ordered Fuller to get a pair of spurs from Bedard's harness shop across the street, but the stable owner instead jumped behind a pole, pulled a revolver out of his pocket and aimed it at Young. He pulled the trigger three times but all that was heard was the snap of the firing pin. Laughing, the Confederate leader said, "Now will you get me the spurs?"

"Yes, but I thought you were joking," replied Fuller.

The St. Albans square was now in a tumult. A man from Highgate, driving a two-horse wagon, passed the bank and was stopped and deprived of his motive power. L. A. Cross, the village photographer, appeared at his doorway and called out, "What are they trying to celebrate?"

"I will let you know," Lieutenant Young shouted, and put a couple of slugs into the door of the photography salon. The raiders threw a phosphoric compound of Greek fire against the wooden buildings, which in all instances happily failed to ignite. A man named Morrison was fatally shot in the abdomen. Mrs. John Gregory Smith was alone with her maids in the governor's mansion. When a neighbor rushed in and told her that the rebels were shooting up the town and were on their way up the hill to burn her house, Mrs. Smith directed her maids to pull down every shade. At first she thought she would run up the flag, but instead began a search for weapons and ammunition. She at length found a large horse pistol and took her station in front of the house. At this point a horseman galloped up the hill. He turned out to be not one of the raiders but F. Stewart Stranahan, her brother-in-law, a member of General Custer's staff on sick leave in St. Albans. Mrs. Smith gave him the horse pistol and shouted, "If you come up with them, kill them! Kill them!" Meanwhile the raiders, firing in every direction as the streets filled with people, had mounted their twenty-two stolen horses and galloped out of town to the north.

St. Albans rallied from its paralysis of surprise rather quickly. While the raid was in progress the telegraph operator sent out emergency messages. From Montpelier and from Burlington, where the bells were ringing, the militia was rushed to St. Albans by rail. The side-wheeler *United States,* with a guard on board, proceeded north under full steam. Bridges, docks and roads in the northern area were guarded. In St. Albans Captain George Conger rounded up men, guns and horses and quickly rode off to the north in pursuit.

On the road from St. Albans to Sheldon the galloping Confederates met a farmer astride a king-sized horse. They drew up quickly and without explanation pulled the flabbergasted man from his saddle. One of their number now mounted the strong horse, leaving the farmer with the old and dejected mount he had been riding. Then the bandits were off again. As the farmer stood examining the jaded plug he had thus suddenly acquired, the St. Albans posse headed by Captain Conger galloped into view. They recognized the horse, thought the farmer was one of the Confederates and at once opened fire. Fleeing across a field the astounded Vermonter managed to reach safety in a swamp.

The St. Albans posse pursued the Confederates across the border and in the small hours of the next morning traced two of them with a large number of bank bills to a Stanbridge hotel room. Eleven others—who, like these two, had been forced to stop because their bareback ride had chafed them badly—were soon in the hands of the Canadian authorities.

An inquiry was begun immediately to gather facts for the impending trial and revealed that the raiders were all young Confederate officers or enlisted men who had been sent under orders from the Confederate secretary of war to attack northern towns. The tall and notably good-looking commander, Lieutenant Bennett H. Young, was a native of Kentucky. He had been in the North for quite some time and with two subordinates had come to St. Albans as early as October 10 to make plans for the raid. Five others had drifted into town that day and the next, registering under assumed names at either the American Hotel or the Tremont House. Circulating about unobtrusively, they had checked on the number of privately-owned weapons and noted the habits of the people and the location of the railroad shops, banks and the stables. They learned that Tuesday was market day and unfavorable for a raid, but that on Wednesday afternoons the streets were empty—and that on Wednesday, October 19, many villagers would be in Montpelier attending the legislature. Thus the day was chosen and that morning the rest of the Confederates had arrived from various points.

With over half of the raiders and about $80,000 (of a total of $208,000 stolen) now in the custody of Canadian officials, the question to be decided by the courts was whether this had been a legitimate act of war. If it was, neutral Canada would have to release the prisoners and return the booty to them. The trial took place before Justice Coursol of Montreal, who heard every prisoner, employees of the robbed banks and all the other St. Albans witnesses. Thomas Collins, one of the raiders, testified that he was a native of Kentucky and a commissioned Confederate officer. At the battle of Cynthiana, Kentucky, he had been separated from his troops. Managing to escape capture by the Union Army he had gone to Chicago where he had joined Lieutenant Young. He swore that he was an enemy of the northern government because his father had been imprisoned by the Yankees with resulting impairment to the elder Collins's mind and body. He told how Yankees had stolen Negro men with the result that their women and children had starved. They had also burned and plundered homes, banks, villages and whole districts. Collins said he was retaliating not as a murderer or thief but as a soldier. The raiders considered that they could do the most damage by holding up St. Albans banks and in this way rudely touch the sensitive "pocket nerve" of the Yankees. Declaring that nine thousand dollars of lawful booty had been taken from him plus some of his private funds, he pointed out that under international law his money and freedom should be returned to him.

Lieutenant Young said his heart was steeled against the invaders and oppressors of his beloved native land, and asked if anyone could wonder that fires of revenge burned within him. He related that the parting words of James A. Seddon, secretary of war for the Confederate States had been: "Lieutenant, you go upon a dangerous mission, and you and your command shall be fully protected." In conclusion Young confessed that he was not fully prepared to defend himself and his men because he had not been in touch with his government in Richmond.

The prosecution based its attack upon the principle that "all damage done to the enemy unnecessarily, every act of hostility which does not tend to procure victory and bring war to a conclusion, is a licentiousness condemned by the law of nature."

The judge took three and a half hours to deliver his opinion on December 13, 1864. He observed that "acts of war by the law of nations are just such acts as the belligerents choose to commit within the territories of each other. These acts are done upon the responsibility of the nation, and the soldier committing them can in no way be held punishable for them. They may be what is termed unlawful acts of war . . . but I, as a judge in a neutral country, cannot sit in judgment upon them. Being committed within the territory of the belligerent, this is no violation of our law . . . I have come to the conclusion that the prisoners cannot be extradited. . . . I am of the opinion therefore that [they] are entitled to their discharge."

Cheers from the throats of British subjects, who, like the English Crown, were sympathetic toward the South, now filled the courtroom, the lobby of the building and the street outside. A second trial followed, but the judgment of Justice Coursol was sustained. The stolen money was given back to the prisoners, who were set free. However the Canadian government later paid the Vermont banks that part of the booty that its court had returned to the Confederates. As it happened this was but a small fraction of the total haul because much of the money had been carried away by the raiders who had not been caught.

In such a manner ended the events of the northernmost action of the Civil War.

You would think Vermont would have been ready to settle down after the war. She had lost over five thousand men in battle and had drawn nearly ten million dollars from her treasury to toughen the sinews of the North. Thousands of young men raised in the mellow valleys of her hinterlands were already moving west.

After, during, and even before the war, though, many of her citizens were involved on the Canadian frontier in a backyard fight that had been going on since the War of 1812. At that time Vermont-owned ships traded northward with the Canadian ports of Lake Champlain. The 1809 edict of the United States government forbidding our vessels to land in British-dominated waters very nearly wrecked the economy of western Vermont. The resulting expedient employed by Canadians and Vermonters was smuggling. Many were the ships fitted out with secret compartments in which raw materials and finished products were exchanged right under the eyes of the revenue officers.

Then the canal from the lake to the Hudson River was opened in 1823 and the Champlain valley began to look to the south for its welfare. Weakening economic ties with the north undermined the position of Green Mountain Tories, and the predominant Vermont sentiment was to start something on the Canadian border. The warships of Britain had twice sailed into the United States from Canada. They might do so again unless Canada was delivered from her helpless subservience to the Crown.

When the citizens of lower Canada rebelled against Britain in the so-called Patriots' War of 1837 enthusiastic Vermonters pitched in to help out. Collecting arms under the leadership of L. J. Papineau they moved up to the "line," as the boundary is familiarly called, and early in December crossed into Canada several hundred strong. There they were routed in an ambush by Canadian loyalists.

Green Mountain sentiment for the rebels now flared openly. Thousands of Vermonters gathered at rallies, filled collection boxes with their dollars and supplied the insurgents with powder and ball despite the fact that the governor had ordered an end to the movement. In early 1838 two thousand patriots met in St. Albans to see what could be done to repeal the neutrality laws and to study the border terrain as a base for military operations. General Winfield Scott, sent by President Van Buren to put down the disturbance, arrived during the meeting and cautioned the citizens not to flout the neutrality laws. Ignoring the general the irate assembly recorded their sentiments:

"That as friends of human liberty and human rights we cannot restrain the expression of our sympathy when we behold an oppressed and heroic people unfurl the banner of freedom.

"Resolved, that we hope that the time will come when the bayonet shall fail to sustain the last relic of royalty which now lingers on the Western Continent.

"Resolved, that it is the duty of every independent American to aid in every possible manner consistent with our laws the exertions of the Patriots in Lower Canada against the tyranny, oppression and misrule of a despotic government."

General John E. Wool (later prominent in the Mexican War) was also sent to Vermont by Van Buren to prevent the Vermonters and Canadian refugees from organizing. He was successful only in seizing some supplies which they had gathered for the new attack on Canada. A force of patriots variously estimated at between one and six hundred men crossed into Canada on February 28, 1838, hoisted a flag and proclaimed the Independent Republic of Canada. The new state was stillborn. Caught between a strong British force in the north and the United States militia under General Wool in the south, the insurgents went down in quick defeat. Although surrender to Wool was almost as distasteful as to the British, the patriots reluctantly laid down their arms before the American general. He made subsequent mobilizations impossible, thus forcing an end to the Patriots' War.

Yet anti-British sentiment did not wane—it merely went underground. Beginning in the 1840s thousands of bitter Irish refugees, fleeing from famine and oppression in their homeland, crossed the Atlantic and found their way into America along the St. Lawrence River and Lake Champlain. Many settled in Vermont to add more discordant voices to the historic chorus of Green Mountain rebellion. Within twenty years the bellicose society known as the Fenians had begun to flourish in the northern United States, despite the opposition of the Catholic church. In susceptible Vermont they had only to light the fuse of anti-British sentiment. The favor that the cause of the South found with the British and Canadian governments (displayed in 1864 by the St. Albans raid) was all that was needed to ignite a Fenian revolt in Vermont.

On May 17, 1866, revenue officers at Rouses Point across the Lake seized two hundred stands of Fenian arms. Eleven days later one thousand men in civilian clothes crowded the streets of St. Albans in anticipation of the long-planned invasion of Canada. Their leaders possessed carefully plotted maps and plans of battle complete even to the fortifications of St. Johns and Montreal. They expected that the moment their forces crossed the border Canadians by the thousands would rally to their side and the British government would fall like a house of cards.

While the couriers of the Fenians carried nocturnal messages back and forth across the border and small task forces hid ammunition in barns and farmhouses, the United States troops under General George Meade, hero of Gettysburg, arrived in St. Albans. For some time the town was again a noisy pageant of the military. United States officers adorned the Welden House, their troops camping on the green, and the variously clad Fenians circulated about, their Irish voices raised, undoubtedly, in the strains of the Fenian national anthem:

> Away with speech and brother, reach me down that
>   rifle gun.
> By her sweet voice, and hers alone, the rights of man
>   are won.
> Fling down the pen; when heroic men, pine sad in
>   dungeons lone,
> 'Tis bayonets bright, with good red blood, should
>   plead before the throne.

Unhappily for the Fenians the projected 1866 invasion failed to come off, owing to the intercession of United States government forces.

There was action in June along the Niagara frontier to the west, but the thrusts from Malone, New York, and from Vermont died a-borning.

Nevertheless the movement did not collapse. Drilling, parading and recruiting continued into 1867 at many points along the boundary. Then there was a period of relative quiet, followed, in the spring of 1870, by great activity all the way from northern Vermont westward to St. Paul, Minnesota. On May 23 of that year large numbers of Vermont Fenians were seen moving north, some on trains, some along the roads with bundles over their shoulders and others accompanying teams of supplies, artillery and ammunition. The next day hundreds more arrived from points as far south of the frontier as Troy, New York. Their national commander, General John O'Neill, who had led previous skirmishes at many points along the frontier, appeared incognito in Franklin. St. Albans on the 25th was the scene of another rally, during which citizens, guests and press representatives from New York and Boston were urged to visit the front.

Early on the morning of the 25th the Canadian government, aware of what was going on in the Green Mountains, dispatched the royal troops to St. Johns. There they detrained to form a defensive line opposite Franklin Center, Vermont, the mobilization point of one thousand Fenians. The United States marshal, General George P. Foster, tried to dissuade the insurgents. Realizing that his plans were going in one Irish ear and out the other he crossed the border and informed the commander of the British force that he was powerless to prevent the Fenians from advancing because he had no troops. The redcoats, installed in rifle pits behind a protective pile of rocks and brushwood, prepared for action. Just south of their entrenchment on a prominent knoll was a gully through which ran Chick-a-Biddy Brook. Eight rods further south beyond the border lay Alva Richard's farm, from which the Fenians launched their attack shortly before noon. In high spirits General O'Neill ordered his troops into battle with the words: "Soldiers:—This is the advance guard of the Irish-American army for the liberation of Ireland from the yoke of the oppressor. For your own country you now enter that of the enemy. The eyes of your countrymen are upon you. Forward, march!"

As the Fenians advanced the Canadians opened fire from their well-concealed position. Returning the volley, the Fenians moved across the line, then circled back to a hill from which they could fight to better advantage. The battle was an hour old when a reporter, viewing its progress from Richard's farmhouse, received a bullet through his hat. He and his colleagues retired to the rear. Shortly thereafter General O'Neill, aparently mistaking the United States marshal, General Foster, for one of his own officers, wandered into a trap—a misfortune which removed him completely from the scene of battle and the command of his troops. Foster thrust him into an enclosed carriage, drove him through the advancing and unsuspecting Fenian troops, and never stopped until he reached St. Albans.

The loss of their general so discouraged the rank and file that the battle of Richard's farm ended with one dead and one severely injured and with no ground gained or lost. When President Grant learned of the arrest of the duped and disheartened Irish general he remarked that it was one of the most ludicrous things he had ever heard. An Irish-Canadian, apparently out of sympathy with the Fenian movement, cruelly indulged himself in the following verses:

> The bloody day at length was done,
> The Faynians wanted dinner,
> So o'er the line they bravely run
> Beneath their waving banner.

> The mane Canadian crew were sold,
> They darstn't follow after,
> But kept their drooping spirits up
> Wid raising shouts of laughter.

> O'Neill's campaign so bravely fought
> Was gloriously inded,
> The IRA their courage proved.
> Their pathriot cause defended.

> And the Faynian bhoys, wid little noise,
> Retreated from the front,
> As brave O'Neill through prison bars,
> Saw Burlington, Vermont.

XIII. The Vershire Riot

THE name of the town had been changed from Vershire to Ely and from Ely back to Vershire. The miners who labored in the hill near the ragged village of Copperfield had little to do with it— they were not influential enough to change anything. Actually no one in Vermont cared to have the name of old man Ely or his frivolous grandson perpetuated. As one newspaper remarked, "The rings on E. Dude Ely Goddard's fingers would amount to something handsome if sold—and it is worthwhile to remark that if he had been differently constituted, or if Smith Ely had attended to business instead of encouraging the grandson in idiocy the trouble would probably have been avoided."

In 1882 the Elys cheated the miners out of three and a half months' wages. Hunger visited the mining families on Copperfield's crooked and treeless street, but they had existed through it. Most of them were immigrants—English, Welsh, Irish, a few French Canadians—to whom mining was familiar. It was almost easier to starve a little than to look elsewhere for different work. If lack of business had been distressing the company their burden might have been lighter, but even the more ignorant of the miners realized in their dull way that such was not the case: all the copper that they mined was sold at a good price. Greed was slowly crippling the business. Aged Smith Ely, who had come from New York, sat in his fancy house devising ways to wrest even more dollars from the mountain and the ugly buildings where the ore was smelted, while young Ely Goddard squandered the money before their eyes.

In July 1883 hard times were upon them again, for they had been paid nothing in May and June. On July 2 the West Fairlee telegraph clicked to the outside world that the laborers had entered the company store when it was opened for mail Monday morning and had cleaned the place out. Work in the mines had stopped. The company and the town were in the possession of the miners. Civilian authorities were powerless.

Since urban readers were unaccustomed to riots, insurrections or strikes, the metropolitan papers featured the Vershire affair prominently. They reported that the miners' wives were gathering stones in baskets. The men had gone to Smith Ely's house with the intention of hanging the old man and might have done so if General Stephen Thomas had not hastened there and stood in the doorway. He had talked to them and later they had gone away. The laborers thirsted for the blood of Ely Goddard but he had fled town six months previously. Though they had now broken into his house they had taken nothing as yet—they had merely posted guards. Armed with knives, clubs and revolvers they had driven Superintendent F. M. F. Cazin out of town. The head of the company, ex-Governor Farnham—an honorable man who had inherited the ills of the previous management and the odium of the Elys (still the principal owners)—was their prisoner. They had seized the mine powder, one hundred fifty kegs in all, and had threatened to blow up West Fairlee. If the money due them was not paid by Thursday night, they promised, the mine buildings would be razed. Also, "somebody would get hurt."

For the first time in over thirty years the National Guard was summoned by unwilling Governor John Barstow. Except for preventing violence he determined that any action he took would be on behalf of the rioters. On Friday four companies of soldiers from St. Albans, Rutland, Northfield and Montpelier rumbled to the scene on a special train of six coaches, a freight car loaded with weapons and equipment, and the Central Vermont Railroad's parlor car, the *Garfield*, carrying the governor, his staff and officers.

In the blackness of early Saturday morning the train chuffed into the Ely station, a drab frame waiting room eleven miles from the mines where a wagon train was formed for the remainder of the trip. The soldiers clambered into four- and six-horse mine carts, and the governor and his staff into a miscellany of other conveyances. It was very dark with only the glimmer of the stars and a few lanterns to light the path as the caravan slowly advanced into the hills. The voices of the soldiers, an occasional command to the horses and the sharp sound of hoofs and wagon wheels seemed to profane the night. Morning would bring a melancholy task—every man felt that a certainty.

When the caravan reached Lake Fairlee the stars were going out and the mist was rising. Colonel William Greenleaf formed his men into a marching column and they entered the Vershire hills as light filled the eastern sky. The troops soon reached the outskirts of the village. Above them the single street threaded steeply upward between the tenements. Beyond stood the still-intact mine buildings, dreary structures black with smelting gases that had rendered the hill bald of trees and vegetation. The emptiness of the place increased the soldiers' anxiety as they filed up the street. Only the tramping of their feet disturbed the hostile stillness, which the miners, from ambush, might end at any moment.

Quite contrary to their expectations, next to nothing happened. The sound of crying presently reached their ears. Then through the smudgy windows of the tenements they saw the distraught faces of the women. A giant of a man smoking a clay pipe and carrying a sun umbrella was the first miner they saw. As they seized him and snapped handcuffs over his wrists he said cheerfully, "I beant done nothin', but if you want me it's all right."

The mission of the troops was all but accomplished before they left the street. The weary miners were all in their beds with the exception of the guards they had posted in various places such as the powderhouse. The leaders surrendered peacefully. There was no violence, no insolence, not even discourtesy, unless the remark of one of the laborers could be interpreted as such. When asked if he were a miner he replied, "No, sorr. I am at prisint a gentleman of indepindint laysure." While rations of canned beef, bread and cheese were distributed to the soldiers, the miners and their families crowded about, their children snapping up and devouring each discarded crust of bread. The Montpelier company shared its surplus of food.

Governor Barstow ordered the tills of the concern emptied of every dollar of cash. Accordingly the miners received one fourth of the sixteen thousand dollars due them in back wages; the rest was to be given them in installments. But the state was not running Smith Ely's copperfield, and many of the miners wandered away without ever being paid.

XIV. Artists of the Upcountry

SOME of the wildest land in Vermont surrounds the little village of Huntington. A rugged stream of the same name running through the town gathers its waters from the woodlands of north-central Vermont and from the springs on the western slopes of Mount Ethan Allen and Camel's Hump and Burnt Rock Mountain. If the wildcat still lives in the Green Mountains he lingers in this country or in the wilderness farther to the north.

In the early 1800s when the inhabitants were still struggling to thrust back the forests it is surprising that anyone in Huntington had the opportunity to print a newspaper. Of course the *Vermont Autograph and Remarker* was not much of a paper, but James Johns considered it as important a purveyor of news as Greeley's *Tribune:* woe to the editor of any urban daily who received a copy of the *Autograph* and did not acknowledge it by sending his journal to Huntington by return mail.

Johns was born in 1797. Only thirteen years later he got the idea for his handwritten newspaper and began to circulate stories, historical essays and poems among the neighboring farmers and woodsmen. A volume of his collected poems, valuable only as a curiosity, was published when he was thirty-one. It is clear that the public was little impressed by his work since his printers sued him for nonpayment of the publishing bill two years later. He seems, however, to have made at least one other excursion into commercial printing in 1839 when he arranged to publish an essay titled: *Sunday not holy or a brief investigation of the first day of the week wherein the idea of its being holy time is examined and refuted.* In later years Johns became an agnostic. He could not be called a teetotaler because he spurned all stimulants. He liked to play the violin at country dances, so he was not a recluse.

The *Autograph and Remarker,* his delight, was a small, verbose and often ungrammatical four-page journal with double columns, which he printed entirely by hand and sold for twenty-five cents. The task of making the numerous copies of each issue required exacting penmanship yet he formed his letters with almost typographical clarity, earning notice among the pen printers of the nineteenth century. Of the *Autograph's* editorial policy he wrote in 1834, "As it is composed wholly of original matter, it is of course the channel through which we occasionally express boldly without fear or favor of any man or set of men." Johns was anti-Jackson, antislavery, anti-imprisonment-for-debt, and antifiction, except when the story dealt with historical figures.

In 1866, seven years before his publication ended its sixty-three-year life, he remarked: "A word or two about the *Autograph* and how it should be received and treated . . . there are those among the type and press publishers who turn up their nose at, and give the cold shoulder to any production of paper that [does not] come in the imposing form of great sheets as big as a table cloth, printed on types in thousands of copies. . . . Now I desire all to whom the *Autograph* [goes] to know . . . that it is the only way I can afford to spread myself on paper for others' perusal. Talk hifalutingly as some do about having press and type and sneer or wonder at my taking the pains to print with a pen!"

For a long time it was Johns's ardent ambition to receive *Our Young Folks* in exchange for the *Autograph.* When he finally did get the magazine he criticized its stories and began a new campaign to receive a copy of the *Atlantic.*

Johns wrote the chronicle of Huntington for Hemenway's *Vermont Historical Gazetteer*. In it he tells the following story, which almost certainly appeared in the *Autograph* at one time or another.

"In December, 1824, occurred a remarkable instance of preservation of life, amidst a fearful accident involving manifest danger of its sacrifice: Charles Swift, son of Lot Swift, then a lad 12 years old, on remounting a horse (which his father had borrowed to send him to mill with) on his return, to take him home (the horse having on a saddle one of the stirrups of which being lost off, had a looped leather strap to supply its place), a pair of bars intervened between the horse and the road, over which the horse, impatient as he was, made a bolt, ere they could be all let down, and by the sudden leap threw the boy from his seat clear, except unluckily his foot hung fast in the looped stirrup, by which he was dragged head downwards, the horse going at a brisk jog, for the distance of 100 rods, and this over a road lined on either side with stumps and trees. Fortunately for him, Mr. Swift's dog, which accompanied him, with the sagacity peculiar to that faithful animal, on seeing Charles thus dragging, seized him by the collar of his coat, and thus in a manner kept him from the ground; and it was probably owing to this interference of the dog that his life was saved, as well as their limbs, and he escaped without a bone of him broken or otherwise harmed."

Abby Hemenway was the fourth of ten children, all born in a two-room log cabin in Ludlow. In 1842 at the age of fourteen Abby was teaching in a district school. Ten years later she was still absorbed in the education of both herself and others at the Black River Academy in Ludlow. A pillar of the Ladies' Association for Mental and Other Improvement, she appeared in such of its theatrical productions as *A Farmer's Wife, A Circassian Mother* and *One of the Ladies of the Harem*.

However suggestive these titles were, Abby was destined to remain Miss Abby and spend her life not in the production of children but of books. At the age of thirty she edited an anthology titled *Poets and Poetry of Vermont*. It had not been completed very long before she got the idea that kept her busy for the rest of her life. She felt strongly that "our [Vermont] historic material is becoming and will continue to become daily more indistinct and irrecoverable; and that our past has been too rich and, in many points, too unique and too romantic to lose." Her plan was to visit every corner of the state and collect the stories of the Revolution while there were veterans' sons still alive to tell them, to hear of the hardships of the wilderness from those who endured them—to collect all of that vast body of town and country folklore crowded out of traditional histories by the marching and countermarching of armies and by the descriptions of the military and political great. She would publish a magazine in which the chronicles of the towns would appear separately, each one assembled by local authorities or old residents. Eventually these histories would be brought together into volumes to form a large and comprehensive *Gazetteer*. The project was admirable but overwhelming, launched as it was without resources in the midst of the Civil War. The august professors of Middlebury College informed her that her idea was impractical and unsuitable for a woman. How did she "expect to do what 40 men had been trying for 16 years and could not?"

Not easily diverted she went to see ex-Governor Hiland Hall in Bennington and emptied her carpetbag of manuscripts before him. Hall, a historian to whom such original materials were as impelling as a row of green peas to a vegetarian, promised his warmest support. She needed it, too. She was having trouble with a Mr. Wadleigh who had been asked to write a history of his home town of Arlington. Correspondence had been unavailing and she therefore appeared at Wadleigh's house one day. The person who answered the door said Wadleigh had gone to a distant funeral and would not be back until late. Furthermore, if this was Miss Hemenway, Mr. Wadleigh had left word that he had decided not to do Arlington for her history.

"I will wait if it takes three days," said Abby, taking a chair in the parlor. "I have come a good way to see Mr. Wadleigh and I should not think of leaving town without seeing him." Within an hour Abby overheard someone in the next room say, "Mr. Wadleigh has come." The gentleman soon entered, obviously quite put out to think she had been admitted, and proceeding to the bookcase he searched among the

volumes with contrived nonchalance while Abby presented her arguments. The tension in the room grew more acute as the minutes passed
and Abby sensed that some of the principal families in town objected
to the writing of the history, and as their pastor he saw no reason why
he should create dissatisfaction by doing it. In fact, he would not do it.

"Well," said Abby, "I might as well have spared myself the trouble
of coming. Governor Hall said it would be no use, that I would not
get Arlington."

There was a start at the bookcase. "He did, did he?"

"He did," said Abby.

"What did Governor Hall say was the reason?"

"Because you at Arlington are so ashamed of your Toryism." Abby
could see that great forces were now at work. Wadleigh knew that
others must think what the governor was thinking, and that if Arlington was to be saved from the taint of Toryism he had better get busy
right away.

"You may tell Governor Hall," he announced, "that we think we
can manage the Arlington history."

Another hard-won victory for the *Gazetteer*. Abby managed to get
six issues of the quarterly published before capitulating to the Civil
War. For lack of support she was forced to suspend publication for a
time while she went to work on an anthology of war poetry. Meanwhile she became a convert to Catholicism. Her conversion might
easily have strained her relationships with her Protestant contributors,
particularly the ministers, but there seem to have been few dislocations.
On the contrary she received a proposal of marriage, curiously enough,
from a Protestant minister. From Burlington in 1867 she wrote her
sister: "I have had a renewal of the proposition of marriage from the
Methodist clergyman since I have written you. He shows himself
somewhat persevering, considering I have never given him the least
encouragement. . . . He says that he will not ask me in religious matters to go against my conscience and that he would take hold with me
on my history & try & make it a splendid success . . ."

But Abby could not be married—she was already betrothed to her
Gazetteer, for better or worse, in sickness and in health. Through the
1860s and 70s it justified her best hopes, although it was never anything

but a crushing financial millstone. The state legislators had appropriated a sum of money that might have helped Volume IV had they not attached conditions that were difficult to fulfill, such as an impossibly early date for completion.

Though Volume IV was attached by a Montpelier publishing firm to satisfy the printing bill, Abby still considered the books hers. She did not care about the legal side of it—the *Gazetteer* was the fruit of her labor and her only means of support. She entered the press one night and removed the books. A dispute of large proportions arose in which Abby did not fare too well, as usual. Although Volume I was hers, Volumes II and III were owned by Samuel Farnam of White River Junction, and Volume IV was not of much financial help because it was so encumbered with debt.

To Abby the most important fact about the *Gazetteer* was that it was still unfinished. If she could not afford a printer she would set type herself, so she moved into a single large room which she subdivided with red curtains. Among the many items in the largest section were cases of type, a printing press, a cupboard, stove and sink. Then there was what she called the reception room where she placed her few fine heirlooms, and finally there was the sleeping section. In the first compartment Volume V began to take form, with her Ludlow relations helping to set type and other assistants appearing later when she could afford to pay them.

By this time she was obsessed with the work of the *Gazetteer,* pursuing it even under the handicap of a broken collarbone which she received when run down by a sleigh. She had not been in Ludlow long, however, when the pressure from her Montpelier creditors became so strong that she packed up and moved to Chicago in 1885. There she rented two rooms where she edited her material at night and during the day set type for the printers downtown. In 1886 when she had 857 pages of Volume V finished, the building burned down. None of the material in her rooms was insured, but even if it had been, much of it could never have been replaced.

"We are sorry for the disaster of the fire," wrote the son-in-law of Abby's Wardsboro compiler, "and before I undertake to replace the lost material, I would like to know what could be done if it is not replaced? Of course, I could not entirely supply the articles but I could do something towards it by writing to Mr. Robbins' friends and Hazelton's friends and Kidder's. . . . We all feel bad over your loss, but it is not quite so bad as when Carlyle lost his whole copy of the French Revolution and had to write it over again. What a bright wife he had! You have no husband to be sorry over the loss, but there are many who will."

The fire hastened the aging of both her body and mind, although she managed to sustain herself by selling single histories of the various towns. In 1890 she died, unattended, of apoplexy in a shabby Chicago room, leaving seven hundred dollars and debts worth more than that.

Thirty-three years later the state spent twelve thousand dollars to index her works, which have no counterpart in the country. Today if a person is interested in the early life of any Vermont town, he will of course turn to the six thousand invaluable pages of Hemenway's *Vermont Historical Gazetteer*. There will never be a Vermont history written that will not owe a profound debt to these bulky volumes.

The creator of Oliver Twist and Nicholas Nickleby was dead quite unexpectedly at fifty-eight, and no one had a right to expect that his last book, *The Mystery of Edwin Drood,* would ever be completed.

Had Drood been murdered that Christmas Eve when he disappeared in the storm that blew in on England from the sea and moaned with ghostly premonition through the buttresses of the ancient cathedral? Perhaps his uncle Jasper knew; or Durdles, the dusty alcoholic who was familiar with all the "dead 'uns" in the myriad crypts beneath the cathedral; certainly the old woman who peddled dope, the Princess Puffer, possessed some clues—but the reader was as ignorant of Drood's fate was as Miss Rosa Bud, his pretty fiancée.

It remained for Thomas P. James, a young tramp printer who arrived in Brattleboro in the early 1870s with his alleged wife to assist the departed Charles Dickens in untangling the mystery of Edwin Drood. James, who has been described as a "free and easy fellow—good tempered, well dressed with his boots always blackened and smoking a cigar with the ease of a lord," never held a job very long and his employment in the Brattleboro printing shops was of equally short duration. He soon announced that he was retiring into deep seclusion as the earthly medium of Charles Dickens in order that he might complete *The Mystery of Edwin Drood*. This created a flurry of specualtion both in spiritualist circles and in the press of the north-country, but when James withdrew to commune with Dickens and emerged after each trance with a fistful of manuscript that was as unmistakably Dickens as the early chapters written by the master himself, consternation struck the reporters.

Prior to 1872, they found, James had known nothing of spiritualism. In October of that year he had attended a séance held by his landlady and h-d fallen into a trance in the course of which he had received messages from residents of Brattleboro who had died before his arrival there. On this same occasion he had intercepted a message from Charles Dickens directing that James should be his earthly agent and the instrument through which *The Mystery of Edwin Drood* should be completed. On November 15 James had started to write. His custom was to go into a room alone, either at six in the morning or seven in the evening, and sit until he fell into a trance. Sometimes if atmospheric conditions were unfavorable he found it difficult to do so, but he reported that the moment he dropped into the trance he was always aware of a grave figure seated beside him. As soon as he awoke from his spell he would find the floor covered with sheets on which were scrawled succeeding chapters of *The Mystery of Edwin Drood*.

What confounded the reporters of metropolitan dailies and those who rejected spiritualism as a fraud, was the fact that James was known to have neither any literary ability whatever nor even any schooling beyond the age of thirteen. In the setting of type he was a competent craftsman; but this was merely a mechanical process which had nothing to do with writing. It was said that he had never written as much as an obituary notice for a newspaper, let alone anything with literary merit. He was reported in at least one interview as having said he had never even read the first part of *Edwin Drood*. "Those who know the medium," declared a correspondent for the Boston *Post*, "all agree that he could not do this work unaided even if he were ever so close a student of Dickens. He has not the power, and even if he had he has not the education. Even those who are most skeptical are acknowledging that . . ."

Within a few months James had accomplished a labor that few established authors would have dared to undertake—a labor which would have consumed years if they had attempted it. *The Mystery of Edwin Drood*—complete—was published in Brattleboro on October 31, 1873, with a Medium's Preface and a Foreword by Dickens which he had transmitted to James through his departed spirit. Revealing some of the charges brought against him while finishing the book, James says in his Preface:

"One statement was, that the manuscript of this Second Part was left completed by Mr. Dickens at the time of his decease, and that one of his heirs, with a view to creating a sensation, thought it would be a capital plan to send it to this country and have it published in this way, and had selected me as his agent to carry out the project.

"Another theory,—and the most popular of any,—was that the Evil One was at the bottom of the whole business; and it was said that, at a certain hour every night, his Satanic Majesty could be seen emerging from the chimney of my house and flying away into space, leaving behind him such a strong odor of brimstone that one could smell it for an hour afterwards; and, I suppose, no chimney ever attracted so much attention, or inspired such feelings of awe as that one did, in consequence of this libel upon its fair bricks and mortar.

"I am knowing to one instance where two or three of the more superstitious stationed themselves near my house, and patiently awaited the phenomenal or diabolical (whichever you please) display; and yet these very people would not believe it possible that the departed spirit of some loved friend could return to earth, even when they could obtain satisfactory evidence of the fact, with much less trouble . . ."

Dickens, in his Foreword, cautions those who would ridicule the manner in which his book was completed not to dismiss lightly the force of spiritualism, and ends his remarks with "I cannot close this page without assuring the dear ones to whom I was so much attached on earth,—family and friends,—how anxiously I await their coming, that they may realize, by experience, how truly I speak concerning this other life . . ."

Prior to his death Dickens had completed some twenty chapters. James, in well over one hundred thousand words on twelve hundred pages of sermon paper, added as many more to bring the mystery to a satisfactory conclusion. Much later Arthur Conan Doyle, reviewing the weird circumstances in an article titled *The Alleged Posthumous Writings of Great Authors,* found James's writing much like that of Dickens, but Dickens gone flat. Yet, he pointed out, "the trick of thought and manner remains. If it be indeed a parody it has the rare merit among parodies of never accentuating or exaggerating the peculiarities of the original. It is sober and restrained . . ." Indeed Doyle noted that many relatively obscure characteristics of Dickens's style were to be found in the James chapters—even English spelling and the English use of the plural in such words as "coals" and "basements"—which an authority, to say nothing of a New England journeyman printer, might easily overlook in writing such a parody.

As for the metropolitan reporters who had come to Brattleboro in 1873 to investigate James and perhaps expose his work as fraudulent—they went away, according to the correspondent for the *Springfield Union,* "absolutely stumped."

The Mystery of Edwin Drood—complete—is on the shelves of many libraries today for all the world to see and wonder at. For the layman, at least, the best passages of the James chapters are quite as good as Dickens at his best, and the lesser portions are very little worse than Dickens in a lull—which is very good indeed.

Dickens on Mr. Grewgious: ". . . He was an arid, sandy man, who, if he had been put in a grinding-mill, looked as if he would have ground immediately into high-dried snuff. He had a scanty flat crop of hair, in color and consistency like some very mangy yellow fur tippet; it was so unlike hair, that it must have been a wig, but for the stupendous improbability of anybody's voluntarily sporting such a head . . . he had certain notches in his forehead, which looked as though Nature had been about to touch them into sensibility or refinement, when she had impatiently thrown away the chisel, and said, 'I really cannot be worried to finish off this man; let him go as he is.'"

James on Miss Keep: "Miss Keep is rather tall and very slim. She has what was probably intended for a blue eye, but the blueing material evidently ran low; hence it would be difficult to state the color—though Miss Keep's enemies—those of her own sex we mean—every lady has these—said Miss Keep's eyes shaded on the milky. She wears her hair pressed tight to her temples in the form of a half-circle, and an artist with his brush could not carry the curve with a more perfect line. Her chin protrudes to about the same angle with her nose. Add to all this a maiden lady with a great love for poetry, and you behold Miss Keep as she is to-day."

The turbulence Brattleboro had known in the skirmishing of the early Vermont republic with New York had long subsided. Three quarters of a century had lent the town the atmosphere of tranquillity and tradition that still pervades so many upland river communities off the highroad of commerce. In 1844 a German physician and author, Dr. Robert Wesselhoeft, wrote Horace Greeley that he had found the Brattleboro temperature milder than that of the New England seacoast and the spring water the purest of any he had tested from Virginia to the White Mountains.

The next year, 1845, the doctor opened a Brattleboro house of health known as the Wesselhoeft Water Cure. So quickly did he eliminate poisons from the systems of his first fifteen patients that he shortly had one hundred fifty; and within a year, three hundred ninety-two, filling the boarding-houses, inns and hotels. To his original building Wesselhoeft hurriedly added a cluster of others—the west building exclusively for the gentlemen and Paradise Row for the ladies, with a connecting salon for dancing, a dining hall, laundry, carpenter's shop, icehouse, courtyard and fountain. Forty-five- by ninety-five-foot indoor plunges of spring water were installed. Tree-lined paths up and down the hillsides led to outdoor springs near the aqueducts, the woolen mill and along Canal Street. On their way to the bathhouses patients might tarry, if they wished, at the Eagle's Nest, a thatched-roof summerhouse.

Dr. Charles W. Grau, a German physician whom Wesselhoeft had brought to Brattleboro to help with his burgeoning clinic and with such journals as *The Brattleborough Hydropathic Messenger* and *A Green Mountain Spring Monthly Journal*, described the water treatment as follows:

"The patient is waked about four o'clock in the morning, and wrapped in thick woolen blankets almost hermetically; only the face and sometimes the whole head remains free; all other contact of the body with the air being carefully prevented. Soon the vital warmth streams out from the patient, and collects around him, more or less according to his own constitution and the state of the atmosphere. After a while he begins to perspire, and he must continue to perspire till his covering itself becomes wet. During this time his head may be covered with cold compresses and he may drink as much fresh water as he likes. . . . As soon as the attendant observes that there has been perspiration enough, he dips the patient into a cold bath. . . . As soon as the first shock is over he feels a sense of comfort, and the surface of the water becomes covered with clammy matter, which perspiration has driven out from him. The pores, which have been opened by the process of perspiration, suck up the moisture with avidity, and, according to all observations, this is the moment when the wholesome change of matter takes place, by which the whole system gradually becomes purified."

Wesselhoeft was a homeopath who relied less on pink pills than on wholesome outdoor living with the baths as the central feature. The meals were plain—bread, butter, mush and milk, soup and lean meat, fruit and pudding. Horseback riding, mountain climbing, archery, or boating on the Connecticut absorbed younger patients while needle-work (on the three-hundred-foot piazza), billiards and bowling occupied the older and less active. In the evenings all could merrily gather at what were termed the Hydropathic Balls. The tonic effects of Wesselhoeft's treatments and those of a second establishment, the Lawrence Water Cure, were so widely heralded as the years passed that the great and near-great from far and wide congregated at Brattleboro. Among the names that dotted the cold-water register prior to the Civil War were Julia Ward Howe, Henry Wadsworth Longfellow, Katherine Beecher, James Russell Lowell, Jared Sparks, Richard Henry Dana, William Dean Howells, Generals George McClellan and William Sherman, Martin Van Buren and a multitude of governors, senators, diplomats, businessmen and European royalty.

Many patients arrived for the social life in their liveried coaches, for which the Wesselhoeft establishment had thoughtfully mapped a different drive for every day in the season. Many others were persons of culture and it was they who imparted to Brattleboro's cold-water period its most distinctive feature. A member of the Germania Band who had given the first trombone solo ever heard in New York, Charles F. Schuster, was imported by Wesselhoeft to take charge of the musical program. For those who wished them there were lessons on the pipe organ, piano, violin and wind instruments, plus vocal and instrumental concerts for the entire assemblage. Guests and local people co-operated in theatricals. There were lectures and literary round tables. All contributed to make Brattleboro a physical and cultural mecca in the decade before the Civil War.

This lustrous environment helped awaken several local boys to their talents. An artist stopping at the water cure admired a marble pig, and finding its creator was a shy young man not yet nineteen, suggested that he leave his job in Williston and Tyler's hardware store and take up sculpturing. Accordingly young Larkin Mead, nephew of John Humphrey Noyes (the prophet of complex marriage), went to study in a Brooklyn studio for two years, after which he returned to Brattleboro in 1856. On the last night of that year Mead could be seen laboring in a snowdrift outside John Burnham's foundry, where his friends Edward and Henry Burnham were tending a hot fire. Mead was making an eight-foot statue of a maiden, moulding her in the foundry and assembling her in the snowdrift outside. Water, dashed over each completed section, froze quickly. After several feverish hours of activity the snow maiden came to life.

When the citizens of Brattleboro arose to the bright cold of New Year's morning they found Larkin Mead's Recording Angel standing in the snow at the corner of North Main and Linden Streets, a graceful figure in icy robes looking for all the world like a statue chiseled from marble. Her face wore a thoughtful expression, as if she were pondering the events of the dead year to be written down with her quill pen in the book she was carrying. She made a deep impression on the villagers, not only because she was made of snow and might melt, but because she possessed such artistic merit that correspondents of the city newspapers came to view her. "As a first work—the genius to conceive and the art to express the spirit of the recording angel—

this is a success," reported one newspaper. "The record of the year is made up, is finished, and the angel seems lost in meditation."

This was the same Larkin Mead who later appeared in Venice in the American consulate and whose sister married the American consul, William Dean Howells. It was also in Venice that the young Vermonter saw in the piazza of San Marco an Italian girl whose beauty was even greater than that of the Snow Angel. This girl, Marietta de Benvenuti, became his wife. William Rutherford Mead, Larkin's brother and also a product of the Brattleboro water-cure period, became the founding architect in the firm of McKim, Mead and White. From the Brattleboro of the pre-water-cure period also came the painter William Morris Hunt, close friend and champion of Jean François Millet and of John La Farge. Hunt's brother, Richard Morris, born in Brattleboro in 1828, was appointed *inspecteur des traveaux* by the French government and gained renown in the work of uniting the Tuileries with the Louvre. He helped remodel the United States capitol and built the administration building of the Columbia World's Fair in Chicago (for which he earned the gold medal of the Royal Institute of British Architects) and also the famous two-million-dollar house of William K. Vanderbilt on Fifth Avenue, New York.

The nineteenth-century figure for whom the tranquil river town is best remembered was not a native. Yet the green hills must also have worked their magic on him, for he did his best work in Vermont. He came to Brattleboro owing, indirectly, to the water cure and to the fact that Mr. and Mrs. Joseph Balestier, two stanch devotees of Wesselhoeft and perennial summer visitors, had bought land three miles from Brattleboro. In 1872, while T. P. James was finishing *The Mystery of Edwin Drood,* they built a residence there. Two of the Balestier grandchildren, Wolcott and Caroline, passed most of their early years in Vermont, the former showing an early flair for writing as editor of a weekly and author of two romances. In 1888 his publisher, John W. Lovell, sent him across the Atlantic as representative from his firm to England. Wolcott shortly made, according to Henry James, an "unparalleled conquest of literary London." The rare possessor of both literary and business judgment, he soon had his own firm and an office near Westminster Abbey that daily reflected the luster of the gathered literati. To this place came Rudyard Kipling from India, in the flush of acclaim for his *Plain Tales from the Hills*. Kipling and Balestier became not only fast friends but collaborated on a novel titled *Naulakha*.

In 1891 Balestier fell victim to typhus in Dresden and suddenly died. Shortly thereafter Caroline Balestier, who had been keeping house with her brother in London, announced her engagement to Rudyard Kipling. They were married a few weeks after the death of her brother, and within two months were aboard the *S.S. Teutonic* on their way to America. Caroline ardently looked forward to Brattleboro. Would Rudyard share her love for the northcountry hills that she and Wolcott had perhaps overglorified in the clammy chill of London? Vermont might prove disappointing, buried as it now was under snow which her husband had never seen except on distant Himalayan peaks.

As they alighted from the train in the subzero Brattleboro cold of February 1892 and entered a sleigh piled high with buffalo robes, Kipling found the countryside "beautiful beyond expression." The natives, he reported (not disparagingly, for he liked them), were "unhandy men to cross in their ways, set, silent, indirect in speech, and as impenetrable as that other Eastern farmer who is the bedrock of another land."

The newlyweds set up housekeeping in the hired man's cottage on the estate of Caroline's grandparents. Here Kipling wrote the Mowgli stories and with the royalties financed the building of Naulakha, his first real home since childhood. Tucked away in the hills just over the town line in Dummerston, this spacious, gray-shingled structure with its three stories and hip roof was the prototype of the summer home of the period. Kipling liked to point out that the interior was like a ship, with the captain's cabin—his study—forward, and the power plant or kitchen in the stern. Since it afforded a life uncluttered with details and disruptions, he was immensely pleased with it. Caroline sat with her sewing in "the dragon's chamber" outside his study, intercepting visitors during his working hours from nine to one.

In the afternoons, which served as intervals of thought or regeneration, Kipling hiked about the countryside, storing his remarkable memory with details of the brooks, trees and wildlife, with Indian names on the land and Yankee ways. In winter he climbed over the hills on snowshoes, rejoicing in the indigo sky and brittle cold. He found the Vermont environment admirably satisfying to a writer's needs. It was not difficult to live up to the motto which his father had inscribed over the studio fireplace during a visit in 1892: THE NIGHT COMETH WHEN NO MAN CAN WORK.

Kipling's four Vermont years were his most fruitful. The *Jungle Books*, *The Seven Seas* and *Captains Courageous*—all were products of the captain's cabin. The New England hill country was also a splendid place to raise children and there were now two in the Naulakha household. There is little doubt that Kipling would have permanently forsaken England had it not been for the lamentable dispute with his brother-in-law.

Certainly one tradition of Vermont life that appealed to Kipling was that of live-and-let-live. He shared with most Englishmen a dislike for the boisterous familiarity of Americans and he had no desire to discard his English reserve while living in America. Brattleboro had no objection to this, but the symptoms of caste he displayed did not set too well. Brattleboro had heard that the Kiplings, even before Naulakha was built (when they were living alone in the hired man's cottage), dressed for dinner each night as if they were going to the opera. Mrs. Kipling, who had acquired a Mayfair accent, rode around town in a two-horse basket phaeton driven by an English coachman dressed in a fancy uniform. Kipling had his own post office and it was said that he was even making plans for his own railroad station. There was nothing very democratic about any of this. Still, rare birds were plentiful in Vermont and some of the natives liked Kipling, for all his English mannerisms. They and the Brattleboro children did not find him, as others had, abrupt, tactless and aloof, but rather saw him as a gentle figure in a buffalo coat, fur cap and high boots like "some weather-beaten farmhand, bent from much hoeing on Vermont hills," following his curiosity about the town. The local doctor, James Conland, who had helped Kipling with the material for *Captains Courageous,* was a lifelong friend. He and others passed many stimulating evenings in the companionship of the captain's cabin at Naulakha. There the talk ranged from India to the American West, from Yankee politicians to rajahs. Sometimes, touched off by the remark of a guest, Kipling would make up a verse on the spur of the moment—witty lines that he would tear up after they had served their purpose.

Beatty Balestier, the brother of Caroline and of the deceased Wolcott, found Kipling more offensive than anyone else in the community. Beatty was the noisy Balestier black sheep, a drunkard and idler who nevertheless possessed some of the family charm. He was a Brattleboro fixture whose deficiencies were known to all but who enjoyed public favor just the same, since he would usually help out in a pinch and could always be counted on for a laugh. Rudyard and Caroline thought him disgraceful and made the mistake of trying to put him on his feet. Beatty did not wish to be put on his feet, at least not in this patronizing manner.

The relationship between Balestier and Kipling became tense as the seasons passed. Psychologically there was little hope—an alcoholic ne'er-do-well living next to a proud and famous brother-in-law. However things had gone well enough at first. Beatty had helped build Naulakha and, with cordial sentiments all round, had offered the Kiplings a piece of land for a dollar to protect their view, providing he retained the haying rights. Later, with their friendship already cooling, Beatty heard that Caroline had sent for a landscape architect to come and make a formal garden out of his field. One evening when the Kiplings were dining at his house he asked Caroline if this were true and she replied that it was. A bitter argument ensued, during which Beatty told his sister that after she left his house that night he would never speak to her again. Kipling remained quiet during the dinner but was later reported to have said disparaging things about Beatty. They met one night in the woods, each driving a buggy. Beatty told Kipling that if he found him discussing family affairs in public, he would "knock his block off." Heated threats were exchanged. Beatty was shortly arrested for "assault with indecent and opprobrious names and epithets and threatening to kill." He would not furnish bond and Kipling, who saw that Beatty would become a martyr if he went to jail, offered to post it. Beatty would not hear of this and gloriously looked forward to jail, rejoicing in the sympathy he would receive from the townspeople and the contempt with which they would regard Kipling for his inhumanity. Beatty, however, was released pending a full-dress hearing before the justice of the peace.

For the sensitive Kipling, who hated publicity and newspaper reporters, the hearing was a dreadful ordeal. It was held in the Brattleboro town hall before a packed audience of villagers, curious outsiders and correspondents from the metropolitan newspapers. During the course of the testimony, while all of the family wash was hung out, Kipling could not have suffered more if he had been on the rack—but the torture was not yet over. Beatty was held on four hundred dollars bail for a hearing before the September 1896 grand jury, a sideshow which, he anticipated, would further humiliate his brother-in-law. To the latter the nightmare of a second hearing was the last straw. He and his wife packed up their things in August and left Naulakha and Vermont forever.

Bidding good-by to his good friend Dr. Conland at the train was the hardest thing Kipling ever had to do. For, despite his troubles, his roots had gone deep during his four years in the northcountry.

". . . We talk about Naulakha—the wife and I," he wrote Conland from London in 1897. "Josephine holds her tongue about it for weeks at a time. Then we hear her telling little Elsie about the summer-house under the trees and the fun of going barefooted. I wonder when we shall come back. There are times when I feel like taking the first boat and getting you up to dinner straight off. Keep an eye on the place for our sakes. I tried to offer it for sale once but I took damn good care to put a prohibitive price on it. . . . Now write me a letter . . . you've no notion, as they say in Vermont, what a store I set by you."

And later that same year: "A doctor's entertainment to congratulate Sir William Gowers upon getting his Knighthood . . . Gowers is the deuce and all of a specialist. I was asked to make a speech. I pulled through somehow, and in the middle of the festive spread with the electric lights and waiters and plush and flumididdle, I suddenly had a vision of you, with your nose inside your collar, whipping along the road in half a blizzard—out Chesterfield way. I didn't go out of my way to do it, but somehow I found myself describing a country doctor's life in America."

XV. Six Thousand Miles in
an Automobile Car

THE automobile was an unreliable novelty, agreed several men in
the San Francisco University Club. For trips within a reasonable
radius of a spare parts depot it was an uncertain means of locomotion.
For longer journeys it was worthless. Dr. H. Nelson Jackson, a physician far from his home on the Vermont shore of Lake Champlain,
felt his blood rising at the injustice being done to the horseless carriage. It was possible, he declared, joining the group from a near-by
table, to bridge the continent in an automobile. With this reckless
statement the discussion suddenly became a controversy from which
Dr. Jackson found he could not honorably withdraw without placing
a fifty-dollar bet that he could drive an automobile across the United
States.

He was glad that his wife did not think his age—thirty-one—was too
advanced to stand the rigors of the trip and that Sewall K. Crocker, a
young mechanic from Tacoma, Washington, agreed with him that it
could be done. The wager was made on May 18, 1903, and Jackson lost

no time in locating a Winton car which Crocker thought would have the best chance for survival. There were not very many of these in California and Jackson, a man in comfortable circumstances, paid L. C. Rowell of the Wells, Fargo Company a handsome premium for his new 1903 Winton two-chair touring car.

With no less care than a quartermaster staff equipping a division of infantry for the field, Jackson and Crocker, who had signed up for the trip, selected their equipment and accessories: waterproof sleeping bags with blankets, rubber mackintoshes, leather coats for cold weather, corduroy suits and canvas outer suits, a telescope valise, a rifle, shotgun, two automatic pistols, fishing poles, a set of tools and spare parts, block and tackle, a vise, two spare tires, a five-gallon tank of extra cylinder oil, a twelve-gallon tank of extra gasoline, a fireman's ax, two tin canteens and a canvas bag of water. The car weighed two thousand five hundred pounds and with Jackson, a six-footer scaling over two hundred, Crocker, one hundred fifty, and the accessories several hundred, the total weight of the expedition came to well over three thousand pounds.

Cheerfully accepting the estimated time for the trip at between six weeks and six months, Mrs. Jackson took the train for the East. At one p.m. on Saturday, May 23, only four days after the bet was made, the two pioneers were off—the two-cylinder engine under the seat firing with reassuring regularity, the sight-drip oiler on the dashboard dripping, the compressed-air throttle compressing, and the clacking chain from the engine to the rear wheels delivering a speed of something under twenty miles an hour. Previous horseless cross-country expeditions having ended unhappily in the southern deserts, Jackson and Crocker resolved to take a northerly route, a thousand miles longer and perhaps much rougher, but far more sensible for man and machine.

The early miles were delightful, the broad hard roads of clay and sand affording maximum co-operation with the frail tires and busy mechanism. Because the *Vermont,* which the Winton had been christened, was encumbered by neither windshield nor top, its passengers were treated to a bouquet of poignant sights and smells as they rolled northward to Sacramento. At dusk it was apparent that the two fitful side lamps would not afford 20/20 vision, even with the co-operation of the moon, and so a day was spent in Sacramento securing and attaching an acetylene headlamp. Then they were off again, northwest up the Sacramento valley for two hundred miles past farming and fruit country, vineyards and mining camps.

As the menacing Sierra Nevadas loomed near, the road degenerated into a disgraceful compound of ruts, bumps and "thank-you-marms," with clouds of dust enveloping the travelers in choking invisibility. The *Vermont* jounced and staggered along, catapulting the cooking utensils into the road one by one. When Jackson and Crocker discovered their loss they determined that living off the countryside with its danger of temporary starvation was less to be feared than a return trip. Soon they were chugging along over adobe clay, which was all right when dry but when wet built up on the spokes of the wheels and the mudguards so that the *Vermont* would no longer go until it was cleaned off. Attempting to negotiate one of the earliest of many bridgeless streams, they splashed into the fordway in high and stalled in the middle. The block and tackle was now anchored to a tree on the far side and the mud-caked Winton gradually hauled from its mountain bath. The rocky ascent and descent of the mountains was easily the most harrowing part of the entire trip. Sometimes the road narrowed to a mere ten feet, hugging a cliff, while the right of way was strewn with boulders which had to be removed by hand. The Winton's feeble brakes were no match for the steep and tortuous descent of the eastern Sierras and as Jackson and Crocker jolted helplessly around hairpin turns above thousand-foot precipices, their hair rose on their heads and their teeth ground together. By the time the *Vermont* reached Alturas, California, its tires consisted mostly of patches. Although the triceps of the adventurers were hard as flint from having pumped hundreds of pounds of air, the objective of the expedition was not that of body-building; the Goodrich people in San Francisco were telegraphed for new rubber.

After waiting fruitlessly for two days Jackson and Crocker decided to move on despite the poor tires. With a serious list to starboard owing to a broken front spring, the *Vermont* labored ahead like a prize fighter, bruised but neither down nor out. A toot from the bulb-horn on the outskirts of each isolated Rocky Mountain town would end every game of roulette and twenty-one as the inhabitants—cowboys, sheepherders and traders—crowded into the streets to see their first automobile. The novelty of the *Vermont* proved as vexing to Jackson and Crocker as the hazards of the road. It was bad enough to have to drive sixty-nine miles to avoid a ravine, but detours caused by human frailty were even more distressing. Already on one occasion a redheaded woman on a white horse had sent them fifty-four miles out of their way so that they would pass her house and give her family a chance to see an automobile. Some natives of the hinterlands had never even heard of a car, let alone seen one. They thought the *Vermont* was a small railroad engine that had somehow got off the track and was now following the horse paths.

Until the new tires arrived the transcontinentalists measured their progress not in miles but in yards. There was so much scar tissue on one of the four remaining tires that they abandoned it and ran on the burlap in which the spares had been wrapped. Gasoline was usually available in the villages but the price was never less than thirty-five cents a gallon and there was no ceiling. On one occasion Jackson had to pay $5.25 for a five-gallon tin of gas. (He later learned, somewhat unhappily, that the man responsible for this holdup was a native Vermonter.) Only once, near Silver Springs, Oregon, did the supply of this vital fluid become exhausted. Almost as if they were standing on the gallows waiting to hear the trap sprung, Jackson and Crocker listened as the final medicine-dropperful of gas filtered through the carburetor. The *Vermont* fired irregularly a few times, belched, wheezed and was still. The sounds of the forest now replaced the turmoil of the motor. Here, clearly, was a chance for leg work. The durable Crocker obliged with a fifteen-mile all-night trek to the nearest settlement, returning in the morning with ten gallons of gas and three of benzine.

Slowly and unsteadily the *Vermont* negotiated the Rockies, pulsing forward through the mists of early morning, through yellow patches of afternoon sun and the deep shadows of twilight; through mountain windstorms and slanting rains, over roots and gullies, through red clay and over the dry beds of boulder-infested streams. A twelve-hour day driving the *Vermont* over such unwilling terrain left hardly an ounce

of energy in either Jackson or Crocker, and they much preferred sleep-
laden mountain nights to those passed in the towns amid the all-
night whooping, tumult and gunfire.

It was at Caldwell, Idaho, that Bud, the third member of the expedition was added. There was not enough room on the driver's seat for a
Great Dane, a collie or even an Airedale—there was just about enough
for a bulldog, and Bud was of that hardy variety. After a few miles he
became a seasoned passenger, sharing in all the excitement of the road.
At first sudden jolts brought his jaw into contact with the cowling and
his teeth together with an audible clack. Soon he was eyeing the road
for obstructions as intently as his masters and, as the front wheels approached a rock, rut or ditch, he would brace himself skilfully in preparation for the shock. The roughness of Idaho roads fully taxed his
ingenuity. The moment the car stopped he would jump down on the
road and fall into a deep sleep.

Before the *Vermont* had crossed Idaho, the "cyclometer" fell off, so
that the three adventurers no longer knew how fast they were going
or how far they had come. Jackson engaged a cowboy to pilot them
across the endless plains. Near Mountain Home the worst mudhole of
the journey trapped the *Vermont,* the wheels sinking into what appeared to be a mixture of mud and quicksand. Within a few minutes
the water was over the running gear. Finding himself suddenly adrift,
the dog paddled for the bank while Jackson and Crocker hurriedly removed everything that could be dismantled. If there had been a tree
the block and tackle would have solved the problem in the usual manner, but there was nothing whatever to which it could be fastened.
Presently the weary motorists located a strong branch which they succeeded in anchoring in a posthole dug on the far bank. The tackle was
attached and the engine, now scarcely above the surface of the water,
was started. With the working end of the tackle fastened to the rear
axle which acted as a windlass, the *Vermont* customarily wound itself
out of a mudhole; but this time it would not budge. Jackson and
Crocker spent four unavailing hours in the water. A four-horse team
finally dislodged the saturated machine from what the travelers henceforth termed their "twenty-four horse-power mudhole," and the journey was resumed.

Crossing into Wyoming the *Vermont* encountered a wasteland of sand and sagebrush which presented almost insuperable difficulties. Even with ropes wound about them the wheels shuddered helplessly in the loose sand. Adopting the only conceivable measure, Jackson and Crocker cut bundles of sagebrush and laid them down in front of the car for a hundred feet. As soon as they had driven this distance the sagebrush would be gathered up and the process repeated until the worst of the area had been crossed. They thought they were in the vicinity of the Green River and rejoiced when they at last reached the stream, only to continue for thirty-six hours in this desolate terrain without food or sight of any living cerature. Tightening their belts, the famished transcontinentalists began to imagine a meal of roast bulldog and as the hours passed they stole speculative glances at Bud. Fortunately they came upon a lone sheepherder who satisfied their hunger with roast lamb. In gratitude Jackson rewarded the shepherd with his rifle. As for Bud, he had handily survived the long fast. A Wyoming newspaper referred to him as a "tortoise-shell bulldog whose eyes are badly bloodshot from exposure to alkali dust. It is to be doubted if he is enjoying the journey as he spends most of his time resting under the car." Bud's lot was improved when Jackson bought him a pair of goggles. Shortly the dog refused to start out in the morning until his glasses were put on.

Navigated only by compass, the *Vermont* jolted on, plagued by the hazards of alkali faults, boulders, mudholes and bridgeless streams. The latter continued to cause the most trouble. Occasionally they were shallow with firm beds of pebbles affording easy passage. Sometimes the drivers were able to cross on railroad bridges, bumping over the ties between trains. But most of the time they had to block-and-tackle across, an operation which was repeated seventeen times on one particular day as the travelers struggled to reach the Continental Divide. The *Vermont* also foundered regularly in what Jackson called "buffalo holes or wallows." Then there was the constant threat of mechanical failure owing to the pounding delivered to the aging parts. In Montpelier, Idaho, the ball bearings rolled out of one of the front wheels, immobilizing the *Vermont* for a day while Crocker made repairs with some bearings he had taken out of a mowing machine. In Rawlins,

Wyoming, the connecting rod let go, puncturing the crankcase. Five days were consumed awaiting parts from the Winton factory in Cleveland.

Between Rawlins and Laramie the travelers felt the full impact of terrain that had never been adjusted to travel by horseless carriage. Near Medicine Bow for three miles beyond Rattlesnake Canyon and Elk Mountain the natives were using the highway as an irrigation ditch. Cruising successfully through this, the two men now faced the Laramie range, the last obstacle before the great upsweep of the Rockies had been conquered. Beyond the Continental Divide there would at least be fewer occasions when they would have to hoist the *Vermont* over the crest of some craggy ascent by block and tackle. Fortunately their sturdy machine rose to the challenge and they were soon in Cheyenne on the edge of the charitable, if endless, Great Plains.

The enthusiasm of the press and the excitement of the people mounted with the brightening prospects for completion of the trip. An old Wyoming native asked Jackson where he had come from. When told San Francisco, he asked where to, receiving the reply, New York. "Where is your home?" was the next question. When he was told Vermont, the old man said: "What in *Hell* will you Vermonters do next?" In Nebraska a farmer saw the mud-caked Winton chugging toward him carrying its two mud-caked drivers and dog, all wearing goggles. Cutting loose his horse the terrified Nebraskan seized his wife and dived under the wagon for refuge. Another farmer wanted to know "how long the derned thing would run after she was wound up?" One boy rode a horse sixty-eight miles to see the *Vermont*. Asked if he had ever seen a car he replied, "I have seen lots of pictures of 'em but this is the first real live one I ever saw."

Except for sudden prairie thunderstorms with no possibility of seeking cover, the trip along the old Nebraska military highway and stage route was rapid and unmarked by crippling delays. Just west of Omaha the front axle snapped but the ingenious Crocker secured an iron pipe and fitted the broken ends of the axle into it. The Winton literally dashed from Omaha to Chicago in two days. The newspapers heralded the completion of each leg of the journey with headlines such as FROM OCEAN TO OCEAN IN AN AUTOMOBILE CAR, or "BEELISTS" STOP HERE.

Receptions were given by city officials and automobile dealers. In every town crowds gathered to press Crocker and the "mad doctor" with questions, while the village wits indulged in jests that the travelers had already heard dozens of times. Even the dog, it was said, howled with dismay every time he heard the hoary "auto-mow-hay" joke.

The Winton Motor Carriage Company in Cleveland was transported with delight over all the free publicity. In the absence of Alexander Winton who was in Europe, Charles B. Shanks, an executive of the company, assembled a party of well-wishers and motored to Elyria in a cavalcade of new rear-entrance Wintons to greet the transcontinentalists. Jackson and Crocker were escorted to a Cleveland hotel for a testimonial banquet while the dog held inquisitive newspapermen and mechanics at a respectful distance from the *Vermont*. The Winton people wished to replace the front axle and otherwise overhaul and clean the haggard machine, but Jackson wanted no aid from the factory that would brand his tour as a promotional stunt. He insisted that representative mud from every state along their route from California should remain on the vehicle until the towers of Manhattan were sighted. There was good reason for this. Already in some quarters the adventurers were being called agents of the Winton company. They were said to have traded cars, as an equestrian changes his mount. They were accused of having put the *Vermont* on a train and thus covering some of the distance by rail. Subsequently the Winton Motor Carriage Company offered $10,000 to anyone who could prove these allegations. Jackson added an equal amount to the award, but the handsome sum went unclaimed. Meanwhile other motorists groomed their machines and started out across the Rockies in the hope of eclipsing the time being established by the pioneers.

With another range of mountains, the Alleghenies, in their path, Jackson and Crocker elected to favor the *Vermont* with the longer water-level route through Buffalo and Rochester. A choice of the former alternative, however, might have obviated the only real accident of the trip, which occurred east of Buffalo. At a speed of some twenty miles an hour the *Vermont* struck a hidden obstruction and vaulted into the air throwing out both the drivers and the dog and tearing off the mudguards. Since examination revealed that various bones, human and canine, were intact and the motor was still running, the trip was resumed.

The tired and dusty trio at length approached the headwaters of the Hudson. As they forged southward along its banks toward Manhattan on the final leg of their journey, the night editors of New York papers charted their daily progress, hoping that the morning edition of July 26 could carry news of their arrival. A correspondent from *Automobile Topics* and an eastern agent for the Winton company drove Mrs. Jackson north to greet her husband en route. They intercepted the adventurers in Fishkill, and the "mad doctor" embraced his wife in happy reunion. As it was nearly midnight the journey was resumed at once. In Peekskill the *Vermont* suffered one final, maddening puncture. The management of the Raleigh Hotel kindly kept their outside light burning until the patch could be glued on. Tire trouble in the form of a leaky valve delayed the motorists once more in the woods a little further south. As was his custom Bud jumped down the moment the car stopped and stretched out on the road in deep slumber. As Crocker adjusted the valve in the semidarkness, hoot owls broke the silence of the woods, and a passing Albany steamer momentarily flashed its searchlight on the solitary workers. When the motors of the two cars were started again, Bud sleepily jumped into the wrong car. Jackson called out to him sharply. The correspondent for *Automobile Topics* reported that "the dog, hearing its master's voice, looked up sharply, then turned lazily to gaze up into the faces of the men on the car in which he was riding. Half dazed, like a man aroused from a deep sleep, the poor animal seemed at a loss to understand when the transfer had been made or how it happened that there were two cars, he in one and his owner in the other."

At half past four, when the *Vermont* crossed the Harlem River, the correspondent affixed a number of American flags to the battle-scarred machine. Fifth Avenue was asleep as the historic trip across the continent ended at the Holland House. "A mud-becoated automobile," reported the New York *Sun*, "found a haven of rest in an uptown storage station last night after the longest motor vehicle journey on record."

Jackson and Crocker had traveled six thousand miles in two months and nine days, having spent nearly three weeks of this period repairing, resting or waiting for spare parts. Alexander Winton, brightening from the discouragement of the Gordon Bennett race in which his car had not fared well, telegraphed from Europe: "It is now up to me to design cars which shall equal if not excel the great record made by Dr. Jackson and Mr. Crocker." Barney Oldfield, to whom the public was comparing Jackson for enterprise and daring, considered the trip an outstanding accomplishment and the Winton a great car.

After a short rest, Jackson, Crocker and Bud started north, Mrs. Jackson proceeding to Vermont by train. Near Albany the high-speed gear disintegrated, causing a twelve-hour delay. In Shelburne, Vermont, only a few miles from home, the breaker box broke. Crocker made a new one out of old parts, and it was soon the privilege of the *Vermont* to tow Jackson's brothers' welcoming vehicle, which had blown out a cylinder head, into Burlington. The invincible *Vermont* suffered a final mishap just as the doctor was driving it into his carriagehouse. After serving valiantly all the way across the wide country, the clacking chain to the rear wheel snapped in two.

But the epilogue was written in a news dispatch dated October 3, 1903: "Dr. H. N. Jackson, first man to cross the continent in an automobile, was arrested in Burlington, Vermont, and fined for driving the machine more than six miles an hour."

XVI. The Moneygrubber
and the Naturalist

THERE are those people of independent spirit born and raised in Vermont who go out in the world and make a trail marked with rebellion. Then there are those of independent spirit born elsewhere who wish to live in the Green Mountains because they find Vermont a good state to be contrary in. Daniel Shays came to Vermont after his rebellion. Robert Lincoln burned up his father's papers in Manchester. One has only to read the italicized paragraph at the end of a piece of literary criticism to learn that the critic is living on his farm in Vermont.

Of all such people who have gone out and come in, none was more wayward than Hetty Green, the richest businesswoman in the world. She was born into a family whose wealth came from the sea in a fleet of New Bedford whaling ships. "My grandfather's eyesight was failing, and my father's too, and as soon as I learned to read it became my daily duty to read aloud to them the financial news of the world. In this way I came to know what stocks and bonds were, how markets fluctuated, and the meaning of bulls and bears. By the time I was fifteen, when I went to Boston to school, I knew more about these things than many a man that makes a living out of them."

Hetty Robinson is said to have been a lovely girl who hastened the

heartbeat of all the sailors and young men working about the New
Bedford wharves, near which her family lived. She was dark and tall
and well formed. Her skin was the shade of alabaster and her cheeks
had the high color of youth. Yet her beauty was constantly competing
with her dress, which was shabbier than that of many of the orphan
girls whose fathers had died at sea. Perhaps this was because of the
Quaker notions of thrift in her family. But Hetty was more than
thrifty—she was parsimonious. At sixteen she was already peculiar, a
girl who could on occasion be charming and gregarious, but who spent
much of her time planning to be rich.

"My father," confessed Hetty much later, "taught me never to owe
anyone anything, not even a kindness." Philanthropy had had no part
in the making of Black Hawk Robinson's fortune, or that of her
mother's father, old Gideon Howland. To gather a fleet of thirty whaling ships and make them pay it was necessary to dominate one's competitors, one's captains and one's sailors. Shrewdness, even ruthlessness,
paid off. A soft heart and a weak mind could lose the money once it
had been made—Hetty had plenty of opportunity to learn that along
the wharves of New Bedford. "I was forced into business. I was the
only child of two rich families and I was taught from the time I was
six years old that I would have to look after my property . . ."

In the household she proved to be a truculent, antagonistic and un-
truthful girl whose one interest, long before she left her teens, had become that of making money. On her first trip to New York her chaperone, a woman of society, was ashamed of her clothes and since
Hetty would not purchase any, the chaperone, Mrs. Lawrence Grin-
nell, offered to buy her a complete ensemble for a party she was to attend. Accordingly an elegant costume was ordered; but when Hetty
appeared at the party she was still dressed in her frowzy New Bedford
clothes. When she returned home she was carrying her fine garments
in unopened boxes. Tucked away in her bosom were bonds which she
had bought with a thousand dollars her father had given her. Society
was all right but society cost money—that was the trouble with it.

She looked upon young men the same way—fortune hunters, most
of them: if she married, her husband would cost her money. Therefore Hetty was still single in 1860 at the age of twenty-nine, still a

beautiful young woman, engaging and even gay as long as no expense was involved in what she was doing. That year she went to the renowned ball attended by Edward, eldest son of Queen Victoria. Few of the young ladies would have the good fortune to dance even once with the prince. Hetty determined to be his partner twice. After an introduction in which she was presented as the Princess of Whales, they danced. She had heard that he was interested in popular education and just before they parted she said, "Oh, Your Highness, do you know how the great masses of our people are being elevated?" The prince had to know how this was being done and sought her out for the second cherished dance. When reminded of her question she laughed and said: "Go west to the Mississippi. Go aboard a high-pressure side-wheel steamboat, and more than likely you will soon realize how in one tremendous explosion the masses are elevated."

At home Hetty was miserable. She stormed or sulked whenever money was spent in the Robinson household, for she knew some day it would be hers, and she would not get that which was spent. Mrs. Robinson shortly went to live with her sister where she remained until her death. After that Hetty did not get on well with her father, because he had inherited all of his wife's estate. On at least one occasion she tried to break her mother's will. Presently she went to live with her Aunt Sylvia, where she became such a tyrant about extravagance—the number of servants and amount of food they were eating—that her aunt was beside herself. Finally she told Hetty it was her own money she was spending, after all. This threw Hetty into a tantrum and her aunt could get no peace until she had moved to her farm seven miles away. Following her there, Hetty badgered the old lady into drawing up a will which made her the beneficiary of every dollar of her aunt's fortune. Aunt Sylvia doubtless thought this would pacify her, but she was mistaken. Hetty refused to allow a wing to be added to the house and fomented such frightening discord among the servants that Sylvia, invalid that she was, told her to get out of the house

When her aunt died Hetty received a great shock. The old lady had made another will leaving much of her money to the families of shipwrecked New Bedford sailors and other charities. She had left only part of her fortune to her family. While Hetty lived she was to receive the income on this part but on her death the principal was to be distributed to all of Aunt Sylvia's descendants. Hetty, in a great wrath, attempted to break the will. She tried to bribe a probate judge and was involved in a charge of forging her aunt's signature to another will which she claimed superseded the legal one. Her efforts were unavailing. At the end of the litigation she witnessed the distribution of a large portion of Aunt Sylvia's money to New Bedford orphans and to old women widowed by accidents aboard her family's whaling ships. Even so, Hetty did all right. Upon the death of her father, Black Hawk Robinson—who had shrewdly turned to railroads and real estate when the whaling business waned—she received about five million dollars.

Meanwhile she had met and married a Vermonter from Bellows Falls named Edward Henry Green. Perhaps love, so long deferred, dominated her courtship. Possibly the fact that Green was worth a million dollars had something to do with it. In any event they were well suited to each other—except that Green liked to live high. At the age of seventeen he had gone to Boston from Bellows Falls and then to the Philippines where, in twenty years, he had made his money. Hetty found his business judgment so good that she allowed him a great deal of freedom in transacting her affairs. Green supported her as if she were not worth a penny and with enthusiasm helped her labor toward her goal of becoming the richest woman in the United States.

As the years passed her property accumulated from ocean to ocean. From her father she had inherited docks in San Francisco. She acquired railroad interests in many corners of the country. She owned two square miles on the west side of Chicago, great numbers of buildings on Michigan and Wabash Avenues, in the Loop and on other streets. She had stacks of bonds and a tremendous reservoir of cash with which to step in during a depression and buy up distressed properties for a song. She would hold them until she could sell them for high prices at the crest of a prosperous period.

"I believe in getting in at the bottom and out at the top," she said. "I like to buy railroad stock or mortgage bonds. When I see a good thing going cheap because nobody wants it, I buy a lot of it and tuck it away. Then when the time comes, they have to hunt me up and pay me a good price for my holdings. I own a lot of city mortgages in crowded sections. They seem to me as good as anything.

"I don't much believe in stocks. I never buy industrials. Railroads and real estate are the things I like. Before deciding on an investment I seek out every kind of information about it. There is no great secret in fortune making. All you have to do is buy cheap and sell dear, act with thrift and shrewdness and be persistent."

Two children were born to the Greens—a boy and a girl—who somewhat limited the amount of traveling they could do. The son was born in London, where Hetty had gone, it was said, to escape the possible consequences of the forgery charge growing out of the litigation over her aunt's will. As soon as the furor died down she left London (having profited from a couple of banks she had started there) and, returning to the United States, she decided in 1874 to go with her husband to Bellows Falls to live. When her mother-in-law, Mrs. Henry A. Green, heard that her wealthy son was coming home again after so many years, bringing his rich wife and two grandchildren, whom she had never seen, there was a great to-do in the homestead. Mary Cray, the family retainer, bustled around with her dustcloth and brushed up on her best recipes, soon to be tested by one of the wealthiest women in the United States. Mary even promised old Mrs. Green that as a concession to this special event she would wear a starched white apron.

What old Mrs. Green and her excited maid met at the door on the great day gave them the shock of their lives. Instead of an elegant lady dressed in rich clothes they saw a matron who resembled a charwoman just off duty. Her hands were dirty. Her face was dirty. Her children's faces were dirty. (Trains were sooty but they could not have accumulated that much dirt if they had ridden in the coal tender.) Hetty's dress was worse than one Mary Cray would wear to clean house. Hardly had she stepped inside when Hetty began to pass remarks about extravagance in the household, whereupon Mary refused to serve dinner. Old Mrs. Green begged her not to desert in this dreadful hour. By mealtime Mary's Irish temper had subsided enough to enable her to bring on her elaborate dinner.

The people of Bellows Falls quickly suspected that none would profit in dollars by Hetty's presence, but they were somewhat compen-

sated by her priceless bequest to folklore. Soon after her arrival she
sallied forth in her rumpled black dress on a search for a horse and
buggy. In Saxtons River she found what she wanted—an ancient moth-
eaten carryall in whose interior hens had been allowed to roost. The
sway-backed horse that went with it was fit for the pasture in recognition of a life of faithful work. The man wanted two hundred dollars
for the horse and rig. Hetty thought it might be worth a hundred but
departed without comment.

"I went to a man who had a grudge against the owner," she bragged
later, her blue eyes bright with amusement, "and got him to tell me of
every fault of the horse and rig. With the knowledge I gained from
him I succeeded in depreciating the owner's opinion of his property
until he let me have it for $40 less than I should have been willing to
pay the first time I went to call on him."

Hetty was obsessed with the idea that the townspeople—doctors,
lawyers and shopkeepers—were all after her money. This was her defense for her chronic inability to part with the smallest sum. It was not
a question of suffering to pay an exorbitant price: she suffered when
she paid a fair price; she suffered when she paid anything at all. It was
her custom to buttonhole lawyers and doctors on the street to get free
information. "She was a damned nuisance," declared F. B. Pingree, a
Bellows Falls lawyer. "There was a long period during which she
called at my office every day ostensibly to gossip, but for the real purpose of getting free advice. Once she gave me a rent bill to collect from
a man who hired the use of her barn. I got after him and he settled,
but she would never pay me." Pingree finally had to tell her to stop
coming to his office.

Since she was merely interested in the market reports, Hetty found
it galling to have to buy a whole newspaper, but she was able to salve
her conscience by cutting holes in the paper for her head and arms and
wearing it under her dress on cold days in place of investing in a warm
undergarment. In later years she frequently ate lunch in the Bellows
Falls hotel. It was her custom to wrap any food she couldn't eat in a
napkin and stuff it into her dress. She arranged with her laundress to
do her work for less by washing only that part of her dress that trailed
on the ground. After returning from a trip to New York she refused to

pay the keeper of David, her aged horse, eighty-seven cents for horse medicine, claiming that if he had not starved the charger during her absence, medicine would not have been needed. A fondness for dogs was one flaw in her armor of thrift. She had a Newfoundland bitch named Juno, who, in the care of the keeper of her horse, escaped into the street during her absence and was soon discovered to be in a family way. Hetty was furious and commanded that Juno be sent to her in New York. When she found she was able to sell the puppies for twenty-five dollars each, all was forgiven.

In their patched and oversized clothes her children, playing about the streets of Bellows Falls, looked as if they were wards of the town. She allowed her son Ned to drive his friends around in the caryall on the theory that a horse could, after all, eat only so much in a day. Ned, after having earned a dime for washing bottles one autumn, lost it among the leaves in front of the Green home. Late that night neighbors could see a flickering lantern slowly crisscrossing the Green yard. It was Hetty and Ned looking for the lost dime. Its fate is unknown but its loss could not have appreciably weakened the Green finances, for Hetty's income at this time was between five and ten thousand dollars a day.

While sliding at the age of fourteen Ned dislocated his kneecap. Hetty attempted to cure it at home by applying a poultice and various other dressings, but despite her best efforts it would not heal. Hetty reasoned that if she took Ned to a Bellows Fall physician she would have to pay an inflated fee, so she took him to New York. She managed to appear so poorly dressed that the New York doctor, Lewis A. Sayre, who examined Ned's knee, treated the boy in Bellevue Hospital as a charity patient. Several days later Sayre learned with astonishment that the mother of his patient was Hetty Green. He informed her that he would have nothing more to do with the case unless she paid up and also paid for future treatment in advance. Hetty departed without settling and her son appeared no more in Bellevue Hospital. The condition of the boy's knee grew so serious that Hetty took him to many doctors, including specialists, whom she must have paid. She was now worried to distraction and was later seen in Baltimore streetcars carrying the half-grown youth in her arms on the way to doctors' offices.

Five years after the accident the leg was amputated. Much later Green told an acquaintance that a second accident, on a handcar, had resulted in the removal of his leg.

In 1875, a year after the Greens had moved to Bellows Falls, Hetty's mother-in-law died—from despondency over the way Hetty had tarnished the family honor, according to the maid, Mary Cray. Hetty packed up the silverware, china and crystal right after the funeral. At dinner, kitchen forks, knives and glasses were on the table and when Henry Green asked why, Hetty replied that the others were too good for everyday use. In a rare outburst of temper her husband seized a cracked glass and, shattering it against the wall, left the table. A little later Mary Cray left the house after a bitter argument, reporting, among other things, that she had been underfed and had been forced to go to her mother's for a square meal. Hetty was undaunted. Despite the objections of her niece, the daughter of her husband's sister, she arranged to auction off all of the old Green valuables—and carried out her plan.

Ordinarily her husband overlooked, or at least understood, her peculiarities. On matters other than those pertaining to thrift Hetty proved a faithful wife and mother who spared no effort in the interest of her family—but since there were very few aspects of living that did not somehow pertain to the spending of money, life was hard for Green and his children. He could spend his own money, which, of course, is what he did; but when in 1885 he became embarrassed financially, their married life tottered. In January of that year Hetty wrote a letter to her New York banking house, John J. Cisco and Son, 59 Wall Street, directing that her money on deposit there and twenty-five million dollars' worth of securities in the safe deposit vault be transferred to the Chemical National Bank. Young Cisco replied that they could not let her have the money, as her husband owed the bank $702,159.04. He had borrowed heavily for speculation and put up stock in the Louisville and Nashville Railroad as collateral. The value of the collateral had depreciated tremendously and Cisco informed Mrs. Green that she would have to write the bank a check for the half-million she had on deposit to cover her husband's loan. Otherwise she could not have her securities.

This letter sent Hetty into a rage. She sat down and wrote the bank that her husband's debt had nothing to do with her and that if they didn't turn over her money immediately, she would start legal proceedings. The bank, owing to a series of withdrawals, was in poor condition and its resources could not stand a further draft of half a million. Upon receipt of Hetty's letter it went into receivership. This news shook Wall Street and might have led to a panic had Jay Gould not stated that the Cisco failure in his opinion had no bearing on conditions generally, and that he would buy any stocks in decline.

"Mrs. Green," a spokesman of the defunct bank announced tersely, "caused the failure." Hetty, in an even greater panic than when her Aunt Sylvia made a new will, got on the day coach at Bellows Falls and rattled off to New York. Hurrying into 59 Wall Street she marched into the office of Lewis May, who had just been appointed receiver of the bank. "I've come for what belongs to me," she announced breathlessly. May said that was her privilege, except for the amount necessary to satisfy the debt of the Green family. Hetty argued that financially she and her husband were two different people. May informed her that she was just one of eight hundred creditors, that she would have to take her chances with the rest, and that either she would pay the debt or he would keep a bundle of her securities. Hetty now started to cry, to wave her arms and stamp her feet. She argued and stormed until she saw the vault locked up for the night. Then she left. She returned to argue every day for two weeks. Finally she wrote out a check to the bank for $422,143.22, and after making other arrangements to satisfy the balance of Henry Green's debt, she was allowed access to her securities. It took six clerks to help carry them out of the bank and load them into the carriage. Hetty squeezed in and was off with her twenty-five million dollars to the Chemical National Bank.

The Cisco bank disaster brought Hetty and Henry to a parting of the ways. In 1885 Bellows Falls listers credited him with seven dollars and a watch. Even the covered bridge across the Connecticut to New Hampshire, which had been so long in his family, and which Hetty had taken particular pleasure in crossing toll-free, had been sacrificed. Henceforth for many years they lived apart, Green dwelling in obscurity in New York and Hetty shuttling back and forth between Manhattan and Bellows Falls on the day coach. Prior to her husband's death in 1902 there were a few years of reunion, during which she looked after Henry (or Papa, as she called him), who had returned to Bellows Falls during a severe illnes. When he was laid away in the cemetery of the Episcopal church there, she put on permanently a heavy black veil that gave her an even more singular appearance and lent her the title of The Witch of Wall Street.

In her life of moneymaking the decades between 1885 and 1916 were gilt-edged. Her children were maturing and household responsibilities no longer occupied her thoughts. For long periods she lived in New York, a bulky figure in black hastening to and fro on her financial errands. She passed every waking moment watching the ebb and flow of the stock and real estate markets and listening to the economic heartbeat of the country. One day she might be seen sitting on the floor of her vault in the Chemical Bank cutting coupons; the next would find her negotiating a loan to the city of New York at a fraction of a percent less than the banks' lowest rate. Unlike those of many Wall Street figures her operations were rarely spectacular (although she was known to have made two hundred thousand dollars in a single day). The increase in her fortune was mainly the result of many thousands of smaller transactions and the compounding and recompounding of her interest. Under her sole management in the last thirty years of her life, her wealth quadrupled from twenty-five to one hundred million dollars, making her the richest businesswoman in the world.

Meanwhile Hetty grew more and more peculiar. In order to avoid establishing a New York residence, thereby making herself liable to city and state taxes, she lived under assumed names in a variety of cheap hotels and flats, moving every few days so that only her close friends knew where she was. She always thought she was being pursued by assassins who were after her money. She was convinced that the relatives of her deceased Aunt Sylvia (who, upon her death would stand to benefit from the distribution of part of Sylvia's fortune) were after her. If she went to dine with any of them she would bring some eggs in a paper bag. Setting up a spirit lamp which she had also brought with her, she would boil the eggs and eat them with a spoon

which she carried. She would explain that indigestion was the reason for all this. Actually she thought they would try to poison her if she ate their food.

She made her son, who went to Texas to manage some of her properties, promise that he would not marry for twenty years. Before she gave her daughter in marriage to the great-grandson of John Jacob Astor, Matthew Astor Wilks, she forced him to sign an agreement forgoing any part of the money that her daughter might expect to inherit some day.

Hetty went into politics to the extent of trying to ruin the public careers of some of the men who had crossed her. These included judges who had ignored her interests and lawyers who had brought suit against her. She particularly hated lawyers and fought a running battle against dozens of them. To her they were the bane of civilization. To them Hetty was one of the most Machiavellian old women who ever lived. Yet even her worst enemies had to admit that she was a very interesting person. Penurious as she was, she occasionally went to great lengths to help somebody—such as the janitor of the Chemical Bank who was fired because of his ragged appearance. Hetty worked for days to get him another job.

Bellows Falls people thought her a good talker, always well posted on political and financial subjects and often amusing even when she was being cantakerous. Her perennial haggling with the Congregational church for having moved their fence, she claimed, one foot on her property, was as much a part of the local scene as the noon whistle of the Farm Machine Company. She was just peculiar and rich. She could have been a handsome woman, people said, if she had only cleaned up and put on some decent clothes.

Hetty had a Skye terrier named Dewey, after the Montpelier hero of Manila Bay. In the years prior to her death when she was living in boardinghouses and cheap flats in New York or New Jersey, she would sometimes tack up the dog's name on the door to confuse the tax assessors. On one occasion she moved from Hoboken to Manhattan to avoid paying his dog tax, but she always saw to it that Dewey had a good piece of steak to eat. He delighted her with his tricks and served the noble purpose of being able to tell lawyers by their smell. When the dog died in 1910 his mistress failed to appear on Wall Street or at her bank for a number of days. Hetty was sick, too. Her daughter brought her into her Manhattan flat, where she slowly recovered from what appeared to be a general breakdown. "The whole trouble with Mother," announced her son, who had arrived from Texas, "was the death of this dog. I do not know how he died but I got word of it down in Texas, and also that Mother was badly knocked out by the loss of her little companion."

Her last illness was a stroke which she suffered after a bitter dispute with the cook in the house of one of her friends. She died in New York on July 3, 1916. Her son engaged a private car to carry her body back to Bellows Falls. There was no more expense after that. Hetty had joined the Episcopal church, so that she was assured of a free burial in the family lot.

Among the jagged mountains of the West, Camel's Hump would perhaps suffer the ignominy of some nameless foothill, but in Vermont it is majestic, towering four thousand feet above the Champlain valley. It is a lonely mountain, having chosen to rise apart from the neighboring crests of the Green Mountains and thus live, for many million years, a life of isolation. But were it set among shouldering companion peaks it would lose its rank as commander of views. From its summit one sees the White Mountains of New Hampshire to the east, and to the west, the sapphire waters of Lake Champlain and the massive community of the Adirondacks.

The forests surrounding the mountain and ascending nearly to its summit are among the wildest in Vermont. For well over a decade no one has lived on Camel's Hump or at its foot, and before long there will be little evidence that it ever was inhabited. Today, however, if one approaches from the north, ascending a steep road crowded by trees and underbrush, he will find, directly below the mountain where the road ends, a wild garden. Here are pine trees in variety, cedar, hemlock, spruce, maples, oaks, willows and stately poplars in rows, growing now without apparent purpose. One finds flowers and berry bushes gone wild. One finds two cellar holes with their somber remains—an old bed, a fragment of a newspaper bearing news of two decades ago.

And, curiously, a few rods below the cellar holes one comes upon a tiny cemetery surrounded by a rusting iron fence. In this enclosure is a row of small gravestones with the legends:

RICHARD OF ANAHASSITT
29 Jan 1931—1941
HIS MASTER'S DEVOTED SHETLAND

BEBE ALPINE
22 May 1931
26 April 1936
A NOBLE ST. BERNARD

SIR HECTOR OF ARNEN
20 Apr 1930
27 Aug 1934
A BEAUTIFUL COLLIE

LANDSEER OF NEWFOUNDLAND
9-20-1924—11-17-1936
ALWAYS A SMILE

BASQUE DE BASQUAERIE
20-6-1933—1943
FIRST GREAT PYRENEES
BORN IN AMERICA

Among others—Scotty, the gold-and-silver collie, the best beloved, died Oct. 29, 1930—A STAR AMONG STARS. And among them all:

WILL S. MONROE
22 March 1863—29 Jan 1939
TEACHER, AUTHOR, TRAIL BUILDER
COMPANION AND LOVER OF DOGS

He was along in years in 1913 when he first came to lecture at the summer school of the university in Burlington. Two seasons later he wrote from New Jersey that if the officer of the Green Mountain Club would map a trail across the peaks of the Green Mountains, he would blaze a section of it. In the ensuing five summers he and his helpers cut the lofty trail—The Monroe Skyline Trail—fifty miles from the Winooski River to the Breadloaf-Hancock Gap. He had insisted that it be built over the summits, above the slash and blowdowns, up where the mountains touched the clouds and where, in bright weather, the eyes captured grand vistas. He designed special shelters for the trail-weary. And at the end of the trail he found himself a Vermonter. He was born in Pennsylvania. Educated here and abroad, he became, in turn, distinguished both there and here as an educator. He wrote at length on the subject of education, and volumes about other people and other countries: *Turkey and the Turks; In Viking Land: Norway: Its Fjords and its Fields; Sicily, the Garden of the Mediterranean; Bohemia and the Czecks; Belgium and her People.* His services to Bulgaria were such that King Boris III awarded him the Order of Commander's Cross. Behind him in 1925 were forty-four years of teaching in Pennsylvania, California, New York, Illinois and Vermont. Coming permanently to the state of his adoption, Professor Will Monroe, Emeritus, bought the old Callahan place at the end of the road under Camel's Hump.

"No, it is not Camel's Hump!" the Professor would caution one, with an index finger raised in kindly warning. "It is *Couching Lion*— after the French. They named it *Lion Couchant,* you know, and this is *Couching Lion* Farm." Here was his house, with its living room, study and bedroom, and the walls, even in the kitchen, great with a thousand fine books. Here was Scotty, the collie aristocrat, whom the professor, like St. Francis of Assisi, called "brother." Here were the young trees which he had set out, and the beginnings of a flower garden. And here was Scotty's Lawn, Scotty's Barn and Scotty's Path leading steeply up to his own—The Skyline Trail—across the summit.

For fourteen years the professor lived at Couching Lion Farm in a manner as simple and sequestered as the twentieth century would allow—but he did not live as a recluse. His sister stayed there from time to time and there were frequent visitors—professorial colleagues, naturalists, dog fanciers and trail builders. He was never the unkempt and crotchety hermit, but a kindly, white-haired vegetarian in knickers, with a Van Dyke beard and a crimson necktie to match his ruddy Scottish complexion. If there were no visitors, he was not alone. There was Scotty, and his flock of pigeons, every member of which he knew by names such as Lohengrin and Elsa.

Frequently in the spring he conducted a bird census on Couching Lion. At three o'clock on the appointed morning he would arouse the scorekeepers—visiting colleagues whom he had put up in the barn.

With a supply of oranges, peanut butter sandwiches, nuts and perhaps a compote of stewed peaches and prunes, they would start up the mountain on diverging trails. As the blackness of the eastern sky softened to gray and pink, and the birds in each area started singing, the census takers would busy themselves with their tabulations. On quests such as this the professor gratified his deep affection for the out-of-doors. Sometimes he and Scotty would go off on a fern-hunting expedition, for he had discovered that Vermont was the great fernery of the nation. As if meeting old friends he would rejoice to find the rare *Fragrant,* the fragile *Bladder,* or Thoreau's "cheerful community of the *Polypody.*"

The four seasons came with pointed variety to the mountains, as if to parade their handiwork before a particular friend. In the fall the maples and sumac wore their proudest vermillion at Couching Lion Farm. The winter sun of a February afternoon etched a brighter tracery in the snow-topped branches outside the professor's study window. Here the lilacs breathed an even rarer perfume, and in summer the willows which the professor had planted by his brook-fed pond sang special songs in a mountain wind. Sometimes he and Scotty would sit there in admiration for hours.

On October 15, 1930, the professor left Couching Lion Farm for Europe. There were many things abroad for even an old man to learn and see. He had plans, as on many other occasions, to carry back across the ocean seeds that Couching Lion did not know. He would repay the debt in advance by scattering Vermont seeds, as he had also done time and again, along his path through Europe. He arrived at Plymouth October 26. Three days later Scotty died, of loneliness, in the living room of faraway Couching Lion Farm. Upon his return the professor fashioned his tiny mountain cemetery by the pond and placed Scotty in it with a headstone bearing his praise.

Thereafter, he promised himself, there would be more dogs than one, for Scotty's grief could have been no less than his own. Thus he brought other "brothers" to the mountain and as he lost them they went to rest in the hallowed place. And when the professor died in 1939 he joined his friends there by the pond in view of the summit of Couching Lion.

XVII. The Legend of
Calvin Coolidge

WHEN John Coolidge died he left his five children five hill farms around Plymouth, Vermont. The eldest of his sons was Calvin, who was the great-grandfather of another Calvin born in 1872 on the fourth of July. Five generations lend tradition to a Vermont farm, even if the great-great-grandson of the man who cleared it does not become President of the United States. "When we come into the world the gate of gifts is closed behind us. We can do nothing about it. So ᶠ as each individual is concerned all he can do is take the abilities he has and make the most of them."

Calvin Coolidge was always the first to admit that he was not the possessor of rare qualities, and he was silent about the qualities he did possess—understanding, shrewdness, humor, tenacity, faith in his country, religious faith and a capacity for work. He was slight of build, had reddish hair and never said much as a boy for he was shy. When he returned from a dance with his sister, Abigail, his father inquired, "Calvin, did you dance?" Calvin, who had just stood near the wall and watched, had to say "No, sir." Whereupon his father handed him twenty-five cents. Abbie, who had danced, felt very bad for she received nothing, so Calvin gave her two fifths of his twenty-five cents.

They were alone in a way, as their mother had died recently. "It seemed as though the rich green tints of the foliage and the blossoms of the flowers came for her in the springtime, and in the autumn it was for her that the mountain sides were struck with crimson and with gold. When she knew that her end was near she called us children to her bedside where we knelt down to receive her final parting blessing. In an hour she was gone. It was her thirty-ninth birthday. I was twelve years old. We laid her away in the blustering snows of March."

After he went over the hill to the Black River Academy at Ludlow, Abbie died from "inflammation of the bowels," and he became more silent than ever. He didn't join in the games at the academy—he just worked, and that was what he did during vacations at home. John Coolidge had a horse rake and a mowing machine and a pair of oxen, with which Calvin had plowed every spring since he was twelve. He had driven the cows to pasture and back again morning and night, and he had milked them. Grandmother Coolidge spun wool on a spinning wheel and knitted socks and mittens. His father ran the general store in Plymouth. There was an aged aunt who smoked a clay pipe. There was a hired girl who was entitled to Calvin's place in the wagon when she wanted to go anywhere. To Calvin this "was all close to nature and in accordance with the ways of nature." Life in Plymouth may have been narrow, but to him it was deep. "The whole stream of life moved leisurely, so that there was time to observe and think."

At nineteen he went to Amherst College, where he just worked and was silent. He was one of the last eight in the Plug Hat Race and consequently had to spend his board money for oysters to feed the class. Called upon for a speech, young Coolidge methodically turned all his pockets inside out and said, "The last shall be first," and sat down. The remainder of his college life was more distinguished. He gave the Grove Oration and won a one-hundred-fifty-dollar gold medal, awarded to seniors by the American Historical Society, for an essay titled "The Principles of the American Revolution."

Following his graduation he climbed the stairs to the Massachusetts office of Hammond and Field over the drugstore in the second story of an old Northampton block, and simply announced to Judge Field, "Like to study law here." The judge took him on with misgivings, but it was soon evident to Field that he had something more than a sad-faced Vermont Yankee who could pronounce the word cow—c a o u w —in four syllables. The selectman of Hadley bounded up the stairs one day to find out if the body of a man shot while rowing a boat could be moved. "Everybody out," he was told. The visitor was downcast. While he waited he poured forth his troubles about moving the body, and when he had finished young Calvin simply said, "Can move body."

"Are you sure?"

"Yes." Judge Field later assured the selectman that if Coolidge said the body could be moved—it could. His apprentice, Field announced, was a hog for work. "I've found out that when he says a thing is so, it's so."

Coolidge remained in the judge's office nearly a year. When he was admitted to the Northampton Superior Court in the summer of 1897 he went out on a quest for an office, which ended in a cubbyhole near the railroad station. These were lonely days. Because he was incapable of casual talk, hearty laughter and had no other gregarious qualities, he made few friends. He just worked, and spent odd moments in the shop of the shoemaker, Mr. Lucey, who didn't mind his long silences.

It came as a surprise to Judge Field, who had classified Coolidge as the type of lawyer who sits in the back room preparing briefs, when the young Vermonter was elected councilman from Ward Two. But Field, who had become mayor, was not surprised that the Plymouth workhorse served well, once elected. It was Coolidge's philosophy that electioneering, as such, is overrated. Public duties discharged faithfully speak for themselves. The people know. He must have been right, for he ignored most of the time-tried customs of politicking and soon won the clerkship of the courts. After this he went back to his practice until 1904, when he was elected chairman of the Republican city committee.

One morning while shaving he looked out of the window and saw a pretty girl going by. For the moment he put aside Dante (which he had been translating from the Italian) and gave chase. The young woman was Miss Grace Goodhue, a teacher at the Clarke School for the Deaf, and a graduate of the University of Vermont. She didn't seem to mind when Calvin bought a lot of food for a picnic and, when it was over, estimated that there was one less macaroon left than he had thought. As he said later, she bore with his infirmities and he rejoiced in her graces. When she went up to Burlington on her vacation in 1905, he followed her there. On the way to her home he met her father, who asked what he was doing in Burlington.

"I'm here to marry Grace," said Calvin.

"Does she know it?" Goodhue inquired.

"No," he said, "she doesn't. But she will." And on October 4, 1905, they were married.

That year Coolidge lost his first and only election—to the Northampton school board. The reason generally given was because he had no children. By 1908 he had two but he had not run again for the school board, inasmuch as the people had sent him to the state legislature. The ex-senator from Northampton, in a letter he had written for Coolidge, assured the speaker of the house that "like the singed cat he is better than he looks." Coolidge was soon named to four committees —Constitutional Amendment, Merchantile Affairs, Judiciary and Banking. In a dollar room facing the airshaft on the third floor of the Adams House in Boston, he pored over his papers nights—practicing what he later preached, that "we need more of the office desk and less of the show window in politics. Let men in office substitute the midnight oil for the limelight." He went back to Northampton in 1908 to mend his unraveling law practice; but the next year he ran for mayor. He won over a professional joiner by a narrow margin and was re-elected for the term of 1911 and '12.

Then the people sent him back to Boston, this time as a state senator. The airshaft bedroom in the Adams House received him again and late oil burned as before. Now, however, his committee responsibilities were greater and he was beginning to attract notice as a wise and efficient legislator. Northampton returned him to the senate four times, twice in honor of his having been made speaker. The lieutenant-governorship and governorship of Massachusetts were his next offices —astonishing conquests in view of his lack of the traditional qualities of the successful politician. In a state notorious for playing politics, he owed his colleagues no political favors. He promised the voters nothing. He was, if possible, more silent than ever and when he did speak it was, as William Allen White has said, in a quacking nasal voice. Perhaps his secret was that he was an average man who had confidence in average men—and the people returned his confidence. Certainly the faithfulness with which he had done his work had something to do with his popularity. He was present at every session and voted on every measure when not prevented by the pressure of committee work.

In politics, beyond the stanchness of his adherence to the Republican party, he could not be classified, except perhaps as a conservative with liberal tendencies. The texture of his thinking and voting and administrating during his Massachusetts years was progressive. He thought working people should share their employers' prosperity. He voted for putting surgical equipment in factories, for reducing hours of labor, for lowering railroad fares for the workingmen, and other measures for their health and safety. He was for the small oil operators and against the monopolies. "You forbid a labor union to injure a man's business," he said, "but a giant corporation can do exactly the same thing." The Bay State, under Coolidge, throttled the power of landlords and checked rent profiteering. It studied housing problems. It encouraged and aided co-operative banking.

At the peak of labor unrest in the Lawrence textile mills, Coolidge called in an editor of the Boston *American*. "Mr. Fuller," the governor said, "I am being urged to send the militia to Lawrence, and before deciding I want to know more about the real situation. So I wish you would go to Lawrence at my expense, take all the time you need, and study the situation thoroughly—not, of course, posing as my representative, but as a natural part of your duty as a newspaper reporter." Fuller said that since he was inclined to favor the strikers he was not sure he could be impartial, but Coolidge told him to go anyway. Subsequently the governor refused to send the militia and advised the officials of the American Woolen Company to settle, which they did.

A chief executive with less sense of moral obligation to the state and the people would have turned his back on the reorganization bill—the hottest political potato Coolidge handled as governor. He had shepherded through the legislature bills to reduce the number of state departments from one hundred forty-four to twenty. It was then his duty personally to eliminate one hundred twenty-four bureau heads, many of them his friends, and select twenty to administer the new departments. While a great body of anxious politicians clamored and milled about outside the executive chamber, Coolidge sat at his desk for ten days and thought. Finally he summoned his Northampton mentor, Judge Field. When the judge arrived, Coolidge conducted him out past the anxious politicians and into a car. They motored in silence for an hour, at length reaching an ancient cemetery in Watertown. Here the governor led his old friend to two weathered tombstones bearing the names of John and Mary Coolidge. He stood, according to Field "at the foot of his forefathers lost in contemplation," and at length said, "Those are my first ancestors in this country." They then returned to the car and drove back to the state house without a word. Soon the governor announced his list of appointees to the twenty departments, which was confirmed in its entirety by the legislature.

The Boston *Globe* said of him: "Those who have been at the State House in recent years say that Mr. Coolidge is one of the keenest men who have filled that office in a long time. When he first came to the Legislature his nasal twang and other peculiarities made some of his Eastern colleagues laugh."

In a letter to his friend Frank Stearns, Coolidge confided: ". . . I remembered thinking at the time that neither the so-called liberals nor the so-called conservatives would understand me. Perhaps both would think I was dishonest or at least not firm in my convictions, and my career would end with that session of the Legislature."

A Democrat in the lower house, Roland D. Sawyer, wrote: "The next week we rode into Boston together. I had been introduced to Mr. C. the week before, and had not been favorably impressed by his cold exterior. This Monday morning I was walking down the car and merely nodding to Mr. C. when he said, "Representative, I see you have a road bill in; sit in here a minute, perhaps I can help you a little on it." Gladly I sat in and in a few words Mr. C. explained to me, a green legislator and member of the opposition party, the methods of legislation, and the way of getting favorable consideration. The brief and well chosen sentences finished, Mr. C. turned his head to look from the car window, and to smoke his stogie. My estimate of the man was at once changed—I saw at once he was a man of kindly nature, interested in his fellow man, but unable to make trivial conversation and not caring to try."

And a colleague, Robert M. Washburn, said in the house: "No man understands Calvin Coolidge unless he recognizes his silence. No man understands his silence unless he recognizes as its original cause his original diffidence. . . . On the inside he is warm."

The first impression Coolidge had made on Frank Stearns, a graduate of Amherst and owner of a Boston department store, had been unsatisfactory. In 1913 Stearns had visited the Northampton legislator and inquired about sewers for Amherst. "Too late," said Coolidge, turning back to his papers. "The time for consideration of new business has passed." But a year later Stearns learned that Coolidge as president of the senate had secured passage of a bill for sewers in Amherst. From this time on Stearns felt curiously drawn to the intractable Yankee and, without the slightest encouragement from Coolidge, found himself trumpeting his name for lieutenant-governor. To the detriment of his business the merchant became, in effect, campaign manager, with bright visions of Coolidge's accession to the governorship and then to the Presidency of the United States. At least some of the laughter of the Back Bay and Beacon Hill had subsided when a plurality of seventeen thousand voters made Coolidge governor in 1918.

It was an imponderable mystery how this silent and stone-faced man continued to receive support from individuals of influence and the electorate while consistently ignoring the rules of politics. When he had run for lieutenant-governor his Democratic opponent had attacked him with scurrilous newspaper ads showing black hands pointing at his picture and his record. Coolidge would not return the fire. He would not even defend himself and prevented Stearns, who had prepared a fine answering advertisement, from printing it. "It's a good advertisement," he told Stearns, "but I will not get into a controversy of that kind. I will not attack an individual. If the people of Massachusetts do not know me well enough to elect me without my answering every indiscriminate attack, then I would rather be defeated." Later, after he was elected governor, Coolidge found that Frank Stearns was serving in two unpaid state jobs, one on the Pilgrim Tercentennial Commission and the other on a committee to welcome returning soldiers home. Coolidge called in Stearns and said, "I think it your duty to resign from both places." No other comment. Instead of angering Stearns, this brusque treatment strengthened his admiration. Exaggerated an example as it was of a mind sensitive toward corruption in public office, it added to the aggregate of little things that are in sum the measure of a man.

Certainly there was a quality of humanity and pathos under the rigid Coolidge visage which the people enjoyed glimpsing as much as they liked to hear him break his endless silences with some pearl of understatement. When Coolidge was host to the other New England governors in a celebration for returning troops, a platform was erected on which the chief executives stood for five hours at rigid attention—and, on Coolidge's part, in silence. Toward the end of this vigil Coolidge turned to his New Hampshire compatriot and said, "Governor, I think you will find that if you put one foot on the rail and lean in my position a while, then change to the other foot, you will find it will rest you."

It was, of course, the Boston police strike that brought him to the attention of the country. The police wished to join the American Federation of Labor and, when warned against doing so by their Boston commissioner, they struck on September 9, 1919. Hoodlums filled the streets and in a short time the crashing of store windows signaled widespread disorder. The police commissioner and mayor of Boston succeeded in putting down the disturbance with local members of the militia, but the police would not return to work and the crisis erupted in the governor's office. On September 11 a body of labor leaders informed Coolidge that if he did not reinstate the police at once, sympathetic strikes in transportation, communication and business would paralyze the city. Next, a group of his political supporters in business advised him that if he warred against the American Federation of Labor he would never be elected to office again in Massachusetts. After a few minutes' silence Coolidge said, "It is not necessary for me to hold another office." In the face of the warning of A.F. of L. President Samuel Gompers, Coolidge dispatched his significant telegram: "The right of the police of Boston to affiliate has always been questioned, never granted, is now prohibited. There is no right to strike against the public safety . . ." With this pronouncement, the calling out of the national guard and the recruiting of new police to replace the strikers (who were prohibited from reinstatement), the country took heart and carried Coolidge, the symbol of law and order in a period of political and social unrest, to the national capital.

The governor gave no encouragement whatever to those who, in 1920, promoted him as a candidate for the Presidency. He had no designs on the White House because he did not consider himself Presidential or Vice-Presidential timber. He did not think it was right to use the governor's office as a campaign arena for a higher political station. "I have never said I would become a candidate for President," he declared. "I have not been and I am not a candidate . . ." But his supporters, chiefly the unflagging Frank Stearns, were determined to present his name at the convention, despite the wing of Massachusetts Republicans headed by Senator Henry Cabot Lodge. "Nominate a man who lives in a two-family house?" asked Lodge. "Never!" If the senator had anything to do with this convention—and he had had a great deal to do with many—Coolidge (who had aligned himself with the liberal Republicans, Taft, Root and Hughes, in behalf of the League of Nations) would go no further.

If it had not been for Lodge, Coolidge might have been nominated for the Presidency. As it was the convention awarded the laconic Yankee second place on the ticket with a clamor that prompted Chauncey M. Depew to inform him: "I have been present at every Republican Convention beginning with 1856, and I have never seen such a personal tribute paid to any individual, by any convention, as was paid to you in the spontaneous nomination for Vice-President." Soon the governor was engaged in another arduous campaign, and in the distasteful business of speechmaking. While the people of the Midwest did not respond to the homely utterances which reached their ears in a clipped Vermont twang, the effusive and open-hearted oratory of the candidate for President, Warren G. Harding, won their approval. The Republican National Committee switched Coolidge to the South where he gained great favor.

"The greatest peril to our institutions does not lie in a direct assault upon them, nor will it come from those who with evil intent strive for their destruction. Disaster will come from those who possibly with good intentions seek the private control of public action. . . .

"The world today is filled with a great impatience. Men are disdainful of the things that are, and are credulously turning toward those who assert that a change of institutions would somehow bring an era of perfection. It is not that a change is needed in our Constitution and laws so much as there is a need of living in accordance with them.

"We are the possessors of tremendous power both as individuals and as States; the great question of the preservation of our institutions is a moral question. Shall we use our power for self-aggrandizement or for service?

"The age of science and commercialism is here. There is no sound reason for wishing it otherwise. The wise desire is not to destroy it but to use it and direct it rather than to be used and directed by it, that it may be, as it should be, not the master but the servant, that the physical forces may not prevail over the moral forces and that the rule of life may not be expediency but righteousness."

When his term as governor was up, Coolidge relinquished his two airshaft rooms at the Adams House (he had added one when he became governor) and took the coach to Northampton. As he smoked his cigar and looked out of the window over the passing landscape that he had observed coming and going each weekend since he had first attended the legislature eleven years before, he must have thought that the singed cat had done pretty well. Certainly his luck had been good. Work, too—nothing brilliant, as he wrote later; just work, painstaking and persistent. It had been twenty-six years since he had gone into Judge Field's law firm and now, the second highest office in the nation. In February 1921 the Coolidges packed their things in the double house on Massasoit Street, and early in March the Vice-President-elect spent a final hour with his friends along Northampton's main thoroughfare. He stood in the doorway of the shoemaker's shop where he had passed so many hours in silence during his fledgling-lawyer days. When Jim Lucey looked up from his work, Calvin merely said, "Well, I've come to say good-by."

Grace Coolidge captivated Washington and made enough joyous conversation at various state and social functions to lessen the impact of her husband's disapproving silences. But his large experience with legislative bodies and his knowledge of parliamentary matters served him well as presiding officer of the United States Senate. He also sat in on meetings of the cabinet. His independence as Vice-President antagonized many of the Republican politicians who attempted to enlist his services in a multitude of special causes, political and otherwise. Coolidge would relight his expired cigar and act independently. Thus they planned to ease him out in 1924; but as it happened that was not their privilege.

Since the time of Lincoln, the great democratic ideal that a man of humble origin may rise to the Presidency of the United States was never more dramatically represented than in the summer of 1923. The Vice-President and his wife had gone to Vermont for a rest at the home of his father. In the blackness of the first hour of August 3, a car rattled over the dusty road from Bridgewater to Plymouth Notch and stopped outside the white dwelling of Colonel John Coolidge. The driver leapt up the stairs and hammered on the door. Shortly, John Coolidge appeared and asked what was wanted.

The man on the porch said that President Harding was dead. There was a message for the Vice-President. Colonel John turned from the window and in a few moments one oil lamp and then another cast forth their unsteady light. The colonel handed his son two telegrams from the messenger. One of them confirmed the news of Harding's sudden death, the other advised Coolidge to be sworn in as President without delay. Calvin knelt to pray in the bedroom. As soon as his secretary arrived he sent a message to Mrs. Harding: "We offer you our deepest sympathy. May God bless you and keep you." In a short time light began to stream from the windows of other houses in the valley. Telephone linemen strung a wire along the roadside to the Coolidge home. Vermont's Congressman Porter Dale, who had arrived with Joe Fountain, a reporter, observing that the United States had no President, also advised that he be sworn in without delay. Calvin asked his father if he was still a notary. The colonel replied that he was and Calvin then said he wanted his father to administer the oath.

In the downstairs sitting room with its wood stove, rocking chairs and center table, John Coolidge brought out the family Bible. Grace carried in an extra lamp for the table. Outside on the porch the neighbors gathered around the window. In this room where his mother had long ago lain ill, and where his sister had died, Calvin Coolidge now raised his right hand. After the taut voice of his father he repeated: "I do solemnly swear that I will faithfully execute the office of President of the United States and will, to the best of my ability, preserve, protect, and defend the Consitution of the United States." . . . And added, "So help me God." As the elder Coolidge affixed his seal and the oath was signed, there was no sound except the ticking of the parlor clock. It was 2:47 A.M.

Colonel John stayed up all night pondering the fact that his son had become President and that he had sworn him in. The President went to bed at three but was up again at six to talk with his friends who had gathered. Before leaving Plymouth he crossed alone to the green cemetery on the hill and stood bareheaded at the family lot.

In Washington at the earliest moment he sat down and wrote his Northampton shoemaker friend: "Not often do I see you or write to you, but I want you to know that if it were not for you I should not be here. And I want to tell you how much I love you. Do not work too much now and try to enjoy yourself in your well-earned hour of age."

The first thing Coolidge said to the chief usher upon moving into the White House was: "I want things as they used to be—before." These few characteristic words were as a tuning fork, establishing the overtones of living during the next six years. There would be no more poker parties, or shabby politicians as in the Harding regime. Life in the White House would conform as nearly as possible to that of Plymouth or Massasoit Street. At the same time the President felt dutybound, completing the term of Warren Harding, to carry out the latter's policies. As for the nest of thieves who had been stealing the government's oil reserves in the Teapot Dome affair, he allowed them to roast for a while in the broiler of public indignation, as evidence against them mounted. He was criticized for not removing Secretary of the Interior Denby or Attorney-General Daugherty immediately upon his entrance into the Presidency. Certainly, as far as he himself was concerned, it would have been good politics to do so, but that was not Coolidge's way. "I do not propose to sacrifice any innocent man for my own welfare, nor do I propose to maintain in office any unfit man for my own welfare." Out of loyalty to the deceased President he wished to give those whom Harding had placed in his cabinet every chance to clear themselves, and if they could not, then "let the guilty be punished."

The quiet years of his Presidency were in some respects no easier than those of other Presidents faced with a hostile Congress in a national crisis. On the grounds of economy he vetoed the soldiers' bonus bill, and Congress passed it over his veto. In the face of public and Congressional hostility to the League of Nations he abandoned his position in its favor. Henry Cabot Lodge crippled Coolidge's effort to have the United States represented in the World Court. Other such stalemates plagued the President and yet, at the same time, forward steps were taken. The railroads were consolidated. The threatening tangle of Mexican claims was straightened out. He believed that the government can do more to remedy the economic ills of the people by rigid economy in public expenditure than by anything else. And so it was a source of great satisfaction to him to reduce the national debt by billions of dollars. "Economy," the President pointed out, "is idealism in its most practical form."

"Calvin," wrote William Howard Taft, "is having a hard time but he has a wonderful composure and great common sense, great patience and courage, and he towers above everybody in Washington in the political field in this respect." Taft thought that Coolidge, in his peculiar way, was nearly as good a politician as Lincoln. One frequent

White House visitor described him as sitting for long hours at his desk in the White House "thinking and thinking and thinking. He concentrates more intensely and more continuously than any man I have ever known." Others, of course, thought that Coolidge was sitting in a mental vacuum and that his silences were but a camouflage for mental torpor. After studying Coolidge a prominent psychologist declared that he was afraid that he "could not arrive at any satisfactory synthesis whatever."

Whereas his eccentricities could at one time be enjoyed in microcosm by the citizens of Northampton and Massachusetts alone, they could now be shared by people from Maine to California. In a period when the country was throbbing with the Model T Ford, the Charleston and the hip flask, this New England Puritan with his immobile face and remarkable propensity for understatement became, strangely enough, the symbol of an era. The people cherished and preserved the true Coolidge stories, fabricated others and told and retold them all until the man was as much myth as substance.

There was the time, during a visit to Amherst shortly before he entered the Vice-Presidency, when he visited the Emily Dickinson memorial cottage. Looking at one of the manuscripts he remarked, "She writes with her hands. I dictate." There was the Washington banquet at which a society matron gushed: "Mr. Coolidge, I've made a bet—quite a large one—that I can make you say three words." Coolidge riveted his Yankee eyes on her and quacked: "You lose." Or, turning the first spadeful of earth for a public building: "There's a mighty fine fishworm"; or, waking up from his nap in the White House and looking around the room: "Well—United States still goin'?" And his famous tour in Delaware through a vast greenhouse filled with exotic flowers and trees. Coolidge stopped and, indicating a familiar species, announced: "Bananas!" With a sentence he could reduce to ashes a talkative diplomat aflame with his own importance. One such retired potentate talked on interminably of his achievements at a White House dinner, only to hear, upon the completion of his remarks, "Grace, the dog's run around the table three times."

Coolidge liked Vermont and New England history, and if his visitor was conversant enough on these subjects to strike a chord that needed to be resolved, the President would not limit himself to his usual staccato comments. He would discourse at length on such varied topics as English poetry, dogs, book publishing and social aspirants; but conscious efforts to prime the pump were doomed. Depending upon the circumstances he could thus appear cold, almost boorish, or warm and erudite. Similarly, he could seem stern and humorless one minute and display a Puckish quality of mischief the next. He was sometimes known, at the end of a busy day, to push every button on his desk, with the consequent ringing of bells all over the White House and the arrival of secretaries, ushers and butlers. One morning he sent Mayes, a credulous servant, to knock on the door of the visiting Charles Evans Hughes and inquire if the judge was ready for a shave and a haircut.

Under the White House roof during the Coolidge regime, there lived with the President, besides his wife and two sons, a variety of furred and feathered folk—dogs, canaries, a large yellow cat which Coolidge liked to drape over his shoulders when moving about the family quarters, and a raccoon. One admirer shipped a bear to the White House. Coolidge gave it to the Washington zoo and visited it frequently. From the bleak responsibilities of the executive offices the President could thus retire into the bright and fortifying atmosphere of family life.

In the summer of 1924 his younger son, Calvin, Jr., who was sixteen, developed a blister while playing tennis and was soon fatally ill with blood poisoning. In his father's words:

"In his suffering he was asking me to make him well. I could not.

"When he went, the power and the glory of the Presidency went with him.

"The ways of Providence are often beyond our understanding. It seemed to me that the world had need of the work that it was probable he could do.

"I do not know why such a price was exacted for occupying the White House."

Within nine months the President suffered a second blow in his father's death. "For my personal contact with him during his last months I had to resort to the poor substitute of the telephone. When I reached home he was gone. It costs a good deal to be President."

Coolidge was in office six years, during which he rose steadily in the favor of the people while their respect for Congress waned. In 1924 he was renominated and re-elected with great enthusiasm and with no obligations, political or otherwise, to any person or group.

"We have our enormous debt to pay, and we are paying it. We have the high cost of government to diminish, and we are diminishing it. We have the heavy burden of taxation to reduce, and we are reducing it.

"It ought to be understood that there can be no remedy for lack of industry and thrift secured by law. It ought to be understood that no scheme of insurance and no scheme of government aid is likely to make us all prosperous. And above all, these remedies must go forward on the firm foundation of an independent, self-supporting, self-governing people . . .

"Unless the President is sustained by an abiding faith in a divine power which is working for the good of humanity, I cannot understand how he would have the courage to attempt to meet the various problems that constantly pour in upon him from all parts of the earth.

"It is a great advantage to a President, and a major source of safety to the country, for him to know that he is not a great man. When a man begins to feel that he is the only one who can lead in this republic, he is guilty of treason to the spirit of our institutions."

Although he could have had the nomination, Calvin Coolidge "did not choose to run in 1928." Hoping that he would change his mind, his faithful Boston friend, Frank Stearns, labored away on plans for the Republican convention. In December 1927, however, the President announced that his statement stood, that no one should be led to suppose that he had modified it and that his decision must be respected. He said that after he had been eliminated the party should complete the serious task of selecting another candidate from the numbers of distinguished men available.

"A President should not only not be selfish," he wrote in his autobiography, "but he ought to avoid the appearance of selfishness. The people would not have confidence in a man that appeared to be grasping for office.

"It is difficult for men in high office to avoid the malady of self-delusion. They are always surrounded by worshippers. They are constantly, and for the most part sincerely, assured of their greatness.

"They live in an artificial atmosphere of adulation and exaltation which sooner or later impairs their judgment.

"In the higher ranges of public service men appear to come forward to perform a certain duty. When it is performed their work is done. They usually find it impossible to readjust themselves in the thought of the people so as to pass on successfully to the solution of new public problems."

Grace Coolidge reported that her husband told a cabinet member that he knew how to save money. "All my training has been in that direction. The country is in a sound financial position. Perhaps the time has come when we ought to spend money. I do not feel that I am qualified to do that."

By March 4, 1929, the day of the inauguration of Herbert Hoover, every detail of the Coolidge departure had been arranged. The President had crated forty cases of books—over four thousand volumes in all—and sent them back to Northampton. Grace Coolidge, whose beauty and warmth had gained her the position of first lady among the first ladies, bade her many friends good-by and surveyed the White House with New England care. After the inauguration they took the train to Northampton and went back into the double house on Massasoit Street.

Coolidge could not have taken the depression harder if he had been President. "These new ideas call for new men to develop them. That task is not for men who believe in the only kind of government I know anything about. We cannot put everything up to the government without overburdening it. However, I do not care to be criticizing those in power. I've never been much good attacking men in public office. If they succeed, the criticism fails; if they fail, the people find it out as quickly as you can tell them."

The ex-President died very suddenly on January 5, 1933. There were the inevitable immediate evaluations—fifty years before evaluation is possible. There were those who pointed to his remark in 1927 that he did not think stocks were too high, and damned him as the cause of the depression. He was, they said, the implement of business and of

laissez-faire. Some said he was totally lacking in originality or imagination. Some said he was an able man. Many said he was lucky. Others
even said he was great.

After the funeral in the Northampton Congregational church, attended by representatives, senators, supreme court justices, the President, and all the citizens who could crowd in, Coolidge was carried
back home to Plymouth. At each hill town through which the small
cortège passed on its way north, the people gathered, bareheaded in
the rain.

"He was one of the common people whom Lincoln said God loved.
There was something in his makeup that reminded us of ourselves in
the old days when the country was young."

XVIII. Epilogue

SOME people think of twentieth-century Vermont as an old woman sitting by the window watching the rest of the world go by. It is true, perhaps, that she is somewhat sot in her ways, but these are ways that she has tested and not found wanting—hard work, thrift, simple living, plainness of manner and of speech. She is not going to join the crowd outside the window just because everybody else has.

And yet, typically enough, Vermont still starts a procession now and then, as she did in the eighteenth and nineteenth centuries. Before the federal government declared war on Germany in 1917, Vermont appropriated one million of her precious dollars for war purposes. And in 1941 Vermont declared war on Japan before Washington did. In political matters the state shows little less rebellion in its determination to stand by the Republican party. In 1832 it was the only state to go anti-Masonic. Since the Civil War it has been the only state that has always been Republican. If the rest of the states went Republican, that would be the day Vermont would go Democratic.

"Is there a 'lost cause'?" wrote Walter Coates, a hill-town writer. "Then I am for it. Is there a philosophy of life and destiny weak and rejected of men? Then will I examine and tolerate and, if needs be, defend that philosophy in its extremity. . . . Yes, write me down as one who abhors a sham, one who resists limitations, who despises cant; as one who will condemn repression and intolerance of every sort . . . who, for these reasons, and because of an inherent tendency of personality, was ever, and will ever be, ONE OF THE MINORITY."

A Vermont that in the nineteenth century brought forth such a maverick theologian as Orestes Brownson, a pirate like Jim Fisk, or the author of *Ten Nights in a Barroom,* can today produce a William Dudley Pelley, or a socialist poet like Sarah Cleghorn. Quite similarly (for inventors are no less wayward) the nineteenth-century Vermonters who developed the steel plow, the modern repeating rifle, the electric motor, the sleeping car, the steam calliope and laughing gas, have now become the architects of machine tools and the designers of the first ski tow in the United States.

Of the last century's everyday folk there was Dorothy Canfield's Old Man Warner, who refused to come down out of Arnold Hollow; and Walter Hard's straight-backed Grandma Westcott, who went to a revival meeting out of curiosity, and when the evangelist stopped at her seat and said in sepulchral tone:

"Sister, are you a Christian?"
She gave herself a twist and sat up more
straight than ever.
"Not in this church I ain't."

Old Man Warner and Grandma Westcott have become the farmer who defiantly undersold the milk producers, and the Vermonter who insisted on climbing the Empire State Building by the stairs.

Certainly the ancestors of these people were wayward. Rebellion is their birthright. Then there is the land: there is a surprise in every turning of the unmatched landscape of Vermont. And so it is with the people.

Bibliography

In the introductory Chapter I: TREMORS UNDER THE TIMBERLINE. The *History of New Hampshire* by Jeremy Belknap (J. Mann and J. K. Demick, Printers, 1812) was consulted for its very full treatment of the early colonial period. Other histories of New Hampshire such as those of McClintock, Barstow and Ticknor are for the most part based upon Belknap's much earlier publication. The *New Hampshire Historical Society Proceedings* were also consulted.

Chapter II: VOX CLAMANTIS IN DESERTO. Definitive accounts of the establishment of Dartmouth College are to be found in *A History of Dartmouth College 1815-1909* by Frederick Chase (Cambridge, Harvard University Press, 1891) and Volume II of the same history by John K. Lord (Concord, N. H., The Rumford Press, 1913). Leon Burr Richardson's *History of Dartmouth College* (2 vols.) (Hanover, N. H., Dartmouth College Publications, 1932) was the most valuable reference. Other sources were: Eleazar Wheelock's *Narrative of the Indian Charity School* (Hartford, Conn., 1775); James Dow McCallum's *Eleazar Wheelock: Founder of Dartmouth College* (Hanover, N.H., Dartmouth Publications, 1939); *The Letters of Eleazar Wheelock's Indians* (Hanover, N.H., Dartmouth College Manuscript Series, 1932); *Historical Discourse delivered before the Alumni of Dartmouth College, June 21, 1869* by Samuel G. Brown (Hanover, N.H., 1870); "State of New Connecticut" by John L. Rice in *Papers and Proceedings of the Connecticut Valley Historical Society, 1876-1881* (Springfield, Mass., 1881); *A Public Defense of the right of the New Hampshire Grants (so called) on both Sides CONNECTICUT River to associate together and form themselves into an INDEPENDENT STATE* (Dresden, N. H., Alden Spooner, 1779); *History of Eastern Vermont* by Benjamin H. Hall (New York, D. Appleton & Company, 1858), and *Independent Vermont* by Charles M. Thompson (Boston, Houghton Mifflin Company, 1942).

Chapter III: BY DINT OF LABOR. The autobiography of Seth Hubbell, from which this chapter was drawn, is to be found in Volume II of the

Vermont Historical Gazetteer by Abby Maria Hemenway (Burlington, Vt., 1871).

Chapter IV: THE CALIPHS OF CUMBERLAND. The most definitive record of the border war in eastern Vermont is the *History of Eastern Vermont* by Benjamin H. Hall. Other sources were: the Charles Phelps papers in the Vermont Historical Society, Montpelier, Vt.; *Family Memoirs* by John Phelps (Brattleboro, Vt., Selleck and Davis, 1866); *The Natural and Civil History of Vermont* by Samuel Williams (Walpole, N. H., Isaiah Thomas and David Carlisle, 1894); *Vermont in the Making 1750-1777* by Matt B. Jones (Cambridge, Harvard University Press, 1939), and Charles M. Thompson's *Independent Vermont*.

Chapter V: THE CASE OF THE CONTRARY CORPSE. Among the numerous separate accounts of the Boorn "murder," the most thorough is *The Boorn Mystery: An Episode from the Judicial Annals of Vermont* by Sherman Roberts Moulton (Montpelier, Vt., The Vermont Historical Society, 1937).

Chapter VI: FOR ONE PAIR OF STAGS. *Matthew Lyon, the Hamden of Congress* by J. Fairfax McLaughlin (New York, Wynkoop, Hallenbeck, Crawford Company, 1900) remains the best biography of Lyon, although it is markedly pro-Lyon in treatment. Other biographies such as *Two Fighters and Two Fines* by Tom W. Campbell (Little Rock, Ark., Pioneer Publishing Company, 1941); "Matthew Lyon" by Loyal S. Fox in Volume I of *Vermont Historical Society Proceedings* (New Series); "The Life and Services of Matthew Lyon" by Pliny H. White in Volume I of *Vermont Historical Society Proceedings* (Old Series), and *For the Rights of Man* by Carl Carmer (Philadelphia, Hinds, Hayden and Eldridge, 1947) are largely drawn from McLaughlin's volume.

Chapter VII: THE POND THAT RAN AWAY. *History and Description of New England* (Vol. II) by A. J. Coolidge and J. B. Mansfield (Boston, Austin J. Coolidge, 1860); *Pictorial Souvenir of "Runaway" or "Dry Pond" Glover, Vermont* (The Monitor Press, Barton, Vt.); *Vermont Historical Gazetteer* (Vol. II), and "Runaway Pond" by Willametta A. Preston in *The Vermonter* (Vol. 5, 1902-03).

Chapter VIII: HEAVEN ON EARTH. *Unscriptural Discipline Exposed and Detected in a faithful Narrative of the extraordinary proceedings of the Anabaptist Church in Poultney, Vt., towards Mrs. Anna Wells. Published by the request, and at the expense of the Congregational Church in Poultney* (Rutland, Vt., Printed by William Fay).

Material on the religious background of early nineteenth-century Vermont and on revivalism may be found in *Social Ferment in Vermont 1791-1850* by David M. Ludlum (New York, Columbia University Press, 1939); *History of Vermont, Natural, Civil and Statistical* by Zadock Thompson (Burlington, Vt., 1842); *Vermont, the Green Mountain State* (Vol. I) by Walter H. Crockett (New York, Century History Company, 1921); *History of Middletown* (Rutland, Vt., 1867); *No Man Knows My History, The Life of Joseph Smith* by Fawn M. Brodie (New York, Alfred A. Knopf, 1945); *Brigham Young* by M. R. Werner (New York, Harcourt, Brace & Co., 1925); *The Story of the Mormons* by William A. Linn (New York, The Macmillan Company, 1902); *Vermont Prose, A Miscellany* by A. W. Peach and Harold A. Rugg, Editors (Brattleboro, Vt., The Stephen Daye Press, 1931); *Mirror of Calvinistic Fanaticism or Jedediah Burchard & Company During a Protracted Meeting of Twenty-Six Days in Woodstock, Vermont* by Russel Streeter (Woodstock, Vt., Nahum Haskell, 1835).

The following volumes on John Humphrey Noyes and the Oneida Community were consulted: *History of American Socialisms* by J. H. Noyes (Philadelphia, J. P. Lippincott & Co., 1870); *John Humphrey Noyes, The Putney Community* (Oneida, N.Y., 1931) and *The Religious Experience of John Humphrey Noyes* (New York, The Macmillan Company, 1923)—both volumes by George Wallingford Noyes; *Noyesism Unveiled* by Hubbard Eastman (Brattleboro, Vt., 1849); *My Father's House, An Oneida Boyhood* by Pierrepont Noyes (New York, Farrar & Rinehart, 1937); "The Oneida Community Experiment in Stirpiculture" in *Eugenics, Genetics and the Family* (Vol. I, 1923); also *A Yankee Saint: John Humphrey Noyes and the Oneida Community* by Robert Allerton (New York, G. P. Putnam's Sons, 1935).

Chapter IX: LABORERS IN LEARNING. *Emma Willard, Daughter of Democracy* by Alma Lutz (Boston & New York, Houghton Mifflin Company, 1929); "Emma Willard" by Beth Gilchrist in *Vermonters, A Book of Biographies* by Walter H. Crockett, Editor (Brattleboro, Vt., The Stephen Daye Press, 1931); "Old Stone House" by C. E.

Ordway in *The Vermonter* (Vols. 9, 10, 11, 1904-05); "Brownington Old Stone House" by Florence E. Waters in *The Vermonter* (Vol. 34, No. 6, 1929), and the *Vermont Historical Gazetteer* (Vol. III).

Chapter X: STEAMBOATS IN THE GROUND SWELL. *Samuel Morey, a Pioneer of Science in America* by Frederick H. Getman (Bruges, Belgium, The St. Catherine Press, Ltd.); *Vermont Historical Gazetteer* (Vol. I).

Material concerning the steamboat war on Lake Champlain was drawn almost entirely from the files of the Burlington *Free Press* between the years 1848-59, and from two volumes titled *Steamboats of Lake Champlain* and *Steamboats of Lake George* by Ogden J. Ross (The Champlain Transportation Company, Albany, 1930).

Chapter XI: DO NOT FOLLOW BUT LEAD. In David M. Ludlum's *Social Ferment in Vermont* and Volume III of Walter H. Crockett's *Vermont, the Green Mountain State* the temperance, anti-Masonic and abolitionist crusades are dealt with at length. The temperance song is from the *Green Mountain Temperance Songster* by M. P. Parish (Burlington, Vt., 1845).

In the sketch of William Lloyd Garrison the following books were consulted: *William Lloyd Garrison, 1805-1879—The Story of his Life Told by His Children* (4 vols.) (New York, The Century Company, 1885); *William Lloyd Garrison* by Lindsay Swift in The American Crisis Biographies (Philadelphia, G. W. Jacobs & Co., 1911), and *Critics and Crusaders* by Charles A. Madison (New York, Henry Holt and Company, 1947-1948).

The best biography of Thaddeus Stevens is *The Life of Thaddeus Stevens* by J. A. Woodburn (Indianapolis, The Bobbs-Merrill Co., 1913). Also *Thaddeus Stevens* by S. W. McCall in The American Statesmen Series (Boston & New York, Houghton Mifflin Company, 1909). The incident of Stevens and his escapade with the cow at the University of Vermont was drawn from an account in the *Vermont Alumni Weekly* (Volume X, No. 24).

The following books and pamphlets were consulted for the sketch of Stephen Douglas: *The Life of Stephen A. Douglas* by James W. Sheahan (New York, Harper and Bros., 1860); *Stephen A. Douglas: A Study in American Politics* by Allen Johnson (New York, The Macmillan Company, 1908); *American Politicians:—A Study in the Evolution of American Politics* by Samuel P. Orth (Cleveland, The Burrows Brothers Company, 1906); *Stephen A. Douglas* by W. G. Brown (Boston & New York, Houghton Mifflin Company, 1902); *Political Debates Between Hon. Abraham Lincoln and Hon. Stephen A. Douglas In the Celebrated Campaign of 1858 in Illinois* (Columbus, Ohio, Follett, Foster and Company, 1860); *The Lincoln and Douglas Debates* by Horace White (Chicago, The University of Chicago Press, 1914).

For the sketch on Horace Greeley: *Horace Greeley, Founder of the New York Tribune* by Don C. Seitz (Indianapolis, The Bobbs-Merrill Co., 1926); *Recollections of a Busy Life* by Horace Greeley (New York, J. B. Ford and Co., 1868); *Horace Greeley, Printer, Editor, Crusader* by Henry Luther Stoddard (New York, G. P. Putnam's Sons, 1946); *Prophet without Honor, The Story of Alvan Earl Bovay and the Origin of the Republican Party* (manuscript) by Henry Christman; *The Life of Horace Greeley, Editor of "The New-York Tribune"* by James Parton (Boston, Houghton Mifflin Company, 1893).

The details of the relationship between Joshua Young and John Brown were drawn from *The Romance of Old New England Churches* by Mary C. Crawford (Boston, L. C. Page & Company, 1903). A complete account of the underground railroad in Vermont may be found in *Vermont's Anti-Slavery and Underground Railroad Record* by Wilbur H. Siebert (Columbus, Ohio, The Spahr and Glenn Co., 1937).

Chapter XII: DISORDER ON THE BORDER. *The St. Albans Raid* by L. N. Benjamin (Montreal, John Lovell, 1865); "Secret History of the St. Albans Raid" by Bennett H. Young in *The Vermonter* (Vol. 7, No. 6, 1902); "An Incident of the Civil War" by Mrs. J. Gregory Smith in *The Vermonter* (Vol. 4, No. 6, 1899); *Vermont Historical Gazetteer* (Vol. II); *Vermont, the Green Mountain State* (Vol. III); files of the Burlington *Free Press* for October 1864; *The Crisis of 1830-42 in Canadian-American Relations* by Albert B. Corey (New Haven, Yale University Press, 1941); *Proceedings of the Vermont Historical Society*, October 19, 1880; *History of Fenianism and Fenian Raids in Vermont* by Edward A. Sowles (Rutland, Vt., Tuttle & Company, 1880); *The Fenian Movement in the United States 1858-1886* by William D'arcy (Washington, The Catholic University Press, 1947).

Chapter XIII: THE VERSHIRE RIOT. Burlington *Free Press,* July 1883; *Message of John L. Barstow to the General Assembly of the State of Vermont, 1883* (Burlington, Vt., Free Press Association, 1884).

Chapter XIV: ARTISTS OF THE UPCOUNTRY. *James Johns, Vermont Pen Printer* by Robert Vail (Chicago, University of Chicago Press, 1933); *Abby Maria Hemenway, Historian, Anthologist and Poet* (manuscript) by Frances H. Babb (Orono, Maine, University of Maine, 1939); "The Alleged Posthumous Writings of Great Authors" by Arthur Conan Doyle in *Fortnightly Review,* December 1927.

Annals of Brattleboro by Mary R. Cabot (Brattleboro, Vt., E. L. Hildreth & Co., 1922); *Rudyard Kipling in New England* by Howard C. Rice (Brattleboro, Vt., The Stephen Daye Press, 1931); *Rudyard Kipling's Vermont Feud* by Frederick F. Van de Water (New York, Reynal and Hitchcock, 1937); *Rudyard Kipling, A Friendly Profile* by Lucile R. Carpenter (Chicago, The Falcon Press, 1942); *Rudyard Kipling* by Hilton Brown (New York & London, Harper and Bros., 1945).

Chapter XV: SIX THOUSAND MILES IN AN AUTOMOBILE CAR. The material in this chapter was drawn from pamphlets and ewspaper clippings in the possession of Colonel H. Nelson Jackson of Burlington, Vt.

Chapter XVI: THE MONEYGRUBBER AND THE NATURALIST. The sketch of Hetty Green was for the most part drawn from the detailed biography *The Witch of Wall Street: Hetty Green* by Boyden Sparkes and Samuel Taylor Moore (New York, Doubleday, Doran & Co., 1935). Other sources were *Some Queer People* by L. D. Black (London, S. Low, Marston & Co. Ltd., 1931); *The Howland Heirs; being the story of a family and a fortune and the inheritance of a trust established for Mrs. Hetty H. R. Green* by William M. Emery (New Bedford, Mass., E. Anthony & Sons, Inc., 1919); *Men of Wealth: The Story of Twelve Significant Fortunes from the Renaissance to the Present Day* by John T. Flynn (New York, Simon & Schuster, 1941), and *History of the Town of Rockingham, 1753-1907* by Lyman Simpson Hayes (Rockingham, Vt., 1907). The material concerning Will Monroe was received from his executor, Judge Clarence P. Cowles of Burlington, Vt.

Chapter XVII: THE LEGEND OF CALVIN COOLIDGE. *Calvin Coolidge —The Man from Vermont* by Claude M. Fuess (Boston, Little, Brown and Company, 1940); *A Puritan in Babylon: The Story of Calvin Coolidge* by William Allen White (New York, The Macmillan Company, 1938); *Calvin Coolidge* by M. E. Hennessy (New York, G. P. Putnam's Sons, 1924); *Cal Coolidge, President* by Roland D. Sawyer (Boston, The Four Seas Co., 1924); *The Legend of Calvin Coolidge* by Cameron Rogers (New York, Doubleday, Doran & Co., 1928); *President Coolidge, A Contemporary Estimate* by Edward E. Whiting (Boston, The Atlantic Monthly Press, 1923); obituaries of Calvin Coolidge in *Proceedings of the American Antiquarian Society* (Vol. 43, 1933).

Chapter XVIII: EPILOGUE. "A Minority Mind" by Walter J. Coates in *The Free Soul, A Journal of Personal Liberation and Eternal Youth* (Volume VI, No. 1); *Some Vermonters* by Walter Hard (Boston, R. G. Badger, 1928).

Index

Onion River, 62, 65, 133
Orford, N. H., 112

Papineau, L. J., 163;
　see also Patriots' War
Parkman, Francis, 155
Patriots' War, 163-164
Peacham, Vt., 134, 138
Pelley, William Dudley, 236
Pennsylvania, 73, 134-137 passim, 144, 215
Perfectionism, see Noyes, John Humphrey, Jr.
Phelps, Charles, 40-50
Phelps, Mrs. Charles, 41-42, 50
Phelps, Mrs. Timothy, 43-44
Phelps, Timothy, 42-50 passim
Philadelphia, 14, 15, 45, 64, 69, 71, 74
Phillips, John, 16
Phoenix (steamer), 154
Pierce, Franklin, 130
Pilgrims (sect), 86, 87
Plattsburg & Montreal R.R., 121, 122
Plattsburg, N. Y., 108
Plymouth Notch, Vt., 227
Plymouth, Vt., 217-234 passim
Poe, Edgar Allen, 145
Poets and Poetry of Vermont, 174
Poland, Joseph, 153
Polhemus, William, 58
Porcupine's Gazette, 61, 64-65
Portsmouth, N. H., 3, 10, 13, 34
Poultney River, 64
Poultney, Vt., 79-82 passim
Presbyterians, 4, 108
Pring, Martin, 2
Puritans, 65, 82
Putney, Vt., 92, 94-102 passim;
　see also Perfectionism

Quakers, 3, 65, 71, 202

Randolph, Vt., 108, 126, 153
Republican party, 2, 132, 137, 142, 150-152, 236;
　see also Coolidge, Calvin
Revivalism, 86-87, 91, 92;
　see also Great Awakening
Revolution, American, 9, 34, 39, 40, 62, 87, 124, 219
Richelieu River, 113, 122
Robinson, "Black Hawk," 202
Robinson, Hetty, see Green, Hetty

Robinson, Judge Moses, 46
Robinson, Rowland T., 153
Rouses Point, N. Y., 165
Runaway Pond, see Long Pond
Rutland & Burlington R. R., 121
Rutland Herald, 57-58
Rutland, Vt., 68, 127, 129, 170
R. W. Sherman (steamer), 119-121

St. Albans raid, 156-163, 165
St. Albans, Vt., 119, 154, 156-161, 164, 165, 166, 170
St. Johns, P.Q., 113, 122, 154, 165, 166
St. Lawrence River, 164
Salisbury, Conn., 62
Saranac (steamer), 114, 154
Saxtons River, Vt., 206
Scott, Gen. Winfield, 164
Scotty (collie), 214, 215, 216
Seddon, James A., 162
Seven Seas, The, 187
Seventh Day Adventists, 87
Shakers, 87, 104
Sharon, Vt., 84, 85
Shays, Daniel, 201
Sheffield, Vt., 77, 78
Shelburne Harbor, 113, 117, 122-123
Shelburne, Vt., 200
Sheldon, Vt., 160
Sherman, Capt. Richard, 114, 115-116, 119
Sherman, Gen. William, 183
Shurtleff, Roswell, 21, 22, 23
Slade, William, 127
Smith, Capt. John, 22
Smith, Mrs. John Gregory, 160
Spadra Bluff, Ark., 74
Sparks, Jared, 183
Speedwell, 2
Spiritualism, 87, 104
Spiritual Magazine, The, 97
Springfield Union, 181
Stamp Act, 38
State Colonization Society, 127
Steamboats, 111-123, 145, 154
Stearns, Frank, 223-224, 225, 232
Stevens, Thaddeus, 133-138, 151
Stirpiculture, 103-104, 105
Stratton Mountain, 126
Streeter, Russel, 87-91
Stuart, John T., 139
Sutton, Vt., 77, 78

Swedenborgianism, 104

Taft, William Howard, 225, 229
Teapot Dome, 229
Temperance, 84, 125
Texas, 70, 212, 213
Thompson, Daniel P., 125
Ticonderoga, *see* Fort Ticonderoga
Tinmouth, Vt., 71, 81
Tippecanoe-and-Tyler-too, 145
Toryism, 36-39 *passim*, 62, 124, 163, 176
Troy, N. Y., 86, 152, 166
Twilight, Alexander L., 108-110
Twilight, Mercy, 110

Underground railroad, 152-155
Unitarian church, 128, 155
United States (steamer), 117, 122, 154, 160
Universalists, 84, 106

Van Buren, Martin, 113, 164, 183
Van Ness, Gov. Cornelius, 108
Vergennes, Vt., 68, 70, 108, 155
Vermont Autograph and Remarker, 172-174
Vermont (automobile), 190-200
Vermont (steamer), 112-113
Vermont Central R.R., 153
Vermont Historical Gazetteer, 174, 178;
    see also Hemenway, Abby
Vermont, Republic of, 12, 14, 33-34, 39, 49, 62, 182;
    see also Allen, Ethan; Allen, Ira; Allen party; Borders, interstate, disputes over; Connecticut valley state; Cumberland County
Vermont Temperance Society, 125
Vermont, University of, 108, 133, 134, 214, 220
Vershire riot, 168-171
Vershire, Vt., 168, 170
Victoria, Queen, 148
Virginia, 70, 127, 155

War of 1812, 24, 124, 133, 163
Wardsboro, Vt., 177-178
War Hawks, 24
Washburn, Robert M., 223
Washington, D. C., 27, 74, 151, 227, 228-232
Washington, George, 18, 43, 111, 112, 124
Waterford Academy for Young Ladies, 108

Watt, James, 111
Webster, Daniel, 26-28, 91, 113, 126
Wells, Anna, 79-82
Wells, Enos, 80
Wentworth, Benning, 8, 10, 34
Wentworth, John, 10, 12-13, 34-35
Wesley, John, 93
Wesselhoeft, Dr. Robert, 182-184, 185
Wesselhoeft Water Cure, 182-184
West Fairlee, Vt., 21, 169
West Haven, Vt. 142
Westminster massacre, 33-39
Westminster, Vt., 35-39 *passim*, 44
Wheeler, Vt., 77, 78
Wheelock, Eleazar, 5-18, 34, 86;
    Connecticut valley state, 13-18;
    Dartmouth College founded by, 6-8;
    death, 17, 18;
    education of Indians, 5-10
Wheelock, John, 18-26 *passim;*
    see also Dartmouth College case; Dartmouth University
Wheelock, Vt., 77, 78
Whelpley, James, 58-59
Whigs, 37, 38, 62, 126, 135-136, 145, 148, 150
White House, 228-231 *passim*, 233
White Mountains, 213
White River Junction, Vt., 177
White, William Allen, 221
Whitefield, George, 82
Whitehall (steamer), 114, 122, 154
Whitehall, N. Y., 113, 114, 120
Whitingham, Vt., 84
Wilder, Alexander, 98
Wilks, Matthew Astor, 212
Willard, Emma, 107-108
Willard, John, 107
Willoughby, Lake, 109
Willow Place, 103;
    see also Perfectionism
Winans, James, 113
Winans, John, 113
Windsor, Vt., 34, 39, 68, 84, 88
Winooski River, 214;
    see also Onion River
Winton (automobile), *see Vermont* (automobile)
Winton, Alexander, 198, 200
Winton Motor Carriage Co., 198, 199
Wires, Salmon P., 154-155